Price __12__ SKU _TAG1181406_

Title _____

Condition - LN VG G AC Location _v-gen M_

[X] Corners _____ Bent

[ ] _____ Bumped

[ ] _____ Creasing to Cover [ ] _____ Edge Wear

[X] _____ Shelf Wear [ ] _____ Sunned

[ ] Spine Creased [ ] Remainder Mark

[ ] _____ Foxing

[ ] _____ Soiling

[X] No Marks in Text [ ] _____ Underlining

[ ] Pages Yellowed [ ] _____ Highlighting

[ ] Weak Hinge(s) [ ] _____ Marginal Marks

[ ] _____ Tear(s) to DJ [ ] _____ Shelf Wear to DJ

Notes _____

_____

_____

_____

_____

Also by John S. McClure
From Westminster John Knox Press

Claiming Theology in the Pulpit (coauthor with Burton Z Cooper)
The Four Codes of Preaching: Rhetorical Strategies

PREACHING WORDS

144 Key Terms in Homiletics

John S. McClure

Westminster John Knox Press
LOUISVILLE • LONDON

© 2007 John S. McClure

Scripture quotations from the New Revised Standard Version of the Bible are copyright © 1989 by the Division of Christian Education of the National Council of the Churches of Christ in the U.S.A. and are used by permission.

Book design by Sharon Adams
Cover design by RD Studio

First edition
Published by Westminster John Knox Press
Louisville, Kentucky

This book is printed on acid-free paper that meets the American National Standards Institute Z39.48 standard. ♾

PRINTED IN THE UNITED STATES OF AMERICA

07 08 09 10 11 12 13 14 15 16—10 9 8 7 6 5 4 3 2 1

Library of Congress Cataloging-in-Publication Data is on file at the Library of Congress, Washington, D.C.

ISBN-13: 978-0-664-23013-5
ISBN-10: 0-664-23013-X

To my friends in the Academy of Homiletics,
for whom *these words* are of utmost importance.

Contents

Contents   ix

Preface

My editor, Jon Berquist, invited me to lunch three years ago at the Academy of Homiletics meeting in Claremont, California, to discuss possible future publications. In the middle of that conversation he said to me: "Isn't it about time for you to write a basic preaching textbook?" I assured him that there were already several excellent basic texts on the market and in the works. I told him that, if anything, we needed a basic preaching text written by a woman. He then asked if I would consider expanding on a chapter from my recent book *Other-wise Preaching: A Postmodern Ethic for Homiletics*, in which I presented a broad history of ideas within recent homiletics. Would I be interested in writing an intellectual history of modern homiletic theory? Once again I balked. Although academic homileticians love theoretical issues, practicing preachers tend to find them of little interest. Most preachers want to know what difference such theories make in terms of the day-to-day practice of preaching. I was not interested, therefore, in discussing further the debates and conversations within homiletics, unless they could be brought down to earth and made useful. He was kind enough to pay for my lunch after this uneventful meeting, and we decided to chat again soon.

The following year, in Memphis, Jon took me to lunch again and we began where we left off. This time, Jon wondered if we might arrive at an idea for a book that would meet him halfway on both projects discussed the year before. As we talked, we devised a way to put a basic preaching text and a homiletic theory book together in a unique way. By the time the waiter brought the check, we had decided that I would produce a different kind of "glossary" or "word book." It would not be a strict glossary, offering objective dictionary-type definitions. Instead, I would produce an updated list of what I considered the most important and widely used terms in the field of homiletics today, along with a few terms representing the essential interdisciplinary conversation partners for homiletics. Then I would explain these terms, providing enough basic information for a novice to get on board. At the same time, however, I would build in some of the major debates and conversations between and among different schools of homiletic theory. In this way, the reader might be exposed to current homiletic theory in a way that made theory immediately useful and understandable for the practice of preaching. Finally, I would include enough bibliographic material for the curious learner to pursue the meaning of each word further, as desired.

As I wrote this book, I became energized as I revisited homiletic texts I had not read for years and digested a stack of newer books and articles I had not had time to read. At my age, one begins to think there is "nothing new under the sun." In homiletics, this is not the case. The creative energy among preachers and teachers of preaching today is remarkable. I hope the reader will agree that word by word, the building blocks of homiletics are well worth studying and arranging into a coherent whole.

Acknowledgments

As I put together the list of homiletic terms for this book, several friends took the time to look over my list and were gracious enough to make comments. Although I did not take all of their suggestions, they helped me clarify my overall philosophy regarding what should be included, and reminded me of words that were, in some cases, off my radar. These persons are Brad Braxton, L. Susan Bond, G. Lee Ramsey, and Dawn Ottoni Wilhelm. I'm also indebted to Noel Schoonmaker, currently a graduate student in the PhD program in homiletics and liturgics at Vanderbilt, for his extensive and careful research of many of these terms and his commitment to this project. Time and time again, Noel brought to me perspectives and resources that have improved this book. Romney Payne also provided helpful research assistance. In the final stages of editing, Joan Dayton read through the manuscript and provided invaluable suggestions. My wife, Annie, was also kind enough to read many portions aloud, a practice that helped me spot several confusing turns of phrase.

I am deeply grateful to Jon Berquist, who kept after me and helped me to think of a way to integrate a basic preaching resource with substantial reflections on current homiletic theory. Jon is a patient listener and creative conversation partner, qualities that make him a first-rate editor. I also owe a tremendous debt of gratitude to Vanderbilt Divinity School for the sabbatical time to complete this project.

Finally, I must acknowledge all of my colleagues in the Academy of Homiletics and beyond, whose work I shamelessly recapitulate in this book. What a delight and privilege it has been to revisit the last forty years of writing in the field of homiletics and realize again what a profound gift these friends are to me in my work and to the church of Jesus Christ. I count it among the greatest privileges in my life to be in ongoing conversation with this group of scholars regarding what we all consider to be the most important part of the church's witness. Whatever small disagreements I express from time to time pale in comparison to the respect I bear for each and every scholar.

Introduction

Preaching Words treats words the way preachers do: as building blocks. When words are learned, owned, and arranged in a particular pattern, a language is learned, in this case the language of preaching. The goal of this book is to provide an overview of the basic words in homiletics today, so that preachers can arrange them word by word into a coherent design or homiletic theory that will best shape their preaching practice.

Before saying what I have tried to do with each of these terms, allow me to say what I have not done. First, I have not tried to offer a long and exhaustive history of each term. I have made judgments regarding how much historical material is required to adequately understand each word today. For the student who desires more back story for a term, there are high-quality histories of preaching. For many words, Westminster John Knox Press's *Concise Encyclopedia of Preaching* will provide an excellent reading companion.

Second, I have not tried to cover every aspect of conversation or debate concerning each term. The meaning of some words is not contested at all. In those cases, I will outline the consensus of thought about the term. Often I summarize the wisdom of one or two homileticians to provide manageable overviews of a word. In situations where the meaning or role of a word is conflicted, I have tried to indicate the major issues and players in the debate, and included enough bibliographic information so that the reader can pursue the intricate details of the debate as desired. Although I have tried to keep my own opinions in the background, in a few places I weigh in with my considered judgment.

Third, although I have chosen terms to provide good coverage of the field of homiletics, I have not included every possible term. For instance, on matters of delivery, I have selected only those terms I deem most essential. I also decided not to try to represent larger traditions of preaching grounded in denominational, racial, or ethnic identities. I do not have sections on Lutheran preaching or Baptist preaching, on African American or Asian American preaching. Throughout the book, I have included relevant voices from within most denominations and traditions, and especially from African American preaching, both in the conversations about each word and in bibliographic references. Where there are homiletic terms I consider important for understanding preaching in the North American context, such as law and gospel within the Lutheran tradition, or call and response in the African American preaching tradition, I have included them. I believe strongly that conversation with these traditions and backgrounds needs to take place within the classroom on a *consistent basis*, in relation to nearly every major term in homiletics, and should not ever be separated out into individual units, like "African American preaching." I am, therefore, attempting to encourage a more integrated pedagogy with this approach.

Fourth, I have not used footnotes. Each section contains paraphrases, and in some case direct quotations by authors who have written on that particular word. Rather than providing footnotes, I have indicated whose work is quoted or paraphrased and then provided bibliographical references. Although this may create some inconvenience for the reader who chooses to do more research, in most cases it will be easy to find these references by looking at the table of contents and index, and flipping to relevant sections of the book or article.

Finally, the reader should not expect that I have summarized all that there is to say on each of these topics. For the most part, I have tried to stay within homiletic literature itself in order to give the reader a sense of what the community of preachers and teachers of preaching is saying about particular topics. I have not therefore taken the time to move deeply into other fields, such as biblical studies, ethics, and theology, in order to develop larger angles of vision or arguments.

Now let me say a word about what to expect. I have begun each section with a very brief definition of the term. In the definition, I have tried to anticipate some of what will be said in the lines that follow. From there I discuss basic purposes, characteristics, and uses for the term within the field of homiletics. If there is significant debate or conversation within the homiletics guild at large about the word, I try to include the basic contours of this conversation and some of the key current players. I will not be able to include every voice in these conversations, but the bibliography should point toward others. I usually conclude each section with several generalizations or lists of advice that emerge from current homiletic wisdom on the subject at hand. As is true with all advice-giving, the reader will need to weigh the relative merits of the advice in relation to tradition, theological perspective, style of preaching, and under-standing of the nature of preaching itself.

Preaching Words can be used in at least three different ways. First, this book provides working pastors with a good homiletic update. Homiletic resources have changed dramatically in the past twenty-five years, and seasoned preach-ers may not have been able to keep up. In this case, preachers will want to read a resource that charts quickly some of these changes. If you are such a person, you will immediately notice many new words in this book, representing recent changes in homiletics. I encourage you, however, not to stop at these new words, but to read all of the words, since the past few years have brought many changes to the meanings of older terms. I have tried to include most of the important issues and debates in homiletics in a way that will allow you to come to a good understanding of the driving forces in this field today.

Second, *Preaching Words* can be used in an introductory preaching course as a supplement to a basic preaching text. This book provides additional top-ics for discussion and surveys of a range of homiletic views on subjects already under discussion in the class. Each section also provides a basic bibliography to help students do further research on topics of interest.

Finally, *Preaching Words* can be used instead of a basic textbook altogether. Some teachers of preaching will prefer the freedom to create their own course outlines and lectures, arranging the words in this book like building blocks to provide an overview of topics and conversation starters for class. For instance, here is a plan designed for a class in which the teacher wants to begin with a broad overview of homiletic models before moving to the basics of sermon preparation and delivery. I have kept it to ten units, realizing that some units would need to be split into two or three sessions. This syllabus outline also provides a good order in which to read the words in this book, even if not used in a course.

A SAMPLE SYLLABUS OUTLINE

Unit I: The Nature and Purposes of Preaching

Words to read: authority, call, evangelistic preaching, fool, genre, gospel, her-ald, homily, *kerygma* and *didache*, pastoral preaching, proclamation, prophetic preaching, purposes, sermon, theology of preaching, witness, Word of God

Unit II: Preaching in Today's World

Words to read: authenticity, authoritarian, collaborative preaching, congrega-tional study, contextual preaching, conversational preaching, culture, disabil-ity, feminist preaching, gender, listener, multicultural preaching, New

Homiletic, pluralism, postliberal preaching, postmodern preaching, testimony, voice

Unit III: The Homiletic Tool Chest: Interdisciplinary Partners

Words to read: communication, deconstruction, drama, dramatism, empathy, ethics, *ethos*, identification, kinesics, language, *logos*, Nommo, orator, *pathos*, performance, performative language, poetics, rhetoric, semiotics, speech act theory, strategic preaching, structuralism

Unit IV: Models for Sermon Preparation

Words to read: biblical preaching, doctrinal preaching, expository preaching, funeral sermon, itinerant, lectionary, liturgical preaching, occasional preaching, planning, teaching sermon, topical preaching, wedding homily

Unit V: The Process of Sermon Brainstorming

Words to read: anti-Judaism, focus and function, hermeneutics, idea, imagination, inclusive language, law and gospel, memory, modes, text-to-sermon method, theme, theology and preaching, wager

Unit VI: Sermon Materials

Words to read: application, body of the sermon, celebration, code, conclusion, contrapuntal, humor, illustration, image, introduction, metaphor, metonymy, plagiarism, synecdoche

Unit VII: Sermon Organization

Words to read: deductive sermon, design, development, dialogue sermon, form, inductive sermon, Lowry Loop, move, mythic communication, narrative preaching, parabolic communication, plot, point, self-disclosure, structure, style, title, transition

Unit VIII: Polishing the Sermon

Words to read: aural, embodiment, extemporaneous, manuscript, notes, oral, pronunciation

Unit IX: Delivery

Words to read: articulation, audible, call and response, delivery, gesture, hum, inflection, personality, pitch, posture, projection, rate, tone

Unit X: Ongoing Formation of the Preacher

Words to read: character, discipline, feedback, mentoring, relationship, resources

These units could be rearranged and shuffled, of course, to accommodate a range of course or reading plans.

As usual, when a writer finishes a book, there are always questions of whether more or less could have been said; and as always, the answer to both questions is yes. Overall, with this book I am left with the profound sense that there is so much more that can be said, and needs to be said, about each word. But then that is precisely the point. The goal is to give the reader a solid and provocative taste of these many intriguing words, along with bibliographic references, so that, through additional study, preachers can, word by word, improve their preaching.

Preaching Words

anti-Judaism   *The ways in which sermons can communicate intentional or unintentional anti-Jewish messages.*

Typically, there are three ways that preachers interpret Christianity's relationship to Judaism. Although all interpretations contain potential problems, the first, *supersessionism*, has been deemed very problematic, and yet endures (1) in subtle ways by force of habit, and (2) in intentional ways that can become openly harmful. For the supersessionist, Christianity essentially and effectively replaces the religion of Israel, and the church replaces Israel as God's elect people. A hard form of supersessionism absolutely rejects Israel and focuses on converting Jews. In a softer view Judaism represents a religious stage within a hierarchy. Judaism, like other religions, is said to have a partial understanding of God but lack fullness of revelation. Supersessionism has a long history and has been shown to be deeply complicit with anti-Semitism and the supporting arguments leading to the Holocaust. Fortunately there are many new resources warning preachers about this and providing alternative ways of interpreting biblical texts and the relationship between Judaism and Christianity.

A second model is *eschatological mysticism*. In this model, preachers strongly assert that the Jewish faith and people remain within God's plan of salvation, and Israel remains an elect people alongside the church. The church grants Judaism full respect and believes that Israel's refusal of Christ as Messiah is due not to sin, but to God's providential will. These differences will be resolved at the eschaton, when the two faiths will come together in unexpected ways.

A third approach is *forked parallelism*. In this model, Christianity and

1

Judaism are different branches off the same trunk, each valid and authentic in its own right. Both emerged in the first century from the trunk of the same tree: the religion of ancient Israel. For some who hold this view, the two religions stress and develop different elements of Israel's faith. One way of understanding this has been to assert that Christianity draws out the universalism already present in Israel's monotheistic faith. The idea that Christ died for all people gives Christianity a sense of mission that moves ancient Israel's faith outward across cultures and ethnic boundaries. Judaism, on the other hand, preserves and stresses more the particularistic elements in Israel's faith. At the center of this rests Judaism's witness to the Law and the Prophets as the essential grounds for justice and shalom in the world. What Judaism loses by way of universalism and expansionism, it gains by intensity of practice and clarity of message.

These stereotypical characteristics are often considered too broad and sweeping. More recently, taking their cue from radical *pluralism, scholars insist that both Judaism and Christianity can be defined only from within. It is important, therefore, to assess the differences between these two branches by investigating closely the spiritual lives and practices of believers themselves. Only then can their full complementary relationships and distinctions be recognized.

Ronald J. Allen and Clark Williamson, representing this last perspective, recommend several general homiletic practices. First, preachers should carefully study the first-century historical situation. In particular they should study how, throughout the Gospels, negative images reflect *later* controversies between Christians and Jews. These historical dynamics can be referenced and framed in sermons. Second, they advise preachers to call attention, whenever possible, to Jewish "themes, resonances, and echoes" within the text, drawing forth the dependence of Christianity on Judaism in positive ways. Third, they advise accentuating the Roman imperial context within which Christians and Jews shared a common plight. Fourth, they advise preachers to accentuate the relationships Jesus and Paul maintained with Jewish groups at the time, highlighting ways in which both were, in fact, practicing Jews, sharing common ideas, commitments, and memory. Finally, they advise preachers to avoid denigrating the Torah as a legalistic system of law, leveled to a form of works righteousness. This leads congregations to misunderstand the richness, complexity, and depth of Torah as "Way" or "way of life."

Burton Z Cooper and John S. McClure, *Claiming Theology in the Pulpit* (Louisville, KY: Westminster John Knox Press, 2003); Ronald J. Allen and Clark M. Williamson, *Preaching the Gospels without Blaming the Jews: A Lectionary Commentary* (Louisville, KY: Westminster John Knox Press, 2004); Howard Clark Kee and Irwin J. Borowsky, eds., *Removing Anti-Judaism from the Pulpit* (New

York: Continuum International Publishing, 1996); Paula Fredriksen and Adele Reinhartz, eds., *Jesus, Judaism, and Christian Anti-Judaism: Reading the New Testament after the Holocaust* (Louisville, KY: Westminster John Knox Press, 2002); Reimund Bieringer, Didier Pollefeyt, and Frederique Vandecasteele, eds., *Anti-Judaism and the Fourth Gospel* (Louisville, KY: Westminster John Knox Press, 2001); William H. Willimon, "Anti-Jewish Preaching," in William H. Willimon and Richard Lischer, eds., *Concise Encyclopedia of Preaching*, 11–13 (Louisville, KY: Westminster John Knox Press, 1995); Sidney Greidanus, *Preaching Christ from the Old Testament: A Contemporary Hermeneutical Method* (Grand Rapids: Wm. B. Eerdmans Publishing Co., 1999); Marilyn J. Salmon, *Preaching without Contempt: Overcoming Unintended Anti-Judaism* (Minneapolis: Fortress Press, 2006).

application   *Language indicating how a sermon or illustration is to be interpreted or applied to daily life.*

In sermon *conclusions, applications are constituted by some form of mandate, encouragement, or *illustration indicating what the listener is supposed to think or do in response to the sermon. Paul Scott Wilson calls this the "mission" implied or stated by a sermon, some form of action or service that listeners are invited to consider. The word "application" is also used to designate the ways that a sermon illustration should be applied. For instance, following an illustration, the preacher might say something like: "This way of thinking will not do . . ." or "isn't this exactly the way it works . . . ," indicating the particular way in which the illustration is to be applied. Both forms of application are considered by *inductive homileticans to be too directive and denotative, removing the listener's freedom and stifling participation in the preaching process.

H. Grady Davis, *Design for Preaching* (Philadelphia: Fortress Press, 1958); Ilion T. Jones, *Principles and Practice of Preaching: A Comprehensive Study of the Art of Sermon Construction* (Nashville: Abingdon Press, 1956); Paul Scott Wilson, *The Four Pages of the Sermon: A Guide to Biblical Preaching* (Nashville: Abingdon Press, 1999).

articulation   *The movement of the preacher's lips, jaw, soft palate, and tongue to form various sounds.*

Articulation is sometimes called diction. When articulation is done well, the physiological movements of jaw, soft palate, and tongue become recognizable, clear, and distinct speech. One of the goals of good preaching is to be articulate, to enunciate words clearly, without overarticulating in a way that appears affected or overdone. Articulation problems are usually the result of either omitting sounds or syllables ("wanna" instead of "want to"), substituting an inappropriate sound for the correct one ("nucular" for "nuclear"), or adding sounds that should not be there ("athalete" instead of "athlete").

Preaching requires clear enunciation. Enunciation is the physiological and grammatical ways sounds and words are produced so that they make sense. Enunciation includes both *pronunciation and articulation. To enunciate is to understand correctly the pronunciation of a word and physically to create precise sounds so that the word can be heard and understood.

Attaining proper articulation is possible only after warming up the voice. Vocalizing refers to the act of preparing the voice and the body as instruments of *communication. Vocalizing usually includes breathing exercises in which the preacher practices filling the diaphragm slowly and completely before exhaling. Since articulation requires the production of accurate vowels and consonants, the preacher can practice vocalizing vowel sounds and consonants. It is helpful to sing up and down scales (as able), changing consonants and vowels. Special attention should be paid to the proper formation of consonants "m" and "n." Finally, preachers can do exercises that will involve facial muscles and lips. One good exercise is slowly to form very large vowels, feeling the facial muscles stretch in the process. It is also helpful to fill the cheeks with air and, with closed lips, push outward.

Preachers cannot assume that they can make clear and articulate sounds unless they have vocalized before reaching the pulpit. Vocalizing clears the sinuses and relaxes the throat, paving the way so that the entire range of the voice can be used to make the necessary physical sounds required for public speaking. This makes the preacher aware of his or her vocal instrument and ready to use it effectively.

Joseph A. DeVito, *Human Communication: The Basic Course*, 10th ed. (Boston: Allyn & Bacon, 2005); G. Robert Jacks, *Getting the Word Across: Speech Communication for Pastors and Lay Leaders* (Grand Rapids: Wm. B. Eerdmans Publishing Co., 1987); Lilyan Wilder, *Seven Steps to Fearless Speaking* (New York: Wiley, 1999); Roger Love and Donna Frazier, *Set Your Voice Free: How to Get the Singing or Speaking Voice You Want*, book and CD edition (London: Little, Brown & Co., 2003).

audible   *Able to be heard.*

For all listeners, but especially for the elderly and hearing impaired, this is an absolutely crucial aspect of preaching. It is a tremendous challenge to overcome hearing problems created by architecture, street sounds, HVAC noise, and the regular audio interference created by coughing, children crying or fussing, and such. In sanctuaries with inadequate acoustics or public address systems, preachers must provide enough breath support for the *projection of the voice so that it can be heard by all. In most situations, preaching can be assisted by public address systems, audio enhancement equipment, and enough hearing assistive devices for all the hearing impaired. Where possible, public address systems should be of FM quality (making use of speakers with both a woofer and tweeter). Microphones should be of the "condenser" rather than "dynamic" type, in order to cover the broadest possible spectrum (high, mid-range, and low frequencies) of sound.

Jennie Weiss Block, *Copious Hosting: A Theology of Access for People with Disabilities* (New York: Continuum Publishing Group, 2002); G. Robert Jacks, *Getting the Word Across: Speech Communication for Pastors and Lay Leaders* (Grand Rapids: Wm. B. Eerdmans Publishing Co., 1987).

aural *Having to do with hearing the sermon.*

In homiletics, "aural" is often used to refer to all aspects of preaching that pertain to the actual event or process of hearing. This includes all elements of sound (*articulation, whether it is *audible, etc.). The word "aural" can be distinguished from the broader category of listening (see *listener), which includes other aspects of preaching than those occurring directly through the ear (for instance: elements of attention, *memory, and meaning making).

This word is often juxtaposed with the word *oral (oral-aural) to indicate *speaking and hearing.* The doctrine of the *Word of God in preaching is strongly influenced by this oral-aural dimension. Richard Lischer, for instance, argues that the Word of God, as it comes to us in preaching, is acoustical in nature. It comes not by reading, as does the Word of God in Scripture, but by *hearing.* Reflecting on theologian Paul Tillich's idea that symbols help us to participate in the mysteries to which they point, Thomas Troeger argues that the preacher's voice is "an aural symbol" that uses the "physical properties of sound to draw people beyond the message that is being articulated into the presence of God." Every preacher, therefore, needs to become aware of the power and possibility of all of the aural aspects of preaching, including intonation, *pitch, the color of sound or *tone, *inflection, and so on, as ways to move listeners beyond the words themselves toward an encounter with God.

Walter Ong, *The Presence of the Word: Some Prolegomena for Cultural and Religious History* (New Haven, CT: Yale University Press, 1967); Richard Lischer, *A Theology of Preaching: The Dynamics of the Gospel* (Durham, NC: The Labyrinth Press, 1992); Thomas H. Troeger, *Imagining a Sermon* (Nashville: Abingdon Press, 1990).

authenticity *The modern ideal among preachers of being true to oneself.*

The concept of authenticity exists at the core of Enlightenment ideas of individual freedom and self-fulfillment. As Ted Smith points out, the idea of authenticity is also rooted in the distinctive modern assumption that the private self is more real than the public self, and that a union between the public and private self is a moral ideal. Authenticity can be contrasted with an older ideal, sincerity. The idea of sincerity assumed a solid self that could be represented in public. The idea of authenticity, on the other hand, has emerged in late modernity, in which the assumption of a stable, fixed self has receded in favor of a more private, fluid, elusive, and hidden self. Authenticity, therefore, refers to the ways that preaching shows forth the preacher's ongoing search for, or awareness of, a fluid and hidden (real) self.

This word is often used to describe preachers who seem to be openly human, searching, and accessible in the pulpit. Authentic preachers do not represent themselves as removed, perfect, or on a pedestal, but through various forms of *self-disclosure and *identification, attempt to communicate a genuine desire for self-awareness and self-knowledge. The goal is to achieve the relational *authority of one who with listeners is on a search for their real humanity.

At the same time, the authentic preacher does not imitate the style of great preachers but works hard to discover his or her own *voice and *style of presentation. Speaking the same way in and out of the pulpit is one of the signs of homiletical authenticity. The authentic preacher is neither false to self nor imitative of others.

According to Robert G. Duffett, this characteristic is absolutely essential for communicating with today's seekers. He observes that many today are upset with what they perceive to be the hypocritical and phony aspects of the church, especially the church presented in the mass media. The first thing they are looking for, therefore, when they do finally come to church, is leadership by someone who is, above all else, honest, consistent, congruent, and real. Duffett and Richard Ward also argue that it is important for preachers to develop an "emotional memory" through which they are able to true up their experience, emotions, and passion with the biblical text and message they preach. Authenticity, therefore, is also a matter of ensuring that words and emotions match in such a way that the preacher is actually living inside the words that he or she is speaking.

According to Mary Lin Hudson and Mary Donovan Turner, for women preachers authenticity is a key component of voice in preaching. Authenticity is possible only when preachers garner sufficient self-esteem and confidence to claim a consistent pulpit voice that will be recognized as belonging uniquely to them.

Ted Smith, *The New Measures* (Cambridge: Cambridge University Press, forthcoming); Mitties McDonald de Champlain, "What to Do While Preaching," in John McClure, ed., *Best Advice for Preaching* (Minneapolis: Fortress Press, 1998), 99–115; Richard L. Thulin, *The "I" of the Sermon: Autobiography in the*

Pulpit (Eugene, OR: Wipf & Stock, 2004); Lionel Trilling, *Sincerity and Authenticity* (Cambridge, MA: Harvard University Press, 1982); Robert G. Duffett, *A Relevant Word: Communicating the Gospel to Seekers* (Valley Forge, PA: Judson Press, 1995); Richard F. Ward, *Speaking from the Heart: Preaching with Passion* (Eugene, OR: Wipf & Stock, 2001); Mary Donovan Turner and Mary Lin Hudson, *Saved from Silence: Finding Women's Voice in Preaching* (St. Louis: Chalice Press, 1999).

authoritarian   *Preaching that is largely antidemocratic, oppositional, and prejudicial in nature, expressing a concern to consolidate control and power over others.*

The word "authoritarian" was used following World War II by T. W. Adorno to describe the form of personality found in leaders such as Hitler. As a result of Adorno's study, published in 1950 as *The Authoritarian Personality*, there developed a growing public suspicion of unilateral *authority within all institutions, a suspicion that peaked in the 1960s on college campuses throughout the United States. During this period of time, some homileticians and pastoral theologians studied and critiqued *personality in the pulpit and parish. Although few of these homileticians used the word "authoritarian," they were all deeply concerned with preaching that communicated, in both method and message, that power and authority within a church should be consolidated and concentrated in a single person, party, or group. Especially troubling were situations in which an authoritarian preacher operated beyond the rules, regulations, and governance of the congregation, expecting blind submission. In the 1960s homileticians began to create and support models and methods that would include listeners in a more consultative role in the *communication process. *Dialogue preaching in the 1960s and *inductive preaching in the 1970s and 1980s were direct responses to the perceived authoritarian characteristics of the pulpit.

John S. McClure, *The Roundtable Pulpit: Where Leadership and Preaching Meet* (Nashville: Abingdon Press, 1995); T. W. Adorno, *The Authoritarian Personality* (New York: W. W. Norton & Co., 1993).

authority   *The legitimate power of the preacher to speak in such a way as to influence thought or behavior within the Christian community.*

According to Jackson W. Carroll, authority is different from power because it is granted by mutual consent of a group. Carroll asserts that authority is ultimately granted within a group only to an individual whom the group believes represents their core values, beliefs, and common purposes.

There are several ways in which authority is conferred on a preacher. First, there is the traditional authority of the office of preaching within the church.

Because of the exclusion of women from this office through much of church history, women do not yet experience this form of authority as strongly as men. Advocates for the leadership of women in the church continue to work to change institutional commitments to women in offices of leadership. This requires ongoing changes in the structures, expectations, placement, remuneration, and advancement of women as preachers and church leaders.

A second form of authority comes from the relationship between preaching and the biblical text. Inasmuch as the Bible is granted authority within the community of faith, the preacher gains authority by demonstrating a clear commitment to the exposition of Scripture. (See *biblical preaching, and *expository preaching.)

Third, the preacher gains authority through professional competence. This is what Max Weber called the "rational-legal" grounds for authority. If the preacher appears well educated and well prepared in the pulpit, most congregations will grant increased authority.

A fourth form of authority is derived from the perception of a preacher's unique giftedness or charisma. Charismatic authority is granted to preachers who seem to have a special relationship with God and bring a new vision. There is always the possibility for the preacher to abuse charismatic authority and develop *authoritarian patterns of communication. In its worst form, charismatic authority is granted to leaders such as Hitler. In its best form, it is granted to social prophets such as Martin Luther King Jr.

Cleophus LaRue identifies a fifth form of authority in black preaching that is granted when the preacher is clearly committed to God's power and mighty acts in history. Inasmuch as the preacher is able to identify the preached Word with this historical and liberating power, the preacher gains authority in the eyes of the community.

Ted Smith identifies "star quality" as a sixth form of authority that emerged with the revivalist preaching of the Second Great Awakening and the rise of mass communication in North America. In a consumer culture, celebrity has become a powerful, legitimating force used in the promotion of both products and ideas. Preachers from Charles Finney to Robert Schuller have used forms of mass communication to cultivate this form of authority.

In a postmodern context, in which all forms of authority are questioned, what Jackson Carroll calls "relational authority" has become increasingly important. Relational authority comes from developing good pastoral and personal *relationships and fostering a sense of a human quest for *authenticity and shared values so that listeners will trust what the preacher says.

Different homiletic models rely on different forms of authority in the pulpit. In some traditions, the preacher is granted sovereign authority as a living oracle of God. This authority is often reinforced by the authority of office, rational-legal competence, and well-trained powers of biblical interpretation. In some cases, this model is bolstered by charisma. The preacher is perceived as a privileged speaker who mediates God's Word to the community; any speaking of God inevitably leads to the point where God actually speaks. The *prophetic traditions of preaching and traditions centered in *rhetoric and oratory are more prone to this way of viewing the preacher's authority, beyond, and even over against, relational forms of authority.

On the other hand, *inductive preaching and some models of *narrative preaching tend toward relational forms of authority. These forms of preaching imply relationships that are symmetrical or mutual in nature. According to Carroll, "in symmetrical authority relationships power within an organization such as the church is, in principle, available to all members." Inductive preaching assumes that all members are on equal ground. The preacher and the listener are more like one another than different. Preachers can, and must, seek *identification with listeners through empathic forms of *imagination. Inductive preaching says, "We are all in this together," and helps to create possibilities for the experience of solidarity and companionship in congregations.

Proponents of *conversational, *collaborative, and *testimonial models of preaching have pointed out some of the limitations of the relational authority assumed by inductive preaching. Because inductive preachers assume an ideal symmetrical situation in which people's experiences are essentially interchangeable, they can easily disregard actual *differences* between people. The assumption that the listener is "like me" may preclude the realization that the listener can, in fact, be (temporarily) "above me" as partner-teacher. Conversational, collaborative, and testimonial models of preaching try to assert a more dynamic, asymmetrical form of relationship as the key to the preacher's authority.

Jackson W. Carroll, *As One with Authority: Reflective Leadership in Ministry* (Louisville, KY: Westminster John Knox Press, 1991); John S. McClure, *The Roundtable Pulpit: Where Leadership and Preaching Meet* (Nashville: Abingdon Press, 1995); Fred B. Craddock, *As One without Authority*, revised and with new sermons (St. Louis: Chalice Press, 2001); Anna Carter Florence, *Preaching as Testimony* (Louisville, KY: Westminster John Knox Press, forthcoming); Anna Carter Florence, "Put Away Your Sword: Taking the Torture Out of the Sermon," in Mike Graves, ed., *What's the Matter with Preaching Today?* (Louisville, KY: Westminster John Knox Press, 2004); Lucy Atkinson Rose, *Sharing the Word: Preaching in the Roundtable Church* (Louisville, KY: Westminster John Knox Press, 1997); Ronald J. Allen, Barbara Shires Blaisdell, and Scott Black Johnston, *Theology for Preaching: Authority, Truth, and Knowledge of God in a Postmodern Ethos* (Nashville: Abingdon Press, 1997); Cleophus J. LaRue, *The Heart of Black Preaching* (Louisville, KY: Westminster John Knox Press, 2000); Alvera Mickelsen, ed., *Women, Authority, and the Bible* (Downers Grove, IL: InterVarsity Press, 1986); Ted Smith, *The New Measures* (Cambridge: Cambridge University Press, forthcoming); James W. Thompson, *Preaching Like Paul:*

Homiletical Wisdom for Today (Louisville, KY: Westminster John Knox Press, 2000); Alex D. Montova, *Preaching with Passion* (London: Kregel Academic and Professional, 2000); Samuel D. Proctor, *A Certain Sound of the Trumpet: Crafting a Sermon of Authority* (Valley Forge, PA: Judson Press, 1994); Christine M. Smith, *Weaving the Sermon: Preaching in a Feminist Perspective* (Louisville, KY: Westminster John Knox Press, 1989).

biblical preaching   *A *genre in which the sermon originates in the biblical text.*

Often opposed to *topical preaching, biblical preaching allows the biblical text to exert a controlling influence on the sermon's *idea and *purpose. This can be accomplished using a variety of forms of biblical *hermeneutics. Biblical preaching can be *expository or idea-centered (thematic) in nature.

Haddon W. Robinson, *Biblical Preaching: The Development and Delivery of Expository Messages*, 2nd ed. (Grand Rapids: Baker Academic, 2001); Ronald J. Allen, *Preaching Verse-by-Verse* (Louisville, KY: Westminster John Knox Press, 2000); Leander Keck, *The Bible in the Pulpit: The Renewal of Biblical Preaching* (Nashville: Abingdon Press, 1978).

body of the sermon   *The middle portion of the sermon, after the *introduction and before the *conclusion.*

The metaphor of the body is often accompanied by other expressions such as fleshing out one's ideas, giving the sermon legs, giving ideas weight and proportion, adding ornamentation. The body of the sermon is the equivalent of *arrangement* from the five canons of *rhetoric (invention, arrangement, style, memory, and delivery). In the body of the sermon the parts of the sermon are organized and expanded in a variety of ways, by means of divisions or *points (Broadus, Blackwood), *moves (Buttrick), sequences (McClure), pages (Wilson).

John Broadus, *A Treatise on the Preparation and Delivery of Sermons* (New York: Harper & Bros., 1926; Andrew W. Blackwood, *The Preparation of Sermons* (Nashville: Abingdon-Cokesbury Press, 1948); David Buttrick, *Homiletic: Moves and Structures* (Philadelphia: Fortress Press, 1987); John S. McClure, *The Four Codes of Preaching: Rhetorical Strategies* (Louisville, KY: Westminster John Knox Press, 2003); Paul Scott Wilson, *The Four Pages of the Sermon: A Guide to Biblical Preaching* (Nashville: Abingdon Press, 1999).

call   *The divine or ecclesiastical summons to preach.*

Throughout Scripture those who speak God's Word to the community are typically issued a summons from God and the community of believers. This summons or call is sometimes given in spite of a range of protestations, anxious disclaimers, grumblings, and expressions of astonishment by those called (Moses, Jonah, Saul, the women at the tomb). The call to preach can be experienced as a disturbance in one's life, and accompanied by a deep sense of obligation: "Woe to me if I do not proclaim the gospel!" (1 Cor. 9:16). Often there is a sense of urgency, because preaching offers a desperately needed word of transforming power and hope.

The call to preach has been experienced by women as problematic, especially in traditions in which women are not permitted to preach. Over the centuries, women who experienced this call have found other outlets for proclamation: preaching within women's enclaves such as convents, preaching at educational events such as Sunday school classes, proclaiming the gospel or testifying in mission contexts, or preaching in social settings such as women's temperance societies or campaigns for women's rights.

Leonora Tubbs Tisdale, "The Calling of the Preacher," in John S. McClure, *Best Advice for Preaching* (Minneapolis: Fortress Press, 1998), 1–16; John M. Mulder, "Call," in William H. Willimon and Richard Lischer, eds., *The Concise Encyclopedia of Preaching* (Louisville, KY: Westminster John Knox Press, 1995), 58–60; Carol M. Noren, "The Call to Preach," in *The Woman in the Pulpit* (Nashville: Abingdon Press, 1991), 15–29; Eunjoo Mary Kim, *Women Preaching: Theology and Practice through the Ages* (Cleveland: Pilgrim Press, 2004); Mary Donovan Turner and Mary Lin Hudson, *Saved from Silence: Finding Women's Voice in Preaching* (St. Louis: Chalice Press, 1999); Catherine A. Brekus, *Female Preaching in America: Strangers and Pilgrims 1740–1845* (Chapel Hill: University of North Carolina Press, 1998).

call and response   *A back-and-forth verbal *dialogue between preacher and congregation during the sermon.*

A characteristic primarily, though not exclusively, of many African American traditions of preaching, call and response has its roots in African music and is also found in gospel and jazz music. In preaching, a sermonic phrase is followed by a direct commentary or response by a member or members of a congregation. Typically, this response amplifies, encourages, cajoles, directs, or reacts to what is being said from the pulpit. Call and response functions, therefore, both dialogically and imitatively. It constitutes a form of dialogue between preacher and congregation at the same time that preacher and congregation imitate certain dispositions, rhythms, and cadences offered to one another within the dialogue itself. Above all else, call and response makes the preaching event both democratic and participatory in nature.

Evans Crawford, *The Hum: Call and Response in African American Preaching* (Nashville: Abingdon Press, 1995); Bruce A. Rosenberg, *The Art of the American Folk Preacher* (New York: Oxford University Press, 1970).

celebration   *A peak moment of emotional, cognitive, and spiritual release occurring during sermons.*

Henry Mitchell and others have identified celebration as a central aspect of most African American sermons. Although several homileticians have identified celebration as a moment of supreme emotional and spiritual catharsis, some are quick to associate the deepest aspect of celebration in preaching with the experience of *liberation*. For listeners, celebration signifies a holistic deliverance *in the present moment* from various forms of racial, social, and class oppression. The *call-and-response dynamic during the time of celebration is sometimes called "whooping."

Henry Mitchell, *The Recovery of Preaching* (San Francisco: Harper & Row, 1977); Warren H. Stewart, *Interpreting God's Word in Black Preaching* (Valley Forge, PA: Judson Press, 1984); Olin P. Moyd, *The Sacred Art* (Valley Forge, PA: Judson Press, 1995); Frank A. Thomas, *They Like to Never Quit Praisin' God* (Cleveland: United Church Press, 1997).

character   *The personal integrity of the preacher as it influences the reception of the sermon.*

After several decades of disregard, the idea of the character of the preacher has reemerged in recent homiletics. For many homileticians and preachers, especially those influenced by the writings of Karl Barth, the communication of the Word of God in preaching should have little or nothing to do with the character of the preacher. Preachers should focus primarily on preparing biblically grounded messages and do everything in their power to get out of the way so that God's Word might speak *in spite of* their presence.

Increased interest in the relationship between *rhetoric and preaching, including homiletic *ethos*, seems to have had some impact on the revival of character in homiletics. It is important to distinguish ethical issues regarding the preacher's character from issues of *personality, in which the central concern is more the psychology of *self-disclosure and *identification with one's listeners.

Lucy Lind Hogan and Robert Reid, *Connecting with the Congregation: Rhetoric and the Art of Preaching* (Nashville: Abingdon Press, 1999); André Resner Jr., *Preacher and Cross: Person and Message in Theology and Rhetoric* (Grand Rapids: Wm. B. Eerdmans Publishing Co., 1999); John S. McClure, Ronald J. Allen, Dale P. Andrews, L. Susan Bond, Dan P. Moseley, and G. Lee Ramsay Jr., *Listening to Listeners: Homiletical Case Studies* (St. Louis: Chalice Press, 2004); Charles L. Campbell, *The Word before the Powers* (Louisville, KY: Westminster John Knox Press, 2004); Thomas G. Long, *Testimony: Talking Ourselves into Being Christian* (San Francisco: Jossey-Bass, 2004).

code   *A recognizable convention of *communication that shapes the trans-action between preacher and *listener.*

This word comes into homiletics from the field of *semiotics, the study of signs. According to experts in semiotics, the meanings of words depend entirely on the codes or conventions of communication within which they are situated. In *The Four Codes of Preaching* I have argued that preachers make use of a basic set of codes for communication, and that understanding these conventions of communication provides a key to understanding and shaping the kind of transaction that occurs between preachers and listeners.

According to this theory there are four basic codes in preaching: a *scriptural* code or set of conventions regarding the meaning and appropriate function of the Bible in the community of faith, a *semantic* code or set of conventions or expectations regarding how it is that ideas, meanings, and truths should be articulated, a *cultural* code or set of conventions regarding where and how the gospel is to be experienced and enculturated, and a *theosymbolic* code or set of conventions regarding the kind of theological worldview that a particular congregation shares and is willing to tolerate. The theory of homiletic codes is important because it draws attention to the ways that preaching is embedded within an ongoing negotiation for the use of signs and symbols within congregations and cultures.

John McClure, *The Four Codes of Preaching: Rhetorical Strategies* (Minneapolis: Fortress Press, 1991; reprint, Louisville, KY: Westminster John Knox Press, 2003).

collaborative preaching   *A particular form of *conversational preaching in which there is an intentional effort to involve others in a sermon brain-storming and *feedback process.*

Collaborative preachers form small groups of laypersons, from within and outside the church, who meet with the preacher to discuss biblical, theological, and experiential materials for the upcoming sermon. In some cases, an effort is made to meet in different social locations so that sermon messages are not constricted by the worldview of one's congregation. Sermon brainstorming might take place, for instance, in a public place such as a library or shopping mall, or at a women's shelter or homeless shelter. The preacher takes careful notes during the process of sermon brainstorming and prepares the sermon so that it resembles both the form and message of the collaborative brainstorming process. After the sermon is preached, preachers return to these groups for feedback and to begin the process again.

In some cases, the names of those participating in these groups are published in bulletins so that feedback will come into the group by way of all of those responsible for the sermon. The brainstorming group changes regularly to avoid establishing an in-group. The goals of this type of preaching are many: educating congregations on what sermons are and how they function in the community, increasing ownership of the ministry of proclamation in the church, teaching the Bible, widening preaching's audience, promoting a public form of theology in the pulpit, and symbolizing a collaborative form of leadership in the church.

John S. McClure, *The Roundtable Pulpit: Where Leadership and Preaching Meet* (Nashville: Abingdon, 1995); O. Wesley Allen, Jr., *A Homiletic of All Believers* (Louisville, KY: Westminster John Knox Press, 2005).

communication   *The mutual sharing of information, ideas, feelings, attitudes, or behavior through preaching.*

Communication is based upon a set of common rules, practices, and conventions, and designates the actual sharing or communion of ideas, feeling, attitudes, or behaviors. In homiletics, the use of the word "communication" indicates the achievement of a certain level of one-mindedness through preaching. When preaching is considered under the rubric of communication, therefore, homileticans concern themselves with information and life-sharing aspects of preaching.

Often the pastoral aspects of preaching are considered under the rubric of communication. J. Randall Nichols, for instance, encourages preachers to consider how it is that sermons create identity and foster social cohesion, equilibrium, common goals, and a mutually caring environment.

Some homileticians have been concerned with changes in the media of communication from oral forms to literary forms and, more recently, to mass media and technology-driven models. The influence of Marshall McLuhan on homiletics in the 1960s and 1970s spawned homiletic reflection regarding ways preaching can adapt to various communication media as they emerge. This conversation continues today.

Communication theories have brought many new insights into the teaching of homiletics. Perhaps the most important of these insights is the idea that meaning is not transmitted directly from preacher to listener (the tactical theory of communication). Rather, meaning is being constantly constructed and reconstructed by listeners based on any number of variables, not the least of which are the competing messages and worldviews that make up their current life situation (the *strategic view of communication). This concern with communication as a listener-driven phenomenon has had much to do with the turn to the *listener in recent homiletics.

J. Randall Nichols, *Building the Word: The Dynamics of Communication and Preaching* (San Francisco: Harper & Row, 1980); Thor Hall, *The Future Shape of Preach-*

ing (Philadelphia: Fortress Press, 1971); Clyde Fant, *Preaching for Today* (New York: Harper & Row, 1975); Clement Welsh, *Preaching in a New Key: Studies in the Psychology of Thinking and Listening* (Philadelphia: Pilgrim Press, 1974); Myron Chartier, *Preaching as Communication: An Interpersonal Perspective* (Nashville: Abingdon Press, 1981); Thomas H. Troeger, *Ten Strategies for Preaching in a Multi-Media Culture* (Nashville: Abingdon Press, 1996); Tex Sample, *The Spectacle of Worship in a Wired World: Electronic Culture and the Gathered People of God* (Nashville: Abingdon Press, 1998).

conclusion   *The ending of a sermon.*

The conclusion follows the *body or middle of the sermon. Conclusions are a fundamental part of most *deductive sermons and permit the preacher to accomplish several important goals. First, the preacher can let the listeners know what the sermon expects of them, opening up a space in which *listeners can begin the process of responding to the message in some way. Often, this aspect of the conclusion is called the *application. In *evangelistic preaching, for instance, the conclusion typically asks the listener for a response of belief and commitment. A *prophetic sermon might encourage a particular form of action in the community.

Another role that conclusions play is restatement. The preacher uses the conclusion to summarize the main *points or thematic content within the message. This is especially true for sermons that are designed to teach, argue, or defend certain ideas.

Some traditions of preaching encourage exhortation at the conclusion of the sermon. Listeners are invited to consider their lives more deeply and make clearer and more serious commitments to a higher calling.

Homileticians committed to *inductive forms of preaching argue that one way to conclude a sermon is to present listeners with a resolving image or *illustration which rehearses the core or final thought of the sermon. Such an illustration may provide an example of the kind of action or thinking that flows from the sermon's message. For the inductive preacher, however, there is no need to conclude the sermon in the usual sense. The goal of inductive preaching is to permit the listener to conclude the sermon in whatever way seems most appropriate and helpful.

In sermons that shape the message to resemble a narrative *plot, the conclusion acts as a resolution to narrative tension. In what has come to be called the *Lowry Loop, Eugene Lowry speaks of this resolution as an insight or "aha" experience in which a clue to the meaning of the gospel is offered by the preacher, followed by a "whee" in which good news is experienced, and a "yeah" in which the consequences of this good news are anticipated. Again, the listener is encouraged to provide much of the final content of resolution in this approach.

Most homileticians encourage brevity in conclusion, insisting that preachers should never offer conclusions that fail to conclude. Conclusions should never introduce new content. This has the effect of reopening the sermon and moving the listeners away from the message already communicated.

James W. Cox, *Preaching: A Comprehensive Approach to the Design and Delivery of Sermons* (San Francisco: Harper & Row, 1985); Fred B. Craddock, *As One without Authority*, revised and with new sermons (St. Louis: Chalice Press, 2001); Eugene Lowry, *The Homiletical Plot*, expanded edition (Louisville, KY: Westminster John Knox Press, 2001).

congregational study   *Studying the symbolic life of the congregation in order to preach more effectively.*

Over the past two decades, congregational study has become an important practical theological discipline. Congregational study is the *semiotic and ethnographic analysis of the signs and symbols that define both the atmosphere (tone, character, style, mood) of a congregation and its worldview (metanarrative, reality picture). In light of this new discipline, homileticians have begun to consider more carefully what it is that preachers are up against when they attempt to communicate the gospel in particular congregations. What views of Scripture are already present, and how is the Bible used in everyday life? What theological themes already predominate in congregational parlance? What theological worldviews are present in the congregation, and how did they come into being? What cultural and experiential assumptions exist in a congregation?

In order to determine the answers to these questions, Nora Tubbs Tisdale encourages preachers to engage in guided interviews; study archival materials such as church bulletins, old sermons, fundraising brochures and newsletters; conduct demographic analysis of a congregation's neighborhood; analyze architecture, visual art, and space; identify and analyze key rituals, special events, and activities; and observe people in their usual practices of faith. Tisdale encourages preachers to exegete their congregations in much the same way they exegete biblical texts. Preachers then make strategic practical theological decisions regarding what and how to communicate.

Another way to view congregations in relation to preaching is through the lens of pastoral theology. In this model the congregation constitutes a community of caregiving, shaped by sermons that engender both a worldview and an ethos of pastoral care (see *pastoral preaching).

Leonora Tubbs Tisdale, *Preaching as Local Theology and Folk Art* (Minneapolis: Fortress Press, 1997); John S. McClure, *The Four Codes of Preaching: Rhetorical Strategies* (Minneapolis: Fortress Press, 1991; reprinted, Louisville, KY: Westminster John Knox Press, 2003); G. Lee Ramsey Jr., *Care-full Preaching: From Sermon to Caring Community* (St. Louis: Chalice Press, 2000); J. Randall Nichols, *The Restoring Word: Preaching as Pastoral Communication* (San Francisco: Harper & Row, 1987).

contextual preaching *Preaching that responds intentionally and dynamically to the social and cultural location within which the preacher prepares and preaches sermons.*

The contextual preacher never assumes that there is a common form of human experience within which to proclaim the gospel. Rather, there are many socially influenced forms of human experience to take into consideration, each of which impinges on the process of sermon preparation and *delivery. Sensitivity to context encourages preachers to study carefully the immediate social context for preaching, engage in contextual forms of biblical *hermeneutics, purchase commentaries written by persons who reflect that context, and prepare sermons that address directly issues that pertain to life in a particular social and cultural situation. Although sensitized by immediate context, a contextual preacher is aware of the limitations imposed by this context and often seeks for ways to broaden the framework for interpreting and understanding the gospel.

Brad R. Braxton, *No Longer Slaves: Galatians and African American Experience* (Collegeville, MN: Liturgical Press, 2002); Justo L. González and Catherine G. González, *The Liberating Pulpit* (Nashville: Abingdon Press, 1994); Kathy Black, *A Healing Homiletic: Preaching and Disability* (Nashville: Abingdon Press, 1996); Robert G. Duffett, *A Relevant Word: Communicating the Gospel to Seekers* (Valley Forge, PA: Judson Press, 1995); James R. Nieman and Thomas G. Rogers, *Preaching to Every Pew: Cross-Cultural Strategies* (Minneapolis: Augsburg Fortress Press, 2001); John S. McClure, *Other-wise Preaching: A Postmodern Ethic for Homiletics* (St. Louis: Chalice Press, 2001).

contrapuntal *A brief passage within a sermon in which the preacher anticipates and defuses the probable oppositions or exceptions to the message preached.*

The word "contrapuntal" was adopted from musical composition theory by David Buttrick and applied to preaching. Contrapuntal derives from the Latin *contrapunctum*, which means "against note." According to Buttrick, a contrapuntal allows the listener to let off steam by acknowledging, without reinforcing, a likely opposition to the preacher's ideas. Within classical *rhetoric, the anticipation of counterarguments was central to juridical, deliberative, and ceremonial oratory. Orators always analyzed the so-called contraries, and prepared responses. The contrapuntal provides the preacher a way of recognizing or defusing opposition without actually engaging in argument itself. According to Buttrick, every *move or movement of thought in a sermon should take into account potential opposing views.

David Buttrick, *Homiletic: Moves and Structures* (Minneapolis: Fortress Press, 1987).

conversational preaching   *A stress on the embeddedness of preaching within a range of conversations taking place within the academy, congregation, community, nation, and across the globe.*

For Ronald J. Allen, the word "conversation" is used as a broad metaphor for the sermon preparation process itself. Sermons are prepared in conversation with the church's tradition, sacred texts, local church situations and concerns, social context, pastoral issues, the church year, and so forth. Lucy A. Rose encourages one aspect of conversation, personal testimony, as a way of inviting others, especially marginalized voices, into a homiletic conversation. For O. Wesley Allen Jr., the church itself is seen as a form of proclamatory conversation. Preaching stands at the hub of this conversational wheel and encourages a particular set of directions in which the conversation can continue.

Ronald J. Allen, *Interpreting the Gospel: An Introduction to Preaching* (St. Louis: Chalice Press, 1998); Lucy Atkinson Rose, *Sharing the Word: Preaching in the Roundtable Church* (Louisville, KY: Westminster John Knox Press, 1997); O. Wesley Allen Jr., *The Homiletic of All Believers* (Louisville, KY: Westminster John Knox Press, 2005).

culture, homiletic   *All the references to culture within a sermon.*

In an increasingly diverse culture, preachers have become more aware of how their own cultural biases and assumptions influence preaching. This is especially true in sermon *illustration, but a sermon's homiletic culture also includes word choices; clichés; references to manners, morals, food, clothing, hairstyles; regional intonations and accents; and verbal stylistics. Although it is important for preachers to be of the culture that is shared by their congregation, this aspect of preaching can become problematic. Beyond simply betraying personal or cultural prejudices, the way that culture is shaped within sermons carries a powerful set of ideological and theological messages. For instance, if a preacher refers over and over again to the culture of sports and uses sports heroes as exemplars of the faith, there is some likelihood that over time the meaning of the gospel will be identified with the entire spirit of competition within culture at large, an assumption that may be problematic. In some cases this cultural *code works against the preacher's message. It is important, therefore, to monitor references to culture to be sure they are, in every respect possible, congruent with one's theology and message.

Paul B. Brown, *In and for the World: Bringing the Contemporary into Christian Worship* (Minneapolis: Fortress, 1992); Kathy Black, *A Healing Homiletic: Preaching and Disability* (Nashville: Abingdon Press, 1996); John S. McClure, "The Other Side of Sermon Illustration," *Journal for Preachers*, Lent 1989: 2–4; John S. McClure, *The Four Codes of Preaching: Rhetorical Strategies* (Minneapolis: Fortress Press, 1991; reprinted, Louisville, KY: Westminster John Knox Press, 2003).

deconstruction *A form of cultural, philosophical, social, and textual critique designed to keep forms of discourse such as preaching from repressing* otherness *(difference, novelty, relativity, and openness).*

Deconstruction is a decentering form of critique, showing how an excluded *other* (a term, person, idea, or reference) is, in fact, present between the lines or in the margins of texts, cultures, and societies. In homiletics deconstruction can refer to a variety of phenomena. In the first place, it can refer to the decentering of both the preacher and hearer in preaching, the ways in which preaching is a powerful event that lays us open before God and each other. Second, deconstruction can refer to the expressive disaster that is at the heart of proclamation. Preaching takes us to the threshold of the possibilities of language, and then must somehow decenter itself in order to open to the reality and presence of the Holy. In a third context, deconstruction can be used theologically to indicate how God's Word in preaching is *kenotic* or self-giving in nature. Rather than holding onto itself as a metanarrative or totalizing discourse, God's Word in preaching always moves toward the suffering of the world. Fourth, deconstruction can refer to a particular way the Bible is used in preaching. The word denotes a hermeneutic of suspicion and openness, in which the preacher abandons well-worn interpretations and traditional meanings and listens instead to the margins of texts, discerning lost or hidden voices or presences between the lines of texts. Deconstructive exegesis pursues an ever-expanding plurality of meanings for the biblical text rather than foreclosing on a unified or uniform paradigm of meaning. Finally, deconstruction refers to the ethical underpinnings of proclamation, whereby preaching seeks provisionally to purify itself as a form of speech. Preaching deconstructs itself to come clean, to escape the totalizing effect of words, and become an ethical form of communication.

John S. McClure, *Other-wise Preaching: A Postmodern Ethic for Homiletics* (St. Louis: Chalice Press, 2001); John S. McClure, "Preaching and the Redemption of Language," in Jana Childers, ed., *Purposes of Preaching* (St. Louis: Chalice Press, 2004), 83–90; John S. McClure, "From Resistance to Jubilee: Prophetic Preaching and the Testimony of Love," Yale Institute of Sacred Music *Colloquium: Music, Worship, Arts*, vol. 2 (Autumn 2005): 77–85.

deductive sermon   *A sermon that develops from the presentation of a general truth to its division, application, and illustrative support.*

The typical deductive outline looks like this:

I. General Truth
   A. Divisions
      1.
         a.
         b.
II. . . .

For instance:

I. Christianity is monotheistic—a religion of the one true God
   A. Paradoxically Christianity is a Trinitarian form of monotheism
      1. Each part of the Trinity expresses a unique form of God's Love
         a. Creator—creative love
         b. Redeemer—self-giving love
         c. Spirit—redemptive love

II. This one God is the God of all. . . .

Typically, the deductive preacher and sermon listener are not happy with ambiguity in preaching. The preacher does not delay the arrival of the sermon's *idea, but arrests the flow of meaning quickly so that hearers know immediately what is being talked about and why. Themes and ideas are then carefully explained and unpacked.

Haddon W. Robinson, *Biblical Preaching: The Development and Delivery of Expository Messages*, 2nd ed. (Grand Rapids: Baker Academic, 2001); James W. Cox, *Preaching: A Comprehensive Approach to the Design and Delivery of Sermons* (San Francisco: Harper & Row, 1985); Fred B. Craddock, *As One without Authority* (St. Louis: Chalice Press, 2001); David M. Greenhaw, "As One *With* Authority: Rehabilitating Concepts for Preaching," in Richard L. Eslinger, ed., *Intersections: Post-Critical Studies in Preaching* (Grand Rapids: Wm. B. Eerdmans Publishing Co., 1994), 105–22.

delivery   *The entire physical process of giving a sermon.*

Homileticians debate the relative merits of *extemporaneous and *manuscript models for delivering sermons. In both models, however, the physical act of delivery includes such elements as *kinesics (body language, appearance, attitude, posture, etc.), *gesture (movement, *facial expression, stock poses, etc.), vocalizing (audibility, volume, intonation, breath control, *pitch, emphasis, phraseology, hesitation, pause, tempo, rhythm), *articulation (diction, grammar, enunciation, *pronunciation, etc.). Careful attention to all of these elements is required if sermon delivery is to improve.

Mitties de Champlain, "What to Do While Preaching," in John S. McClure, *Best Advice for Preaching* (Minneapolis: Fortress Press, 1998), 99–115; G. Robert Jacks, *Getting the Word Across: Speech Communication for Pastors and Lay Leaders* (Wm. B. Eerdmans Publishing Co., 1987).

design   *The* organic *aspect of sermon *form.*

In the 1950s, homiletician H. Grady Davis described the way that sermons can take the natural, organic shape of the *idea or *theme preached. He decided that, to some extent, sermons are experienced almost visually as having an innate pattern or design. This design is *utterly unique to each sermon.* In many ways, Davis's emphasis on organic design foreshadowed the *inductive preaching movement. He sought to move preaching away from logic-centered concepts such as outlines, or *points, to more aesthetic and visual ways of thinking about the underlying pattern of a sermon.

H. Grady Davis, *Design for Preaching* (Philadelphia: Fortress, 1958).

development   *Aspects of a sermon's *body or *form that amplify the sermon's *idea or *thematic content.*

Elements of sermon development are sometimes called supportive materials. These materials can include a wide range of things: definitions of terms; explanations of words, phrases, or ideas; restatements of ideas or key concepts; examples of an idea or assertion; illustrations; jokes; metaphors; personal testimonials; biblical references and warrants.

James W. Cox, *Preaching: A Comprehensive Approach to the Design and Delivery of Sermons* (San Francisco: Harper & Row, 1985); Thomas G. Long, *The Witness of Preaching*, 2nd ed. (Louisville, KY: Westminster John Knox Press, 2005); Ronald J. Allen, *Interpreting the Gospel: An Introduction to Preaching* (St. Louis: Chalice Press, 1998).

dialogue sermon   *A multiparty sermon constructed and delivered in a dialogical or conversational fashion.*

Following World War II, sovereign models of preaching centered in the personal charisma of the preacher came under a great deal of scrutiny as potentially *authoritarian in nature. Preachers were warned against misusing their *authority and the symbolic power vested in their words. Some psychologists studied the *personality types of preachers, creating typologies to help preachers understand problematic tendencies. Meanwhile, theologians were very interested in the dialogical philosophies of Søren Kierkegaard and Martin Buber, and biblical scholars were unearthing a diversity of forms of communication in the Hebrew Bible and New Testament, especially dialogue, parable, and story. Homileticians began to experiment with models of preaching in which the *listener would be consulted or brought into dialogue either prior to, during, or after the sermon. By the 1960s some preachers were experimenting with two-party or multiparty dialogue sermons. Sometimes these sermons were accompanied by postsermon *feedback sessions or the involvement of laity in sermon brainstorming. Many removed *manuscripts from the pulpits and began to use walk-around forms of *delivery.

The broad use of the word "dialogue" in homiletics refers to this larger movement to incorporate the listener more meaningfully into preaching. Principles of dialogue underlie not only the dialogue preaching movement, but also *inductive preaching, which, though monologue in form, attempts to consult the experience of the listener and to involve the listener in a dialogue by allowing the listener to complete the sermon. Principles of dialogue also find their way into more recent *conversational and *collaborative forms of homiletics.

Reuel L. Howe, *The Miracle of Dialogue* (New York: Seabury Press, 1963); Clyde H. Reid, "Preaching and the Nature of Communication," *Pastoral Psychology* 14 (1963): 40–49; John Killinger, ed., *Experimental Preaching* (Nashville: Abingdon Press, 1973); Browne Barr, *Parish Back Talk* (Nashville: Abingdon Press, 1964); Browne Barr and Mark Eakin, *The Ministering Congregation* (Philadelphia: United Church Press, 1972).

disability   *A physical, emotional, or cognitive loss of ability in human functioning that either hinders one's access to preaching, hearing, understanding, or seeing sermons, or excludes one from messages preached.*

Persons with obvious disabilities are quick to point out that everyone is disabled in some respect and that everyone, by virtue of aging, will experience relative forms of disability in life. For this and other reasons, there is some argument regarding the phrase "person with a disability," with many preferring the term "differently abled."

Listeners with disabilities experience a variety of problems. For the hearing-impaired, it is crucial that preachers address issues of *audibility in the pulpit through hearing assistive devices and, whenever possible, find someone who will sign the sermon. For the visually impaired, audibility issues are also important, since access to body language and gesture is not available. Today, preachers can use computer programs to provide sermon manuscripts or full outlines in Braille.

Perhaps the most egregious breakdown of the pulpit in relation to persons with disabilities stems from exclusionary hermeneutical and theological practices in which "blindness," "lameness," "deafness," "uncleanness" (chronic illness), mental illness (demonic possession), and other forms of disability continue to be tacitly or explicitly associated with human sin, evil, or spiritual ineptitude. Kathy Black has done a great deal to help preachers rethink difficult biblical texts and become more aware of the issues of inclusivity and access that find their way into the content of sermons.

Finally, there are many preachers with disabilities. Many naves and pulpits are wholly inaccessible to persons who are mobility impaired or visually impaired. Many pulpits are not well designed to hold large sheets of Braille manuscript. Seminaries are not well equipped to teach persons with pronounced disabilities. It is, however, possible to overcome these and other exclusivities. Most denominations have resources available for working through architectural issues, and grant money is also available in some instances to assist churches and seminaries willing to address these concerns.

Brett Webb-Mitchell, *Unexpected Guests at God's Banquet* (New York: Crossroad Classic, 1994); Jennie Weiss Block, *Copious Hosting: A Theology of Access for People with Disabilities* (New York: Continuum Publishing Group, 2002); Kathy Black, *A Healing Homiletic: Preaching and Disability* (Nashville: Abingdon Press, 1996).

discipline   *Control over the regular task of preaching, gained by self-enforced patterns of prayer, study, and preparation.*

The various responsibilities given to a preacher by congregation and denomination compete with the time usually allotted for sermon preparation. Preachers, therefore, must bracket regular hours for study and do everything possible to develop a workable weekly system of sermon preparation. They must bracket time, not only for exegesis, but also for reading theology, literature, and news. Working with a *lectionary study group of other pastors who divide up basic exegetical work on the upcoming lectionary texts can prove a time-saving discipline. It is extremely important that preachers keep eyes and ears open, not only to what is occurring within their congregations, but also to local and world events. Preachers must also develop disciplines of *planning, learning to make use of the church calendar, lectionaries, and worship planning resources. Sermon planning usually includes attention to secular and national calendars as well. Preachers need a basic discipline of storing and filing sermonic materials, whether in hard files or computer files. Previous exegetical work on texts that will be preached again should be stored for easy retrieval. Sermon *illustrations and topical references should also be easily at hand. The discipline of filing can save the preacher a great deal of time over the years. Preachers should also regularly work at developing a good library of preaching *resources. Finally, preachers must attend to spiritual disciplines: prayer, sabbatical, retreats, and other practices of refreshment. In some instances, a spiritual director is a good idea.

Thomas G. Long and Neely Dixon Carter, eds., *Preaching in and out of Season* (Louisville, KY: Westminster John Knox Press, 1990); Thomas G. Long, "Patterns in Sermons," in John S. McClure, *Best Advice for Preaching* (Minneapolis: Fortress Press, 1998), 35–59.

doctrinal preaching   *A *genre of preaching in which church doctrine is taught or explained.*

Although all preaching should be theological, communicating intentionally from and on behalf of a theological worldview, doctrinal preaching is a particular form of preaching in which a classical doctrine of the church is explained within a contemporary context. This kind of preaching is especially helpful during those seasons of the church year when catechetical training is occurring, such as the season of Lent. It is also helpful on those few Sundays in the church calendar in which doctrines are central: Trinity Sunday, Reformation Sunday, Christ the King, Ascension, and All Saints.

Mark Ellingsen, *Doctrine and Word: Theology in the Pulpit* (Atlanta: John Knox Press, 1983); William J. Carl III, *Preaching Christian Doctrine* (Philadelphia: Fortress, 1984); Ronald J. Allen, *Preaching Is Believing: The Sermon as Theological Reflection* (Louisville, KY: Westminster John Knox Press, 2002).

drama   *Preaching as the art of staged performance.*

In recent homiletics there is a renewed emphasis on preaching as a performance art. Like music, preaching is performed. Preachers enact their messages, and they communicate best when they embody what they preach. The drama-sensitized preacher always seeks out congruence between the message and the manner of speaking. This preacher will be keenly aware of the role of *embodiment, vocalizing, *inflection, phrasing, and pause, as well as nonverbal factors such as *facial expression, *gesture, and movement. All of these dramatic elements are placed in the service of preaching as a powerful interpretive art. For some, worship itself is viewed as a form of theater involving action, plot, blocking, organization of space, timing, and so forth, in such a way as to enhance the overall performance of the Word.

In many seeker services, preaching is either supplemented by dramatic presentations or scenes, or the entire proclamation of the gospel is supplanted by an interpreted or uninterpreted drama. In these situations, the theories of scene writing and script writing move into the foreground and become a part of homiletic theory and practice. Preachers who use actual dramas as proclamation in worship also need to learn how to integrate a drama team into their congregation's worship planning. This is an aspect of homiletics that will likely be of increasing importance in coming years.

Jana Childers, *Performing the Word: Preaching as Theatre* (Nashville: Abingdon Press, 1998); Richard F. Ward, *Speaking of the Holy: The Art of Communication in Preaching* (St. Louis: Chalice Press, 2001); Charles L. Bartow, *The Preaching Moment: A Guide to Sermon Delivery* (Nashville: Abingdon Press, 1980); Thomas H. Troeger, *Ten Strategies for Preaching in a Multimedia Culture* (Nashville: Abingdon Press, 1996); Jerry Eckert, *In the Carpenter's Workshop: An Exploration of the Use of Drama in Story Sermons* (Lima, OH: CSS Publishing Co., 1997); Alison Stewart, ed., *Drama Team Handbook* (Downers Grove, IL: InterVarsity Press, 2003); Steve Peterson, *Drama Ministry* (Grand Rapids: Zondervan, 1999).

dramatism   *An influential theory of *rhetoric as social drama developed by the renowned twentieth-century rhetorician Kenneth Burke.*

Burke's theory of rhetoric and society is built around five basic elements of drama: the *act*, or what is said and done by the speaker; the *scene*, which provides the context for communication; the *agent* or person who speaks; the *agency* or means of communication; and the *purpose* or goal of communication. All five of these elements are fundamental to understanding the event of preaching.

Burke's work is most important because he saw all of life, especially social life, in these dramatist terms. Preaching, therefore, can be viewed as ensconced within a larger set of dramas that are occurring within congregational and social situations. Each sermon, therefore, is a speech act carried out within a variety of different scenes with multiple purposes. According to Burke, the single most important aspect of communication from a dramatist perspective is the speaker's ability to *identify* with an audience (see *identification). Those who assume a dramatist perspective on preaching tend to emphasize that the preacher must act as if he or she were, in fact, an actor in a social drama or series of social dramas, gaining acceptance for sermon messages by means of identification with listeners, in order to achieve certain cooperative ends.

Kenneth Burke, "Dramatism," *International Encyclopedia of the Social Sciences*, David L. Sills, ed. (New York: Macmillan, 1948), 7:445–51; Craig A. Loscalzo, *Preaching Sermons That Connect: Effective Communication through Identification* (Downers Grove, IL: InterVarsity Press, 1992).

embodiment   *All the ways in which preaching is enhanced by virtue of its presentation through the human body.*

Homileticians who encourage preachers to incorporate elements of drama stress the importance of embodiment. These homileticians typically critique any idea that preaching is to be considered primarily a verbal and cerebral event. According to Pamela Moeller, "preaching is a whole-body activity, dependent as much on a healthy diaphragm, an expressive face, and appropriate gestures . . . as on a clear theme and purpose and a well-constructed form." Moeller argues for the physical bodying forth of the sermon from the first moment of sermon preparation to the last moment of delivery. She encourages preachers to read biblical texts out loud as a part of their exegetical practice, embodying and performing texts in order to better understand their meanings. She also encourages preachers to talk and bodily improvise sermons as they construct them. This same lively process is carried on into the rehearsal of delivery and then into the pulpit.

Pamela Moeller, *A Kinesthetic Homiletic: Embodying Gospel in Preaching* (Minneapolis: Fortress Press, 1993); Jana Childers, *Performing the Word: Preaching as Theatre* (Nashville: Abingdon Press, 1998).

empathy   *The preacher's ability to enter and feel the lived reality of listeners.*

According to G. Lee Ramsay Jr., one of the key qualities of pastoral preaching is the ability to establish "communion" with one's *listeners, demonstrating that the preacher knows something of what their world is like from the inside out. Empathy is similar to Kenneth Burke's idea of *identification, except that with empathy, the rhetorical goals of cooperation or persuasion recede into the background. The goal of empathy is to deepen and enrich the sense in which preaching expresses pastoral care and becomes an extension of the community as a network of caring relationships.

Empathy is also an important aspect of *inductive preaching. Fred Craddock encourages inductive preachers to develop an "empathic *imagination" in order to relate the gospel to the lived experiences of listeners. In inductive sermons, preachers empathize with listeners in order to get them on board a shared journey toward the meaning of the gospel.

G. Lee Ramsey Jr., *Care-full Preaching: From Sermon to Caring Community* (St. Louis: Chalice Press, 2000); Fred B. Craddock, *As One without Authority*, revised and with new sermons (St. Louis: Chalice Press, 2001).

ethics *Those things that promote the welfare of the preacher and congregation and the obligations or duties preachers owe themselves and listeners.*

In the first instance this word refers to the preacher's ethical obligations or duties. In many ways preachers can demonstrate that preaching is an ethical act. First, they can do their own sermon preparation and avoid *plagiarism, giving brief but adequate credit to sources for ideas or illustrations. Second, they can avoid devious tactics or manipulative techniques of communication. This includes such things as illustrations that manipulate emotions, sensational *rhetoric that overstates the problems of an opponent or overextols the virtues of one's own ideas, and *self-disclosure that turns the focal point of preaching away from the gospel message and onto the preacher in self-promoting ways.

In the second instance, homileticians discuss preaching as a form of communication that imparts a distinctly ethical vision and encourages a set of ethical practices. For Walter Brueggemann, this means the proclamation of an alternative script or vision for the world that derives directly from the biblical text as it voices its fundamental concern for peace and justice. For others, such as liberation theologians Justo González and Catherine González, ethical preaching identifies vested interests of power in biblical interpretation, church practices, and culture, proclaiming a word of liberation that calls forth a new community of hope. More recently, Charles Campbell and Stanley Saunders have proposed a form of preaching "to the powers." In this model, the preacher preaches to the principalities and powers identified in the book of Ephesians, rather than to a human audience. Ethics in preaching is an extension of the ways in which the Word of God is always confronting structural evil in the world. In yet another model, I have considered ethical preaching that arises from the preacher's awareness of mutual vulnerability and responsibility.

Raymond H. Bailey, "Ethics in Preaching," *Review and Expositor* 86 (1989): 533–37; Walter Brueggemann, *Cadences of Home: Preaching among Exiles* (Louisville, KY: Westminster John Knox Press, 1997); Justo L. González and Catherine G. González, *The Liberating Pulpit* (Nashville: Abingdon Press, 1994); Stanley P. Saunders and Charles L. Campbell, *The Word on the Street: Performing the Scripture in the Urban Context* (Grand Rapids: Wm. B. Eerdmans Publishing Co., 2000); Charles L. Campbell, *The Word before the Powers* (Louisville, KY: Westminster John Knox Press, 2004); John S. McClure, *Other-wise Preaching: A Postmodern Ethic for Homiletics* (St. Louis: Chalice Press, 2001).

ethos *Persuasive appeals based on the preacher's *character.*

Ethos is a Greek term borrowed from the field of *rhetoric, referring to the ways in which appeals to a preacher's character, knowledge, and intentions function to persuade or dissuade listeners. Aristotle identified three persuasive appeals in rhetoric: appeals based on the character of the speaker (*ethos*), appeals based on logical reason (**logos*), and emotional appeals (**pathos*). Although the word *ethos* is sometimes used to refer to the atmosphere or tone prevailing in a situation, this is not what is usually meant when this word is used by a rhetorician or homiletician. Typically, in homiletics, this word refers to the ethical character of the preacher, the ways in which the preacher's *authority, credibility, trustworthiness, and virtue are established. Clyde E. Fant once referred to this as the *incarnational* element in preaching. Fant argued that the earthen vessel through which the message is communicated is integral to the message itself.

Lucy Lind Hogan and Robert Reid refer to two loci for *ethos*: "internal" *ethos* or *ethos* established *within* the sermon itself, and "external" *ethos* or *ethos* established in the larger congregational context. Although appeals to *ethos* can occur throughout a sermon, it is typical for a preacher to use the initial portion of a sermon to establish credibility with listeners. This practice dates back to the time of Cicero, who suggested that the introduction or *exordium* of a speech was the best place to accomplish this task. In some instances, preachers discuss their own prior experience or expertise with the subject matter for the Sunday sermon, establishing their knowledge or wisdom about the sermon's *theme. Another strategy is for the preacher to identify clearly his or her intentions so that listeners recognize that the preacher is honest and working in good faith, or feel that they are being included or allowed to stand alongside the preacher. If a preacher has a long established honorable character in a congregation and community, this element within preaching may need less conscious effort.

In some cases, too much attention to *ethos* can appear as self-promotion or egocentrism. J. Randall Nichols once distinguished between helpful *self-disclosure, in which the preacher risks a modest and healthy availability to listeners in order to communicate a positive regard for their well-being, and self-display, in which the lens of the sermonic camera turns all eyes toward the preacher, making a sermon, in essence, *about* the preacher. Appeals to *ethos* should always be done in service to the larger task of communication (see *authenticity and *personality).

Clyde E. Fant, *Preaching for Today* (New York: Harper & Row, 1975); J. Randall Nichols, *The Restoring Word: Preaching as Pastoral Communication* (San Francisco: Harper & Row, 1987); Lucy Lind Hogan and Robert Reid, *Connecting with the Congregation: Rhetoric and the Art of Preaching* (Nashville: Abingdon Press, 1999); Dennis Hollinger, "The Ethics of Persuasion in Preaching," in David B. Greiser and Michael King, eds., *Anabaptist Preaching: A Conversation between Pulpit, Pew, and Bible* (Telford, PA: Cascadia Publishing House, 2003), 186–99.

evangelistic preaching   *Preaching for conversion.*

The New Testament word *evangel* simply translates as "good news" or "glad tidings." Evangelistic preaching announces this good news and encourages immediate personal and social transformation.

Proponents of evangelistic preaching are divided on the nature, method, and goal of preaching for conversion. For some, following in the tradition of revivalist Charles G. Finney, evangelistic preaching is focused strongly on convicting the individual listener of sin and insisting on a decision or verdict. The goal is to win from the listener an immediate decision for Christ, if at all possible. Virtually any and all means to this end are considered appropriate. Finney, an *extemporaneous preacher and tremendous dramatist in the pulpit, would go to great lengths to move the hearts and minds of listeners. Craig Loscalzo, an inheritor of this tradition, closely associates apologetics and evangelism. According to Loscalzo, evangelism proclaims the *what* of the gospel and apologetics proclaims the *why*. For Loscalzo, it is crucial for the preacher to make a case for the gospel, presenting the Christian faith as the best alternative in the marketplace of religious ideas.

Those who preach for individual conversion need to be certain that the conviction under which the nonbeliever stands, and the new life in Christ, includes awareness of social sin and the gospel requirements for justice. Historically, separating conversion from its fruits has led to a pronounced focus on the personal to the exclusion of the social.

In a very different approach, William Willimon insists on the separation of evangelistic and apologetic impulses in preaching. Preachers should be careful not to dumb down the gospel, arguing for its viability. Rather, evangelistic preaching should straightforwardly present the gospel in all of its ancient peculiarity and permit God to do the converting. Willimon also argues that evangelistic preaching is important for those who are already believers, encouraging them to recommit to Christ and to their baptismal vows. According to Willimon, the Christian gospel is not only concerned with individual salvation. The biblical narrative as a whole is deeply concerned with a conversion to justice and peacemaking. Walter Brueggemann calls this "world-switching." The preacher invites the nonbeliever into a strange new world that is rooted in the biblical narrative's prophetic witness.

In recent years, liturgical scholars such as Robert Webber and Patrick Kiefert have promoted a communal and liturgical model of evangelism. This approach takes its cue from pre-Constantinian liturgical texts such as the *Apostolic Constitutions*. In these ancient texts, it appears that some churches celebrated a series of liturgical rites of passage through which a catechumenate or group of novices in the faith were incorporated into the church community.

This was a deeply communal practice in which the liturgy and ritual of the community did most of the task of proclaiming the faith, with preaching in an assisting role. This communal, incorporation model of evangelism culminated, during the season of Lent, with an intense period of preparation during which the central mysteries of the faith were taught to catechumens. Preaching during the season of Lent played an important role in this final process, expounding and teaching the basics of Christian faith to those who were novices. Finally, at an Easter vigil, the catechumens were fully incorporated into the church through baptisms and the preaching of resurrection faith.

Within liturgical evangelism, part of the training of the catechumens is social witness. Learning the faith communally and liturgically does not mean only learning *about* the faith in the abstract; it also involves practicing the faith. The catechumens should be involved in social witness, acts of charity, and advocacy. The preaching that occurs during liturgical rites of passage should integrate reflections on this social mission.

In the last analysis, every preacher is an evangelist. The great preacher Henry Sloane Coffin once asserted that evangelistic preaching is "the supreme duty of the Christian preacher." Often misunderstood, evangelism, or preaching for conversion, is nonetheless at the heart of all Christian preaching.

Lewis Drummond, "Charles G. Finney and His Impact on Evangelistic Preaching," *Preaching* 7, no. 1 (Jul.–Aug. 1991): 42–43; Alan Walker, *Evangelistic Preaching* (Grand Rapids: Francis Asbury Press, 1988); Craig A. Loscalzo, *Evangelistic Preaching That Connects: Guidance in Shaping Fresh and Appealing Sermons* (Downers Grove, IL: InterVarsity Press, 1995); Craig A. Loscalzo, *Apologetic Preaching: Proclaiming Christ to a Postmodern World* (Downers Grove, IL: InterVarsity Press, 2000); William H. Willimon, *The Intrusive Word: Preaching to the Unbaptized* (Grand Rapids: Wm. B. Eerdmans Publishing Co., 1994); Robert Webber, *Ancient Future Evangelism: Making Your Church a Faith-Forming Community* (Grand Rapids: Baker Books, 2003); Robert E. Webber, *Celebrating Our Faith: Evangelism through Worship* (New York: Harper & Row, 1986); Patrick R. Kiefert, *Welcoming the Stranger: A Public Theology of Worship and Evangelism* (Minneapolis: Augsburg Fortress, 1992); Priscilla Pope-Levinson and John R. Levinson, "Evangelistic Preaching at the Beginning of the New Millennium," *Journal for Preachers*, Pentecost 2000, 3–9.

expository preaching   *A *form of preaching in which a message is derived from Scripture and made as accessible as possible to contemporary hearers.*

The main principle for expository preaching is the centrality and authority of Scripture in the task of preaching. Generally this translates into two principles. First, preachers strive to understand the biblical text on its own terms as much as possible, apart from their own personal or doctrinal agendas. So the task of sermon preparation will begin with the careful exegesis of a biblical text. The preacher strives to allow the text to define the sermon's subject matter. The use of a *lectionary in preaching is predicated, to a great extent, on this expository principle.

The second principle of expository preaching is clarity in communication. The goal of expository preaching is to make biblical truth accessible. Expository preachers, therefore, tend to use plain, understandable language in order to make biblical ideas as clear, concise, and relevant as possible.

Although there are many expository methods, the two primary types are verse-by-verse exposition and thematic exposition. Verse-by-verse exposition is sometimes called "running commentary." The preacher divides a biblical passage into small units of meaning and moves through those units in a sequential fashion. In thematic expository preaching, the preacher derives a central *idea from a biblical text, and then allows the sermon to take its shape and sequential ordering from that idea. The text is used, as necessary, to shore up the unit of thematic meaning the preacher is developing. Sometimes expository preachers will preach sermons on biblical characters such as Moses, Jesus, or Paul. Another expository practice is the continuous exposition of a book of the Bible.

The primary weakness of expository preaching is its tendency to narrow a preacher's engagement with culture or human experience. Since the text defines the arena of experience to be addressed, many current issues that are not dealt with by biblical writers are excluded from the pulpit. Preachers can also develop a rather utilitarian approach to the Bible; the Bible becomes something that must always be applied to daily life. This can lead the preacher to an overly pragmatic sense of the biblical text's purpose.

The great strength of expository preaching is its reinforcement of the centrality and authority of Scripture in the pulpit and congregational life. It also respects the deep desire of listeners today to understand both the claims and the usefulness of the biblical text for life in today's difficult world.

Haddon W. Robinson, *Biblical Preaching: The Development and Delivery of Expository Messages*, 2nd ed. (Grand Rapids: Baker Academic, 2001); Ronald J. Allen, *Preaching Verse-by-Verse* (Louisville, KY: Westminster John Knox Press, 2000); Harold T. Bryson, *Expository Preaching: The Art of Preaching through a Book of the Bible* (Nashville: Broadman & Holman, 1995); Fredrick C. Holmgren and Herman E. Schaalman, *Preaching Biblical Texts: Expositions by Jewish and Christian Scholars* (Grand Rapids: Wm. B. Eerdmans Publishing Co., 1995).

extemporaneous   *Delivering a sermon without a *manuscript or *notes.*

Extemporaneous does not mean impromptu. The extemporaneous sermon is not preached off the cuff. In fact, in order for extemporaneous preaching to avoid rambling, *more* preparation is required than in manuscript preaching. Although some advocates of extemporaneous preaching insist that the entire sermon preparation process should be kept in the oral domain and never committed to writing, most extemporaneous preachers engage in a *text-to-sermon method identical to their counterpart manuscript preachers, including exegesis and the development of an outline. Though it is often discouraged, some extemporaneous preachers actually write a full-blown manuscript, only to abandon it once they have developed an oral *delivery.

Typically, the extemporaneous preacher will take at least some form of outline into the pulpit. According to James Cox, extemporaneous preachers must learn the importance of an "orderly sequence of thought," commit themselves to a regular regimen of sustained practice, and learn to make good use of key words, phrases, and mnemonic devices in order to adequately recall where they are in their message and what they are prepared to say.

One of the key questions asked by the extemporaneous preacher is: "What if I forget?" Kirk Byron Jones argues that this question can be answered best by cultivating a healthy craft of improvisation. He points out that the word "improvisation" comes from the Latin words meaning "not provided" or "not foreseen." In the world of jazz, improvisation means that one learns to play in a way that trusts openness, spontaneity, and moving with the music. According to Jones, this requires cultivating a sense of playfulness, variation, and "having more than enough to say." One must also develop enough self-confidence and spiritual openness to be daring or risk taking in the pulpit. All of this, he argues, requires the *discipline of mastering one's craft, which involves practicing the basics of *communication and delivery, endless experimentation or "woodshedding," and cultivating trust that the excellence of prior preparation will not let the preacher down during the sermon event itself.

The debate regarding whether preachers should preach without manuscript or notes has a long history. Typically, the choice of one or the other form of delivery depends largely on one's audience, purposes, and native gifts. There are many reasons to choose extemporaneous preaching. This method of delivery maximizes rapport with the congregation, increases congregational participation, promotes the *oral dimensions of preaching, makes the preacher more aware of organization and thus promotes clarity, and increases natural *tone and feeling in delivery. With the renewed interest in *authenticity, availability, and presence in the pulpit, extemporaneous styles of delivery have become more widely used across preaching traditions. If preachers can keep this method from reducing the range and depth of their preaching messages, manage the stress that comes with leaving one's notes behind, and become comfortable with some loss of exactness, extemporaneous preaching can go a long way toward bringing the pulpit ministry alive in dynamic and exciting ways.

James W. Cox, *Preaching* (San Francisco: Harper & Row, 1985); Joseph M. Webb, *Preaching without Notes* (Nashville: Abingdon Press, 2001); Kirk Byron Jones, *The Jazz of Preaching: How to Preach with Great Freedom and Joy* (Nashville: Abingdon Press, 2004); Ralph Lewis, "Preaching with and without Notes," in Michael Duduit, ed., *Handbook of Contemporary Preaching* (Nashville: Broadman & Holman Publishers, 1993), 409–19; Charles W. Koller, *How to Preach without Notes* (Grand Rapids: Baker Publishing Group, 1997).

facial expression   *The appearance of the face during communication. (See *gesture and *kinesics.)*

feedback   *An evaluative response by listeners to a sermon or to the preacher's overall preaching ministry.*

Typically, there are three purposes for sermon feedback. The first is the formal evaluation of the preaching ministry in a congregation as part of a job performance review or congregational study. The second purpose is preacher education. When preachers leave seminaries, they typically have no way of receiving feedback on their sermons. Instituting a formal feedback process can provide ministers with valuable information about how their sermons are being received. The third purpose is to create better and more active listeners. Listeners who expect to be asked questions about sermons tend to become more active listeners on Sunday mornings.

There are several types of sermon feedback. The most common is immediate and informal: a comment in passing at the church door or sometime later that day. Preachers can create a set of ready questions for such situations designed to elicit this kind of feedback or to increase its range or depth. There is usually not enough time, however, to pursue such feedback beyond a casual level. Sometimes informal feedback will be delayed. The preacher will receive a phone call sometime during the week or hear a comment at a later date about a sermon that was either troublesome or helpful. In these situations it is always important to pursue in a nondefensive way the line of feedback the listener is attempting to communicate, in order to gather more information and ensure clarity.

The second type of feedback is content-based and designed to encourage active listening. In some congregations, an adult Sunday school class following worship can be linked directly to the sermon. Listeners are invited to engage the preacher in conversation about the ideas preached. Preachers can receive excellent feedback in these forums regarding sermon content. Listeners also become far more active if they know that they will have this opportunity for interaction with the preacher.

Another option is to get feedback through a sermon preparation brainstorming group or sermon round table. In this *collaborative preaching model, preachers receive feedback from a small group concerning the previous week's sermon. At the same time the group is invited to "feed-forward" information regarding what the preacher might preach the next Sunday. It is appropriate to print the names of persons involved in this sermon feedback/feed-forward group in the bulletin, so that feedback from the congregation can be offered to anyone in the group. This tends to broaden the scope of feedback and increases ownership of the preaching process by those involved in the sermon round table. The members of these round tables can be rotated so that the feedback/feed-forward process can involve many church members over an extended period of time.

A third type of feedback is focused on sermon coaching. In this model, the preacher puts together a group of experts who will provide feedback on every aspect of preaching. This group typically does not meet on Sunday, but at a time shortly after the sermon is preached. This could be on a Monday morning or lunchtime. Feedback can be offered with varying degrees of specificity regarding the sermon just preached. In some mega churches, or churches with an alternative service earlier in the day or on a previous day of the week, preachers select an expert group of listeners, some with degrees in rhetoric, advertising, human communication, psychology, mass media, or theology. This group listens to the first preaching of the sermon and meets immediately with the preacher to offer advice on how to revise the sermon before the other services. In this situation the sermon feedback group is actually counseling the preacher regarding the sermon's content and delivery, suggesting things to be changed, deleted, or embellished to make the sermon more dynamic and effective.

A fourth model of feedback exists as part of an entire *congregational study. This model is outlined by the Listening to Listeners project team in chapter 9 of *Listening to Listeners: Homiletical Case Studies*. The preacher conducts several interviews with focus groups and key individuals of different ages, races, and social backgrounds in the congregation in order to determine key patterns, expectations, and issues among sermon listeners. The preacher then adjusts to meet or modify listener concerns.

The final form of feedback is self-feedback. Preachers can make good use of audio and video technologies to listen to and watch themselves. Regular self-analysis allows preachers to catch bad habits as they are forming, modify gestures, pitch, and intonation that have become predictable, and work on a range of problems related to sermon organization, language, and style.

Receiving sermon feedback is absolutely crucial to improving one's preaching and increasing the involvement of listeners in the sermon process. Sermon feedback, of course, can be either negative or positive, and it is important that the preacher is prepared to listen to and hear both. This will require a certain level of self-esteem, as well as the ability to separate one's ego from the process when necessary. One of the worst things a preacher can do, however, is to avoid feedback altogether, preaching in isolation from the responses of listeners.

Reuel Howe, *Partners in Preaching: Clergy and Laity in Dialogue* (New York: Seabury Press, 1967); Craig Loscalzo, "Feedback," in John S. McClure, ed., *Best Advice for Preaching* (Minneapolis: Fortress Press, 1998); Ken Untener, *Preaching Better: Practical Suggestions for Homilists* (New York: Paulist Press, 1999); John S. McClure, *The Roundtable Pulpit: Where Leadership and Preaching Meet* (Nashville: Abingdon Press, 1995); John S. McClure, Ronald J. Allen, Dale P. Andrews, L. Susan Bond, Dan P. Moseley, and G. Lee Ramsay Jr., *Listening to Listeners: Homiletical Case Studies* (St. Louis: Chalice Press, 2004).

feminist preaching   *Preaching practices designed to overcome gender oppression and injustice.*

Contemporary feminism took its shape from the women's liberation movement of the late 1960s and early 1970s and has since then blossomed into a comprehensive rethinking of epistemology, psychology, culture, race, and theology. This has had a pervasive influence on theological education in the United States. From early liberationist models of feminism, which included a strong focus on unique and powerful forms of advocacy for women, feminism has more recently experienced some fragmentation. Womanist and black feminist movements have gone separate ways, and postmodern critiques have exposed subtle forms of essentialism (the idea that there is a feminine essence) and stereotyping (regarding all women as a single type) in earlier feminist literature.

Feminist homileticians have struggled with these issues. Several characteristics of feminist preaching can be distilled from this complex movement. First, feminist preachers tend to be critical of overtly persuasive forms of communication and favor forms of *authority in the pulpit which are less hierarchical and more mutual and relational in nature. Second, feminist preachers are cautious with so-called objective, historical readings of biblical texts and tend to bring to the exegetical process a *hermeneutic of suspicion, and a concern to listen for the social and ecclesial presence and interests of women. Third, feminist preachers tend to make use of liberationist and feminist theologies to rethink the theology that is preached from the pulpit. Every major doctrine is reconsidered from a feminist perspective: evil, sin, Christology, soteriology, ecclesiology, eschatology, and so forth. Fourth, feminist preachers pay careful attention to the language and cultural references used in preaching. Biblical texts are studied for a wider range of references to God beyond the usual male-gendered language. Inclusive language with respect to people is likewise employed. At the same time, cultural references in preaching, especially *illustrations, are considered carefully in order to avoid gender stereotypes, implicit violence against or condescension toward women, patriarchal assumptions, and exclusive language. Sixth, feminist preachers address subjects from the pulpit that pertain to the lives of women in today's society: sexual and domestic violence, single-parent families, issues of power and empowerment in the workplace, gender discrimination, poverty, and so on. Finally, feminist preachers are sensitized to the intersection between the oppression of women and all other forms of oppression, interpersonal or systemic, including racism, classism, ageism, and handicappism.

Beyond these explicit homiletic concerns, feminist preachers also attend carefully to the broader vocational elements that impinge upon women in ministry. This includes promoting the ordination of women, creating new homiletic models grounded in the actual practices of women preachers, furthering research into the history of women's public speaking and preaching, carving out new spaces within society and the churches for women as preachers, and nurturing relational networks that support women in ministry.

Christine M. Smith, *Weaving the Sermon: Preaching in a Feminist Perspective* (Louisville, KY: Westminster John Knox Press, 1989); Christine M. Smith, *Preaching as Weeping, Confession, and Resistance: Radical Responses to Radical Evil* (Louisville, KY: Westminster John Knox Press, 1992); Lucy Rose, *Sharing the Word: Preaching in the Roundtable Church* (Louisville, KY: Westminster John Knox Press, 1997); Roxanne Mountford, *The Gendered Pulpit: Preaching in American Protestant Spaces* (Carbondale: Southern Illinois University Press, 2003); Jane V. Craske, *A Woman's Perspective on Preaching* (Peterborough: Foundery Press, 2001); Mary Catherine Hilkert, *Naming Grace: Preaching and the Sacramental Imagination* (New York: Continuum, 2003); Mary Donovan Turner and Mary Lin Hudson, *Saved from Silence: Finding Women's Voice in Preaching* (St. Louis: Chalice Press, 1999).

focus and function   *What the sermon intends to* say *(focus) and* do *(function).*

These two terms were coined by Thomas G. Long to describe the final stage of the biblical preacher's exegetical process. According to Long, before writing a sermon, the preacher must decide on these two principle "aims." He advises preachers to develop a "focus statement" as a brief statement of the sermon's *idea or what it will be about, and a "function statement" or brief description of what the preacher desires the sermon to "cause to happen" for the hearers.

The process of deciding on a sermon's focus and function is extremely useful, especially for preachers engaging in some form of *expository preaching. Long encourages an integral *relationship* between what a sermon says and what a sermon does. Preachers should attend, therefore, not only to the need to have a clear and unified sermon theme; they should also be certain this message is integrally related to a particular purpose. Unlike those who would bind the purpose of a sermon to the sermon's genre (*evangelistic, *prophetic, *pastoral, etc.), Long's approach allows each sermon to have a very specific, textually grounded, and congregationally sensitized purpose.

Thomas G. Long, *The Witness of Preaching*, 2nd ed. (Louisville, KY: Westminster John Knox Press, 2005).

fool   *A biblical image of the preacher as one whose message is scandalous and foolish when measured by the standards of human culture.*

The tradition of the preacher as a holy fool extends back to the scandalous behavior of Jesus in relation to the religious establishment of his day. Paul contrasts "God's foolishness" with the "wisdom of the world" and tells the Corinthian church that "God decided, through the foolishness of our proclamation, to save those who believe" (1 Cor. 1:21). Probably the best-known holy fool was St. Basil the Blessed, or Vasily, a Russian Orthodox saint known for his rebukes of Ivan the Terrible. Basil became a street preacher who went about naked and weighed himself down with chains. Preachers in the tradition of the holy fool have seen this identity as an invitation to confront those who consider themselves worldly wise, especially those who are in positions of wealth and power, with the foolishness of the cross, which is found in weakness, peacemaking, and charity.

The preacher who takes on the identity of the fool is also keenly aware of what John B. Rogers calls the "impossible possibility" of preaching, the strange mystery that God will work for the salvation of the world through the paltry words of a handful of preachers. The sense that preaching is foolishness is increased by the fact that, in today's context, in which empirical quantification of results in terms of numbers is the measure of effectiveness, there is no real way to measure this salvation. As Ian Pitt-Watson points out, preaching becomes even more of a foolish impossibility in a postmodern age in which all forms of authoritative speech have come under suspicion. And yet, in the midst of this, preachers continue to say, "Thus saith the Lord."

More recently, the image of the preacher as fool for Christ is being attached to more countercultural forms of homiletics. Stanley Saunders and Charles Campbell, for instance, encourage students and preachers to engage in street preaching, confronting head-on the principalities and powers of this world, proclaiming the foolish gospel of love and peace in an apocalyptic context.

Ian Pitt-Watson, *Preaching: A Kind of Folly* (Philadelphia: Westminster Press, 1976); John B. Rogers Jr., "The Foolishness of Preaching," *Interpretation* 45, no. 3 (July 1991): 241–52; Robert Farrar Capon, *The Foolishness of Preaching: Proclaiming the Gospel against the Wisdom of the World* (Grand Rapids: Wm. B. Eerdmans Publishing Co., 1998); Peter C. Phan, "The Wisdom of Holy Fools in Postmodernity," *Theological Studies* 62 (2001): 730–52; Stanley P. Saunders and Charles L. Campbell, *The Word on the Street: Performing the Scriptures in the Urban Context* (Grand Rapids: Wm. B. Eerdmans Publishing Co., 2000); Charles L. Campbell, *The Word before the Powers: An Ethic of Preaching* (Louisville, KY: Westminster John Knox Press, 2002).

form   *The overarching shape of a sermon, based upon the arrangement or ordering of the sermon's parts.*

Midcentury homiletician Grady Davis strove for a deep, organic understanding of form, along the lines of the sermon's essence, with his concept of the sermon's *design. For most homileticians and preachers, however, a sermon's form is defined by the way that the parts of a sermon are arranged. In the field of *rhetoric, this is sometimes called the disposition of the elements of a speech.

In homiletics today, a wide variety of forms persist: *deductive, *inductive, *plot, verse-by-verse *expository, and so on, as well as a number of stock forms such as problem-solution, *law-gospel, spatial forms such as "on the one hand . . . on the other hand," and "in Ephesus . . . in Jerusalem," conditional forms such as "if this . . . then this . . . and also this," forms of indirection such as "not this . . . or this . . . but this," ambiguity/clarity, story forms (preaching as story), and so on. Basic homiletic textbooks are replete with descriptions of many of these forms.

In recent years, Leander Keck, Thomas G. Long, David Buttrick, and others have encouraged preachers to pay special attention to the literary forms in the Bible before deciding on the form of a sermon. If the biblical text takes the form of a hymn, parable, teaching, or story, preachers are encouraged to carry this same form into the pulpit.

More recently, conversational forms are being encouraged. These can be learned by listening to talk radio, or from the natural give and take of interpersonal or group conversations. The field of conversation analysis has also established a range of conversational forms. It is possible, for instance, to hold a collaborative sermon brainstorming session or "sermon round table" with laity and then allow the shape of that conversation to provide the form for this Sunday's sermon. For example, if the group argued about some aspect of meaning from a text, the shape of that argument might become the form of the sermon.

Whether derived from the biblical text, the shape of one's theme, stock forms, or the rich variety of ways in which human beings converse, the possibilities for sermon forms are virtually limitless. Some homileticians encourage preachers to use a variety of different models in order to sustain interest in the pulpit. Others encourage a narrowing of the range, in order to promote clarity.

Another good reason to narrow one's repertoire of forms issues from a preacher's practical theology of "truth." In *The Four Codes of Preaching*, I argued that the choice of a sermon form is a choice for the way in which truth manifests itself in preaching. Over a period of time, this choice goes a long way toward establishing and supporting a congregation's approach to Christian truth. More apologetic and defensive sermon forms (argument, debate, oppositional rhetoric), for instance, promote a view of truth as obvious, singular, and univocal. On the other end of the scale, more artistic forms (narrative, inductive, or imagistic) promote a view of truth as hidden, ambiguous, and plurivocal. Between these two extremes are two other choices. If the preacher chooses to use conversational forms, truth is tentative, emergent, hypothetical, and multivocal in nature (see *wager). If the preacher chooses assertive forms (deductive, law-gospel, or one of a variety of stock forms), truth is paradigmatic, conclusive, and warranted by traditions and experts. It is possible that mixing these forms unintentionally in one's preaching would over time communicate mixed messages about the nature of Christian truth.

Leander E. Keck, *The Bible in the Pulpit: The Renewal of Biblical Preaching* (Nashville: Abingdon Press, 1978); Thomas G. Long, *The Witness of Preaching*, 2nd ed. (Louisville, KY: Westminster John Knox Press, 2005); Eugene L. Lowry, *The Homiletical Plot: The Sermon as Narrative Art Form*, expanded edition (Louisville, KY: Westminster John Knox Press, 2001); John S. McClure, *The Roundtable Pulpit: Where Leadership and Preaching Meet* (Nashville: Abingdon, 1995); Thomas G. Long, *Preaching and the Literary Forms of the Bible* (Philadelphia: Fortress Press, 1989); David Buttrick, "Interpretation and Preaching," *Interpretation*, Jan. 1981, 46–58; Jolyon P. Mitchell, *Visually Speaking: Radio and the Renaissance of Preaching* (Louisville, KY: Westminster John Knox Press, 1999); Fred B. Craddock, *Preaching* (Nashville: Abingdon Press, 1985); Ronald J. Allen, *Interpreting the Gospel: An Introduction to Preaching* (St. Louis: Chalice Press, 1998); Ronald J. Allen, ed., *Patterns of Preaching: A Sermon Sampler* (St. Louis: Chalice Press, 1998); John S. McClure, *The Four Codes of Preaching: Rhetorical Strategies* (Minneapolis: Fortress Press, 1991; reprinted, Louisville, KY: Westminster John Knox Press, 2003).

funeral sermon   *A sermon on the occasion of a funeral.*

The prototype for the Christian funeral sermon is found at the empty tomb. According to Scripture, early that first Easter morning the women went to the tomb of Jesus, ostensibly to begin the funeral and burial process. When they arrived, they encountered the great mystery at the heart of the Christian faith: resurrection.

The purposes of the funeral sermon are essentially twofold. First, the funeral sermon is designed to help family members and friends confront the reality of the death of a loved one. This means, of course, that the preacher must take with all seriousness the very present grief and sense of loss among all who are mourning. Second, the funeral sermon is to offer comfort and hope. The comfort offered by the preacher is not the comfort of one who is trying to smooth over a difficult situation. Rather, the preacher offers comfort through the proclamation of the mystery of resurrection faith.

There are many issues and concerns confronting preachers at the time of a funeral. First, there is within our culture at large a burgeoning funeral business that, in many instances, has removed funerals from church sanctuaries. Sacred spaces, however, can promote healing and provide a supportive context for mourners. Whether the funeral takes place at the church or at the funeral home, the preacher can be prepared to claim both sacred space and sacred time. This can be accomplished by accentuating the *liturgical aspects of preaching.

A second issue is the public and, therefore, *evangelistic dimension of funeral preaching. At most funerals many persons who have no faith are present. This provides the opportunity for preachers to proclaim Christ as hope in the midst of the one crisis that all human beings inevitably face: death. This privilege is often abused, as preachers peddle fear of eternal damnation at the expense of resurrection hope. It is important for preachers to remain focused on the hope and comfort of the good news, instead of manipulating the fear of death.

A third issue is the strong cultural push toward eulogy in funeral services. The drive to eulogize begins with the obituary process, and preachers are often expected to turn their sermons into eulogies, incorporating a range of biographical and narrative embellishments. Funeral sermons, however, should not be spent canonizing the deceased. The expectation for eulogy that is present in a funeral service can be taken up by the preacher in the style of preaching. This style can be personal, attempting to capture something of the essence of the deceased's life and faith through simple references, inasmuch as these can be placed into service for the proclamation of the good news.

A final issue that confronts the preacher is the powerful emotion present during funerals. The trauma of grief often makes listening to any kind of sermon extremely difficult. The wisdom of most preachers regarding this is that it is sometimes easier to hear images than to hear logical propositions, assertions, or arguments. Brevity is also a good idea, since the attention span of mourners is likely to be shortened.

Robert Hughes counsels that preachers preparing the funeral sermon should remember all of the major players present at a funeral: the deceased, the family, the church congregation, the larger communion of saints, and friends who may or may not be Christians. At the intersection of all of these different stories, in which the deceased has played a particular role, the preacher can ask the question, "What is God doing here?" This process helps the preacher juxtapose the personal reality of the confrontation with death with the comfort and the good news of God's continued presence and mercy.

In the last analysis, as John Allyn Melloh asserts, the funeral sermon is mystagogical in nature. It is the preaching of one of the great mysteries of faith: resurrection. Funeral preaching attempts, in small ways, to break open that mystery and invite others to know something of its comfort and hope. To a greater or lesser extent, the Christian life, from baptism on, is a transition more deeply into this mystery. For the Christian, funeral preaching is always a reminder of what we already know, but need to know more deeply: that through our baptism we are being translated into a new life that is not our own, but resurrection life given to us in and through Jesus Christ.

Robert G. Hughes, *A Trumpet in Darkness: Preaching to Mourners* (Philadelphia: Fortress Press, 1985); Charles Hoffacker, *A Matter of Life and Death: Preaching at Funerals* (Cambridge, MA: Cowley Publications, 2002); R. C. Sonefeld, *Preaching the Funeral Homily: Proclaiming the Gospel of Heavenly Hope* (San Jose, CA: Resource Publications, 2000); John Allyn Melloh, "Homily or Eulogy: The Dilemma of Funeral Preaching," *Worship* 67, no. 6 (Nov. 1993): 502–18; Thomas G. Long, "The Funeral: Changing Patterns and Teachable Moments," *Journal for Preachers*, Easter 1996, 3–8.

gender *The socially and culturally constituted characteristics of preaching attributed to the different biological sexes.*

With the ordination of women by many Christian denominations in the twentieth century, the question of women's and men's distinctive ways of preaching has found its way into many preaching classrooms. This is a highly complex subject, and empirical communication studies are not altogether conclusive. Although one can fairly speak of distinctive characteristics of *feminist preaching, a form of preaching that grows out of strong commitments to justice for women, it is not as easy to speak in any universal or essential way about women's distinctive ways of sermon preparation or preaching.

The great majority of what is known about preaching is still based on an official form of pulpit communication that was, until recently, done primarily by
men. This is not to say, however, that preaching necessarily represents a wholly
masculine form of communicating. What we do know is that women and men
have communicated in very different *spaces* throughout the history of the
church. Men occupied the central institutional roles within the church. Women
preached in convents or other female enclaves, became *itinerant preachers on
the American frontier, or preached as moral advocates during the women's temperance movement, women's voting rights movement, child labor laws movement, and civil rights movement in the United States. These different spaces,
as one can imagine, have helped to shape very different models of communication for men and women, one more formal and attached to hierarchical church
leadership, and the other less formal, more relational, and often some form of
*testimony. In fact, as Roxanne Mountford points out, though we may not yet
be able to speak clearly about gendered *speech* in the pulpit, we can speak with
great assurance about the gendered *pulpit*, or the way that pulpit spaces have
been constructed by and for men to the exclusion of women. Further observation and study may also determine aspects of rhetoric, delivery, and content that
are indeed gendered, but most of this work has yet to be done.

The most important development in recent years has been the production
of books and resources designed to create a community of women preachers
who share their particular homiletic concerns, processes of sermon preparation, ideas about delivery, and finished sermons. By expanding this community of intentional conversation, women in the pulpit are forming a
community of support, mentoring, and learning that will teach us much in the
future about women's ways of preaching.

Roxanne Mountford, *The Gendered Pulpit: Preaching in American Protestant Spaces*
(Carbondale: Southern Illinois University Press, 2003); Jane V. Craske, *A
Woman's Perspective on Preaching* (Peterborough: Foundery Press, 2001); Beverly
Zink-Sawyer, *From Preachers to Suffragists: Woman's Rights and Religious Convic-
tion in the Lives of Three Nineteenth-Century American Clergywomen* (Louisville,
KY: Westminster John Knox Press, 2003); Jana Childers, ed., *Birthing the Ser-
mon: Women Preachers on the Creative Process* (St. Louis: Chalice Press, 2001);
Mary Donovan Turner and Mary Lin Hudson, *Saved from Silence: Finding
Women's Voice in Preaching* (St. Louis: Chalice Press, 1999); Elaine J. Lawless,
God's Peculiar People: Women's Voices and Folk Tradition in a Pentecostal Church (Lex-
ington: University Press of Kentucky, 2005); Teresa Fry L. Brown, *Weary Throats
and New Songs: Black Women Proclaiming God's Word* (Nashville: Abingdon Press,
2003); Phoebe Palmer, "The Great Army of Preaching Women," in Richard
Lischer, ed., *The Company of Preachers: Wisdom on Preaching, Augustine to the
Present* (Grand Rapids: Wm. B. Eerdmans Publishing Co., 2002), 90–97;
Eunjoo Mary Kim, *Women Preaching: Theology and Practice through the Ages*
(Cleveland: Pilgrim Press, 2004).

extojewis — *working / commentary*
digging to dele
genre

43

idolojewis — personal idea

genre *A category of preaching derived from long-standing conventions or expectations.*

Preaching genres are often confused with preaching *forms. Whereas forms are derived from the arrangement of the parts of a sermon (*inductive, *deductive, verse-by-verse *expository, etc.), sermon genres are based upon conventions of pulpit communication that have histories within the church. A first set of genres is rooted in conventions about how a sermon message is created or derived. In this instance, genre answers the question, What is most authoritative for the creation of the sermon? If the sermon is grounded primarily in biblical study and reflection, the larger genre is called *biblical preaching. If the sermon is derived from interaction primarily with church doctrine and theology, the sermon genre is *doctrinal preaching. If the sermon is begun through a preacher's interaction with current issues or everyday experiences or needs, the sermon is designated loosely as *topical preaching.

In the second case, sermon genre is derived not from the origins of the sermon, but from its destination or *purpose. If the sermon is designed for the purpose of converting others, it is called *evangelistic. If the sermon's purpose is to educate listeners, it is called a *teaching sermon. If it is meant to offer comfort and care for the community, it is called a *pastoral sermon. If it is for the purpose of promoting justice, it is called a *prophetic sermon.

Within each genre, sermons can take a variety of forms. For instance, biblical sermons might be expository (thematic or verse by verse) or *narrative in form. A doctrinal sermon might be deductive or inductive. A topical sermon might be inductive or deductive, or a problem-solution model might be used, and so on.

Genres of preaching are usually not thought through in great detail in relation to the actual traditions that give them birth and support them. They tend to be loosely descriptive in common parlance. There are, however, long-standing conventions of preaching and listening that accompany each genre, making them of ongoing importance today.

Haddon W. Robinson, *Biblical Preaching: The Development and Delivery of Expository Messages*, 2nd ed. (Grand Rapids: Baker Academic, 2001); Ronald J. Allen, *Preaching the Topical Sermon* (Louisville, KY: Westminster John Knox Press, 1992); Ronald J. Allen, *Preaching Is Believing: The Sermon as Theological Reflection* (Louisville, KY: Westminster John Knox Press, 2002); Ronald J. Allen, *The Teaching Sermon* (Nashville: Abingdon Press, 1995); G. Lee Ramsey Jr., *Care-full Preaching: From Sermon to Caring Community* (St. Louis: Chalice Press, 2000); Walter Brueggemann, *The Prophetic Imagination*, revised and updated edition (Minneapolis: Augsburg Fortress Press, 2001); Walter J. Burghardt, SJ, *Preaching the Just Word* (New Haven, CT: Yale University Press, 1996); Craig Loscalzo, *Evangelistic Preaching That Connects: Guidance in Shaping Fresh and Appealing Sermons* (Downers Grove, IL: InterVarsity Press, 1995).

gesture   *The movement of hands, arms, face, and body to reinforce the preacher's message.*

Preaching is not only *aural *communication. It is also, for those who are sighted, a powerfully visual event. Gesture is, perhaps, the central part of the *drama of preaching and its *embodiment. The amount, size, and role of gesturing in all human communication is highly context and tradition specific. These matters are also bound closely to local congregational expectations and social codes. In Euro-American and African American revivalist traditions, for instance, the use of highly pronounced gestures is common and expected. More reserved gestures are expected within many Euro-American mainline denominational traditions.

In whatever context, the basic rules for gesture remain the same. First and foremost, gestures should be closely integrated with the preacher's message. Nothing seems more contrived than the strange gesture that does not match what is being said. Second, gestures can send subtle, often unintended messages. A perpetually wagging or pointing finger can make listeners feel either put down or accused. A pounding fist or clapping hand can signal angry or even abusive intentions. Third, gestures are best when natural and uncontrived. This does not mean that gestures have to be small or restricted. Gestures are best when they grow out of the preacher's normal way of communicating, even if somewhat exaggerated. There are, of course, certain stock gestures that are expected within some traditions: the wiping of a brow, the removal of one's glasses, the hand on the hip, and so forth. These are exceptions, signaling the overriding power and importance of local expectations or preaching traditions.

Facial expression is also an important part of gesture in preaching. Here congruence with one's message is most crucial. If one is expressing joy or happiness, the face should not be frowning. If the sermon is expressing hopefulness, the face should not look fearful or anxious.

No matter what kind of visual gesture is involved, the preacher must work to discover the deepest possible congruence between word and gesture. Sermons are far more than words, and gestures are vital, visual servants that can make words much more powerful and meaningful for those in the pews.

———

Mitties de Champlain, "What to Do While Preaching," in John S. McClure, *Best Advice for Preaching* (Minneapolis: Fortress Press, 1998), 99–115; G. Robert Jacks, *Getting the Word Across: Speech Communication for Pastors and Lay Leaders* (Grand Rapids: Wm. B. Eerdmans Publishing Co., 1987).

gospel   *The message of good news proclaimed by Christian preachers.*

The heart and soul of preaching is the *good* news of God's redemptive grace and mercy. Whether preaching a text from the Hebrew Bible or from the New

Testament, preachers are fundamentally in the service of a God of redemption and hope. With this in mind, homiletic wisdom offers several suggestions. First, preachers should preach only what inspires them. Robin Meyers speaks of preaching as "self-persuasion." It is easy to finish several hours of exegesis only to arrive at a completely flat, moralistic, or insignificant message. Before preparing a sermon, preachers should take the time to ask whether the message they plan to bring is inspirational good news for their own life.

Second, preachers can examine their motives. Often preachers experience feelings of anger or frustration because congregations do not seem to be conforming to their expectations. These feelings can make them into preachers of bad news, literally or figuratively wagging fingers at listeners from the pulpit. Even in situations where righteous anger is called for, sermons should be motivated by the desire to preach redemption and hope.

Third, preachers can make sure that the good news preached is faithful to the biblical text. There is not only one good news message in the Bible. God's grace and mercy take many different shapes. Preachers can seek out the richness and variety of God's redemptive presence in the Bible. At the same time, preachers should realize that not every text is a bearer of good news. It is often necessary to reach for a hermeneutic of good news that allows for the large witness of the Bible to inform the sermon.

Fourth, although some occasions and biblical texts call for an imperative word from the pulpit, it is best to avoid both the hard and the soft imperative voice in preaching, unless they are first grounded in the solid indicative of God's grace. Preachers can weed out most of the language of "must," "should," "ought to," "let us," "we are called to," and substitute the language of identity, possibility, process, and vision. In this way, every sermon can declare that the church is a powerful agent of grace, living more deeply into its redemptive identity every day.

Finally preachers should regularly rethink their homiletic theology, especially their understanding of Christ in today's world, and the meaning of redemptive good news for their congregation: What do we really believe? What is God doing in our midst? Who is Jesus Christ and what is Christ's good news for our world today?

In recent years scholars have attempted to separate the idea of gospel from a narrow identification with the words of the Bible. Theologian Edward Farley has distinguished between preachers who preach the Bible and preachers who preach the gospel. He separates biblicist and fundamentalist preachers who preach propositions derived from the Bible from preachers who remember that the Bible is a form of witness, pointing to and proclaiming the gospel of Jesus Christ. Gospel then is an ongoing theological and eschatological reality that texts point to, but cannot contain. In another attempt to get at this larger meaning of the word "gospel," Fred Craddock extends the meaning of "gospel" to incorporate elements of natural theology discovered in God's creation and encourages preachers to preach "the gospel of God."

Edward Farley, *Practicing Gospel: Unconventional Thoughts on the Church's Ministry* (Louisville, KY: Westminster John Knox Press, 2003); Fred B. Craddock, "The Gospel of God," in Thomas G. Long and Edward Farley, eds., *Preaching as a Theological Task: World, Gospel, Scripture* (Louisville, KY: Westminster John Knox Press, 1996), 73–81; Burton Z Cooper and John S. McClure, *Claiming Theology in the Pulpit* (Louisville, KY: Westminster John Knox Press, 2003); Robin Meyers, *With Ears to Hear: Preaching as Self-Persuasion* (Cleveland: Pilgrim Press, 1993).

herald   *A biblical image for the preacher as messenger.*

The idea of the preacher as herald of God is rooted in Hebrew prophecy, especially the book of Isaiah. The crucial supporting text for Christian preachers is Romans 10:15: "How beautiful are the feet of those who bring good news." The New Testament word for herald is *keryx*, and the message the herald brings, the *proclamation, is the *kerygma*.

The idea of the herald focuses on the *message* of preaching. The herald is one who brings a message on behalf of another who is greater. The sermon is not the messenger's message, but God's. The image of the preacher as herald is closely associated with the theology of Karl Barth and some forms of *postliberal homiletics. In the words of Karl Barth, "Proclamation is human language through which God himself speaks, like the King through the mouth of his herald." The *personality, *ethos, or *authenticity of the preacher is of very little importance to the task of heralding. *Rhetoric and *poetics, and to some extent *delivery, are also of little significance. The preacher's task is to faithfully present the *message*, getting out of the way and letting God speak.

In African American traditions of preaching, the herald image is understood somewhat differently. Olin Moyd points out that Romans 10:15 includes an idea of "beauty," not the beauty of the physical feet of the messenger, but the beauty of the good news that shines through the messenger. It is important, therefore, that the messenger portray something of the beauty of the message in sermonic speech. Not only the message, therefore, but also the *articulation, *style, and delivery of the preacher, carries the divine *kerygma*.

Homileticians have debated the herald image in our generation. Clyde Fant, arguing that it denies the incarnational element of preaching, asserts that the earthen vessels through which the gospel is proclaimed are vital to the message itself. Thomas G. Long has argued that the image of the preacher as *witness is more balanced, conveying better both the convictional and communal elements of preaching. Lucy Rose notes that the herald image can be used to further deauthorize the importance of experience in preaching, excluding or suppressing the *voices of women and other minorities in the pulpit.

Although inadequate in many respects, the image of herald continues to be important for homiletics, because it expresses the centrality of God's action in preaching and reminds preachers *whose* message they are bringing to the church.

Karl Barth, *Church Dogmatics*, I/1, *The Doctrine of the Word of God*, G. T. Thompson, trans. (New York: Charles Scribner's Sons, 1936); D.W. Cleverly Ford, *The Ministry of the Word* (Grand Rapids: Wm. B. Eerdmans Publishing Co., 1979); Thomas G. Long, *The Witness of Preaching*, 2nd ed. (Louisville, KY: Westminster John Knox Press, 2005); André Resner Jr., *Preacher and Cross: Person and Message in Theology and Rhetoric* (Grand Rapids: Wm. B. Eerdmans Publishing Co., 1999); Olin P. Moyd, *The Sacred Art: Preaching and Theology in the African American Tradition* (Valley Forge, PA: Judson Press, 1995); Brad R. Braxton, *Preaching Paul* (Nashville: Abingdon Press, 2004); Clyde E. Fant, *Preaching for Today* (New York: Harper & Row, 1975); Lucy Atkinson Rose, *Sharing the Word: Preaching in the Roundtable Church* (Louisville, KY: Westminster John Knox Press, 1997).

hermeneutics   *The interpretation of the Bible for preaching.*

Biblical hermeneutics is a complex field of study. For the preacher, hermeneutics becomes the art of placing the biblical text into conversation with contemporary theology and life in order to arrive at something significant to say on Sunday morning. The idea of hermeneutics as conversation between ancient text and contemporary life comes from the philosopher Hans Georg Gadamer, who asserted that the final result of this conversation is a "fusion of horizons" between an ancient text and the modern interpreter.

There are five primary approaches to hermeneutics that have the most impact on preaching today. The first three approaches are *text-centered*; a fourth is *theology-centered*; a fifth is *context-centered*. The first text-centered model is *propositional translation*. In this model the preacher uses in sermons only the obvious language of the English Bible. What is behind the text (the historical, communal, and authorial background) and what is in front of the text (its formal, rhetorical, or literary qualities) recede into the background. The preacher attempts to derive a simple, common-sense proposition or *idea from the surface of the text that can then be translated by analogy into the contemporary context. This translation is best when historical and literary study of the text has already been done, informing the choice of an idea to preach. Historical and literary elements are then left behind and do not show up in the language of the sermon itself.

There are three substyles of propositional translation. In the first, *literal* translation, the preacher wants the listener to act or think in precisely the same terms used in the text. If the Bible says that the early church "spoke in tongues," the preacher reasserts this as a proposition to be literally translated into thought and action. At the other extreme from literal translation is *paraphrase*. In this approach, the translator becomes more aggressive, bringing ideological, allegorical, figurative, arcane, or even numerological interests to bear on the text.

The best form of propositional translation is sometimes called *dynamic equivalence* or *dynamic analogy*. The preacher strives to be faithful to the text while searching for roughly equivalent concepts or situations within the contemporary context. For instance, in the story of Mary and Martha, the biblical text says that Mary was "seated at his (Jesus') feet." In a literal translation, this would mean that *all women named Mary* should sit at Jesus' feet in a posture of learning. This severely distorts the meaning of the text. On the other hand, the preacher might paraphrase the text and turn Mary into a representative of true believers who will one day sit at the feet of Jesus in glory. Again, this distorts the meaning of the text by turning it into an allegory. Using dynamic equivalence, the preacher might notice that Mary, a woman, was being taught by a rabbi, an act that encourages us to consider more deeply the role of women in Jesus' ministry and in the ministry today.

The second text-centered hermeneutical approach is *historical continuity*. In this approach, the preacher will usually pass over the analogies suggested by the obvious features of the text and draw forth an interpretation from what is behind the text, the historical context out of which the words of the page arise. The preacher may even hint at the naiveté of a simple, propositional translation, because it lacks an appropriate understanding of the historical distance between the first century and today. The sermon will typically demonstrate some struggle to get at the meaning of the text, since it is hidden from plain view and requires a special interpreter (hermeneut) to be unearthed. Instead of preaching sermons that ask the congregation to live lives that are dynamically equivalent to biblical characters and thoughts, listeners are invited to be involved in a community striving to live *in continuity* with the ancient community of faith. The preacher will identify historical, social, and cultural coordinates in the biblical text, such as exodus, exile, and empire, or speak about the difficulties of being a believer in "Matthew's congregation," or "in Corinth." Listeners will be encouraged to discover similar historical, social, and cultural issues today, such as oppression, war, cultural displacement, idolatry, and interreligious conflict, and to place today's church into a relationship of historical continuity with its ancient past.

The third text-centered hermeneutical model is *literary transposition*. In the theory of music, the word "transposition" means "to have the same structure, yet in a different key." In literary transposition, the biblical text becomes the rhetorical model for preaching. The sermon strives, in some way, to *do* rhetorically what the biblical text does or intends, but in a new key. Common-sense meanings within the text and historical continuities are pushed into the background, and the *performative aspects of the language operating in front of the text become most important for interpretation. Another way to think of this is to say that the *how* of the text is more important than the *what* of the text. Since language is formative of consciousness, the sermon seeks to promote, through language, the same strange and ancient forms of Christian consciousness expressed by the biblical text (doxology, lament, parabolic reversal, etc.). As David Buttrick puts it, sermons "replot plots" and "reintend intentional language." According to Leander Keck, the sermon should "impart a Bible-shaped Word in a Bible-like way."

The fourth approach, *theological transformation*, is not text centered, but theology centered. In this approach, the preacher goes in search of the theological or christological *claims* of the text. The preacher's understanding of those claims becomes central to the interpretive task. If the preacher is a liberation theologian, those claims will have to do with some aspect of divine justice. If the preacher has what Gustav Aulén calls a "Christus Victor" theology, the preacher will look for the ways the text exposes and confonts the principalities and powers in the world. If the preacher is a conservative evangelical theologian, the claims of the text will center in the need for a personal relationship with Jesus Christ. No matter what text is preached, there is a divine presence between the lines of the biblical text in control of the interpretive process, guiding the preacher toward the deeper theological claims of the text. Theological transformation brings with it a stronger affective element than do the first three approaches. The Scripture bears witness to a living and evocative agent who wants to make a claim on, encounter, confront, shake, break into, or disrupt listeners' lives.

The final hermeneutical approach used by preachers today is a *contextual* hermeneutic. In this approach the Bible contains an inner meaning, hidden from view, awaiting this particular moment in history and this particular situation so that it might be drawn out into plain view. This inner meaning might not be unique. It could have been discovered before, but it is always developing further implications and meanings as it is interpreted in different epochs and situations. For instance, the deeper meaning of the Bible regarding slavery did not come into plain view until the modern civil rights movement came along and brought out latent meanings for Pauline phrases such as "no longer slaves." Hidden meanings for forgiveness in the Bible could not have been discovered until issues of domestic violence and apartheid came into view. The contextual interpreter reads the Bible by peering at it between the lines of today's cultural and social texts, looking for ways in which the context for faith today becomes a catalyst for the discovery of new implications or trajectories of meaning.

The most common contextual hermeneutic is sometimes called the "hermeneutic of suspicion." Justo González and Catherine González demonstrate how an assessment of the current situation and experience of injustice lead the interpreter to be suspicious of traditional interpretations, wondering if they harbor subtexts of oppression or domination. From there, the preacher critiques the current situation, theology, and interpretations of the Bible. Then the preacher decides on a new way of interpreting and experiencing the text, theology, and current situation.

Most preachers are not hermeneutical purists. They range back and forth among these approaches. Some consistently combine two or three in a unique configuration. In some cases, this combination is expected within a preaching tradition. James Earl Massey, for instance, argues that within the African American tradition preachers are expected to combine propositional translation, or "the adequacy and immediacy of the biblical witness," with theological transformation, "the centrality of preaching as an agency for hearing and faith," and a contextual hermeneutic emphasizing "the importance of the hearer's situation in planning the sermon." Leonora Tubbs Tisdale speaks of contextual hermeneutics as an intensely local phenomenon best accomplished through *congregational study, but desires Scripture, or textual models of hermeneutics, to remain the "leading partner" in the "dance of interpretation." Reflecting on Asian American preaching, Eunjoo Mary Kim proposes a hermeneutic that mixes a liberating theological hermeneutic and a more literary "metaphorical" form of interpretation. When writing about hermeneutics in the context of poverty, David Buttrick juxtaposes a liberating theological hermeneutic with a literary, narrative model in which "the stories of God . . . also happen to be our stories." It may well be that preachers should learn all five approaches, and then attempt to become self-conscious and intentional as biblical interpreters, combining hermeneutical approaches that will work best in their situation.

John S. McClure, *The Four Codes of Preaching: Rhetorical Strategies* (Minneapolis: Fortress Press, 1991; reprinted, Louisville, KY: Westminster John Knox Press, 2003); Gabriel Fackre, *The Christian Story: A Pastoral Systematics*, vol. 2 (Grand Rapids: Wm. B. Eerdmans Publishing Co., 1987); Stephen Farris, *Preaching That Matters: The Bible and Our Lives* (Louisville, KY: Westminster John Knox Press, 1998); David Buttrick, "Interpretation and Preaching," *Interpretation*, Jan. 1981, 46–58; Thomas G. Long, "Shaping Sermons by Plotting the Text's Claim upon Us," in Don Wardlaw, ed., *Preaching Biblically: Sermons in the Shape of Scripture* (Philadelphia: Westminster Press, 1983), 84–100; Thomas G. Long, *Preaching and the Literary Forms of the Bible* (Philadelphia: Fortress Press, 1989); Leander Keck, *The Bible in the Pulpit: The Renewal of Biblical Preaching* (Nashville: Abingdon Press, 1978); Ernest Best, *From Text to Sermon: Responsible Use of the New*

Testament in Preaching (Atlanta: John Knox Press, 1978); Donald K. McKim, *A Guide to Contemporary Hermeneutics: Major Trends in Biblical Interpretation* (Grand Rapids: Wm. B. Eerdmans Publishing Co., 1986); Raymond Bailey, ed., *Hermeneutics for Preaching: Approaches to Contemporary Interpretation of Scripture* (Nashville: Broadman Press, 1992); David Jasper, *A Short Introduction to Hermeneutics* (Louisville, KY: Westminster John Knox Press, 2004); Justo L. González and Catherine G. González, *The Liberating Pulpit* (Nashville: Abingdon Press, 1994); Walter Dietrich and Ulrich Luz, eds., *The Bible in a World Context: An Experiment in Contextual Hermeneutics* (Grand Rapids: Wm. B. Eerdmans Publishing Co., 2002); Brad R. Braxton, *No Longer Slaves: Galatians and African American Experience* (Collegeville, MN: Liturgical Press, 2002); David G. Buttrick, "Preaching, Hermeneutics, and Liberation," in Paul Plenge Parker, ed., *Standing with the Poor: Theological Reflections on Economic Reality* (Cleveland: Pilgrim Press, 1992), 95–105; James Earl Massey, "Hermeneutics for Preaching," *Review and Expositor* 90, no. 3 (1993): 359–69; Leonora Tubbs Tisdale, *Preaching as Local Theology and Folk Art* (Minneapolis: Fortress Press, 1997); Eunjoo Mary Kim, "Hermeneutics and Asian American Preaching," *Semeia* 90–91, no. 1 (2002): 269–90; Gustav Aulén, *Christus Victor: An Historical Study of the Three Main Types of the Idea of the Atonement* (London: SPCK Press, 1931).

homily   *A concise *liturgical sermon.*

The word "homily" comes from the Latin word *homilia*, which translates the Greek word for conversation, discourse, or address. This term is primarily used in Roman Catholic and Episcopal contexts. Charles Rice contrasts the "extended sermon" with the "concise homily," and asserts that homilies are short, "liturgy-friendly" discourses preceding the Eucharist. Homilies have often been associated with the teaching of doctrine or moral lessons. Christopher Webber also points out that homilies are closely associated with *occasional preaching, especially *weddings, *funerals, and baptisms. With the renewed interest in preaching in the Roman Catholic Church since Vatican II, the word "homily" is heard more often today. Due probably to increased ecumenical dialogue, *"sermon" and "homily" have become more or less interchangeable in recent years.

Charles L. Rice, *The Embodied Word: Preaching as Art and Liturgy* (Minneapolis: Fortress Press, 1991); Christopher L. Webber, *The Art of the Homily* (Harrisburg, PA: Morehouse Publishing Co., 1992); Robert P. Waznak, SS, *An Introduction to the Homily* (Collegeville, MN: Liturgical Press, 1998).

hum   *Another word for the dynamics of *call and response in African American preaching and in some Euro-American folk preaching.*

humor   *The purposeful encouragement of laughter in preaching.*

Humor has ancient, biblical warrant (Sarah's laughter, Balaam's ass, God's laughter in Psalm 2:4, Jesus' parables, etc.). Both Henry Ward Beecher and

Charles G. Finney in the 1800s used humor to communicate the gospel. The undercurrent of joy that accompanies the proclamation of good news is naturally accompanied by laughter. This does not mean that the preacher becomes a joke teller. Nevertheless, humor can turn the listener away from oneself and toward God. As William Willimon puts it, humor can assist the preacher in "taking God a little more seriously and ourselves a little less so."

Some homileticians connect humor with the way listeners perceive the preacher, arguing that it promotes *authenticity and *ethos in preaching and can function to unite preacher and congregation. Many encourage humor in sermon introductions as a way of "breaking the ice." David Buttrick suggests caution, however; he argues that humor in sermon introductions (and elsewhere) can focus too much attention on the preacher, saying, "Look, I'm a funny, likable person." It can also trivialize a message that is otherwise serious in nature.

Willimon argues that humor is best when it (1) arises out of the interaction between the biblical text and the congregation, perhaps in a way that points up shared foibles, (2) is natural for the preacher's own style and *personality, (3) is congruent with the purposes of Christian communication (as opposed to the barroom or office party), and (4) does not violate the liturgical and congregational context.

In African American preaching, humor accompanies the joy and liberation expressed during times of *celebration. Laughter, shouting, and exclamations of praise become mixed together during these special times of release and doxology.

In all instances, humor should not be used for its own sake, but should be relevant to the *idea expressed in the sermon. It should express the shared humility of preacher and *listener before a God who overturns our expectations and topples our self-serious agendas, and should always embody the joy of the gospel.

John Buchanan, "Punch Line: Sermonic Joke-Telling Is a Precarious Business," *Christian Century* 120, no. 16 (Aug. 9, 2003): 3; Danny Harrell, "This Is Not Your Father's Preaching Style: How to Speak the Language of the 'Whatever' Generation," *Leadership: A Practical Journal for Church Leaders,* Summer 1998, 83–84; Elizabeth Achtemeier, *Creative Preaching: Finding the Words* (Nashville: Abingdon Press, 1980); Walter J. Burghardt, SJ, *Preaching: The Art and the Craft* (New York: Paulist Press, 1987); David Buttrick, *Homiletic: Moves and Structures* (Philadelphia: Fortress Press, 1987); William H. Willimon, "Humor," in William H. Willimon and Richard Lischer, eds., *Concise Encyclopedia of Preaching* (Louisville, KY: Westminster John Knox Press, 1995), 262–64; Thomas E. Troxell, "Humor as a Preaching Tool," *Military Chaplain's Review* 15, no. 1 (Winter 1986): 59–63; Wesley W. Nelson, "Taking Pulpit Humor Seriously," *Covenant Quarterly* 56, no. 2 (May 1998): 3–14; James R. Barnette, "Using Humor in Preaching: An Interview with Bob Russell," *Preaching* 10, no. 5 (Mar.–Apr. 1995):

5–10; James R. Barnette, "A Time to Laugh: Principles of Good Pulpit Humor," *Preaching* 11, no. 5 (Mar.–Apr. 1996): 1–11; Eugene T. Sutton, "And for Preachers . . . Humor," *Perspectives*, Oct. 1991, n/a; John Vannorsdall, "Humor as Content and Device in Preaching," *Dialog* 22 (Summer 1983): 187–90.

idea   *The central *theme of a sermon.*

A sermon's central idea can be derived from the biblical text, as is usually the case in *biblical preaching, or taken from a lively conversation between a pressing social or personal topic and the Bible, as in *topical preaching. Every *genre and *form of preaching *must have a unifying idea or theme*. Although this idea will be divided into several parts, depending on the form a sermon takes, it is important, by the end of every sermon, that a complete idea has been expressed.

At some point during the sermon preparation process, preachers can write down a "theme-statement," "focus-statement," "thesis-statement," "central proposition," "main thought," or "central idea." Haddon Robinson calls this the sermon's "big idea." Most homileticians make it clear that a sermon's idea has both a subject and a predicate. The subject is whatever the preacher will be *talking about*. The predicate, or complement of that subject, is what the preacher will be *saying about the subject*. A preacher, therefore, does not have a theme or sermon idea when there is only a subject: love, hope, peace, faith. These are subjects without predicates, words without complements.

Of course, preachers can arrive at ideas to preach that are untrue, unbelievable, or simply insignificant. It is important for preachers to preach not only their *conclusions*, based upon biblical exegesis and the study of life, but also their *convictions*, ideas they know to be true, believable, and important.

Besides being significant, sermon ideas should be singular and focused. Paul Scott Wilson encourages preachers to develop sermon ideas that express a singular doctrine, address a single need in the congregation or world, and promote a single mission or *application when it comes to the actual living out of Christian faith.

Fred Craddock encourages preachers to shape sermon ideas in the affirmative rather than the imperative, in order to avoid moralistic messages. Paul Scott Wilson broadens this, insisting that sermon ideas should avoid, at all costs, placing the weight of redemptive action on human beings rather than onto God. It is important, therefore, when crafting a sermon idea, to avoid the imperative voice: "we are called to," "let us," "we must," "we should," "we have to," "God calls us . . ."

It is helpful to state a sermon idea in a simple rather than compound sentence. Not everything to be said in a sermon will be said in its sermon idea or theme statement. Much will be implied in the statement and left to the sermon's *development. Avoid questions when shaping sermon ideas. Questions usually indicate that a preacher is not ready to identify a clear topic, has a subject but no predicate, or has something to say, but is reluctant to state it. For this reason, state sermon ideas in theme statements that are declarative and not interrogative in nature.

The idea of a sermon is the central organizing principle for sermon construction. Although some will argue that too much emphasis on idea forces preachers to adopt more assertive and *deductive forms of preaching, this is not the case. *Inductive or *narrative forms that delay the arrival of a sermon's full idea nonetheless require a complete idea.

H. Grady Davis, *Design for Preaching* (Philadelphia: Fortress Press, 1958); Haddon W. Robinson, *Biblical Preaching: The Development and Delivery of Expository Messages*, 2nd ed. (Grand Rapids: Baker Academic, 2001); Paul Scott Wilson, *The Four Pages of the Sermon: A Guide to Biblical Preaching* (Nashville: Abingdon Press, 1999); Fred Craddock, *Preaching* (Nashville: Abingdon Press, 1985).

identification   *The ability of a speaker to speak another person's language through the use of matching forms of speech, gestures, intonations, images, ideas, and attitudes.*

Rhetorician Kenneth Burke used the term "identification" to replace the term "persuasion" as the key to the New Rhetoric. The goal of *rhetoric for Burke is *cooperation*, not persuasion, and this is achieved primarily when a speaker identifies his or her ways with the listener's. Sometimes preachers and listeners use the language of "connection" to express this quality in good preaching: "She connects with me." "He makes a connection with my life." Developmental psychologists attribute this rhetorical element to empathic role-taking skills developed in early childhood, when children demonstrate the ability to "get into someone else's shoes." Identification, however, involves more than *empathy. It involves the ability to actually take on another person's entire mode of being and communicating, at nearly every possible level. Identification, therefore, creates a *rhetoric of listening* that involves a deep level of cooperation between the preacher and the listener.

In many respects, the *inductive preaching movement, attributed to the influence of Fred Craddock, is built around this principle of identification. Inductive method seeks a deep cooperation between speaker and listener through identification, allowing the particulars of shared experiences—such as gestures, intonations, ideas, patterns of thought, and attitudes—to move both speaker and listener toward a common destination. The inductive preacher consults the life world of the listener for experiences that can be incorporated into the sermon. The result is a form of preaching that resembles joint prob-

illustration   55

lem solving, placing preacher and hearer on level ground in pursuit of clues to the solution of common problems. It is easy to see, then, how inductive preaching respects Burke's desire that rhetoric move away from persuasion toward cooperation.

The assumption that speaker and listener can arrive at a place where their experiences are, in some real sense, interchangeable, has been challenged in postmodern rhetorical theories, and by proponents of *collaborative preaching and *testimony. These critics argue that the focus on cooperation, mutuality, and consensus may obscure how different the experiences and life world of two people may, in fact, be. The search for symmetry between speaker and listener may preclude respect for the listener as truly *other*. Although this is clearly not Burke's or Craddock's intention, it is certainly something to keep in mind when thinking about ways to overcome the troublesome aspects of persuasion and promote cooperative models of preaching.

Kenneth Burke, *A Rhetoric of Motives* (Berkeley: University of California Press, 1969); Craig A. Loscalzo, *Preaching Sermons That Connect: Effective Communication through Identification* (Downers Grove, IL: InterVarsity Press, 1992); Fred B. Craddock, *As One without Authority*, revised and with new sermons (St. Louis: Chalice Press, 2001); Lucy Rose, *Sharing the Word: Preaching in the Roundtable Church* (Louisville, KY: Westminster John Knox Press, 1997); John S. McClure, *The Roundtable Pulpit: Where Leadership and Preaching Meet* (Nashville: Abingdon Press, 1995); John S. McClure, *Other-wise Preaching: A Postmodern Ethic for Homiletics* (St. Louis: Chalice Press, 2001).

illustration   *That which "brings light to" or clarifies the sermon's meaning.*

According to Fred Craddock, the sermon illustration answers the question, "For instance?" Illustrations take many shapes in sermons: examples, quotations, descriptions, snapshots of life, brief stories or anecdotes, word pictures, characterizations.

The concept of illustration has been the topic of a great deal of critical conversation in contemporary homiletic theory. The rationalist and utilitarian assumption that illustrations are simply persuasive tools in service of sermon *"points" has been challenged by homileticians with deeper poetic sensitivities. They have argued that illustrations can indeed *be* the point and need not be wholly subservient to a sermon's rational content.

Thomas G. Long argues for three basic types of illustrative material. In the *simile-type*, preachers offer a story or slice of life that is *like* what is being talked about. In the *synecdoche-type*, the preacher searches for a slice of life that is, in fact, a partial picture of the larger idea under discussion. In moving from simile to *synecdoche, the preacher moves from *likeness* to *isness*. In the *metaphor-type*, the preacher juxtaposes an experience with a concept and allows listeners to draw out the connections between them on their own.

Advice regarding sermon illustration abounds. First, the best illustrations come from the preacher's own observations, reading, and experience, not from books or online services of canned illustrations. Preachers need to develop what Leander Keck once called "priestly listening," the ability to identify God's presence within the full range of life experience. Second, illustrations need to closely match the ideas being developed. This is a matter of both content and *tone (positive/negative). If the sermon's thought is serious and ponderous, the illustration should not be humorous or light. If the content is humorous or joyous, illustrations should follow suit. Third, most homileticians, remembering that attention spans are not what they used to be, encourage brevity in illustration. Fourth, illustrations should not be buttressed by long-winded explanations. This is similar to the joke told so poorly that it requires unpacking. Illustrations do not exist to be exegeted. Fifth, preachers should avoid *plagiarism when illustrating. Credit is easily given where it is due. Sixth, illustrations should be in the public domain. Preachers must be very careful not to betray confidences, using stories that disclose intimate details of the lives of persons in the congregation or community. Seventh, sermon illustrations should not be focused entirely on *self-disclosure. The debate on the use of oneself in sermon illustrations is extremely complex. Most homileticians encourage preachers to use themselves sparingly in stories. When they are necessary, illustrations involving the preacher are best done when the preacher remains behind the lens of the camera, rather than getting around in front—and certainly not up close in the zoom lens. Finally, there is some debate over the relative frequency of sermon illustrations. David Buttrick encourages preachers to limit themselves to one piece of illustrative material per sermon *move. Others allow some flexibility, arguing that multiple examples can increase clarity or encourage a broader range of application. In all cases, additional illustrations should not lead to new thoughts or overly complicate the idea illustrated.

The work of illustration is closely tied to the way that *culture is encoded in sermons. For this reason, preachers need to be extremely careful over the course of time about their choices of illustrations, in order to avoid promoting stereotypes or ideologies that run contrary to their best intentions. Preachers can regularly take stock of the various cultural stereotypes and ideologies that are present in their illustrative material.

At the same time, sermon illustrations are the subtle—or not so subtle— bearers of the relationship between what H. Richard Niebuhr calls "Christ and culture." The preacher who tells stories that closely identify the gospel with the very surface features of popular culture is promoting the "Christ of culture" model. The preacher who uses synecdoche-type illustrations that attempt to synthesize the sermon's meaning with deep or profound parts of experience or culture is representing the "Christ above culture" model. If the church or an individual believer is an agent of redemptive change within stories or illustrations, illustrations can represent "Christ transforming culture." Simile-type illustrations, if used over an extended period of time, tend to separate Christ and culture. In this more utilitarian approach, illustrations are primarily analogies to help preachers "make a point"; the gospel of Christ is identified with cognitive points or ideas only, separated from illustrative experience that can *shed light on* but not *be* the point. This tends to support Niebuhr's dualist or "Christ and culture in paradox" model, in which gospel and culture are on two separate tracks. Finally, if examples or illustrations of the good news of Jesus Christ are found only in the church or its witness, and the bad news is located only in culture or "the world," a separatist or "Christ against culture" model is conveyed. Because illustrations subtly communicate this deeper theological ethic, it is a good idea for preachers to become aware of their tendencies and to make clear decisions about the way they usually illustrate sermons based on their ethical commitments.

In the last analysis, sermon illustrations are needed for sermons to be understood and brought home. Like trying on clothes, illustrations allow listeners to see how sermon ideas fit their own lives. Preachers, therefore, need to allow ample time to design and weave illustrations into their sermons.

Thomas G. Long, *The Witness of Preaching*, 2nd ed. (Louisville, KY: Westminster John Knox Press, 2005); Fred B. Craddock, *Preaching* (Nashville: Abingdon Press, 1985); David Buttrick, *Homiletic: Moves and Structures* (Philadelphia: Fortress Press, 1987); John McClure, *The Four Codes of Preaching: Rhetorical Strategies* (Minneapolis: Fortress Press, 1991; reprinted, Louisville, KY: Westminster John Knox Press, 2003); John S. McClure, "The Other Side of Sermon Illustration," *Journal for Preachers* 12 (1989): 2–4; Richard L. Thulin, *The "I" of the Sermon: Autobiography in the Pulpit* (Eugene, OR: Wipf & Stock, 2004); H. Richard Niebuhr, *Christ and Culture* (New York: Harper & Row, 1951).

image   *A visual or sensory representation or presentation of meaning.*

The image has a long history in the field of *poetics. It is also much discussed in media studies. The current generation has been raised in a visual culture replete with movies, television, and computers. Those in church on Sunday mornings expect something of the immediacy, vividness, and sensory engagement that is supplied by images.

In the field of homiletics, David Buttrick and Mary Catherine Hilkert assert in different ways that preaching is grounded in a form of symbolic revelation that is mediated to us through images. For both, the image exists as a unique wedding of thought and imagination having the power to touch people far more deeply than rational discourse. By activating the listener's imagination during preaching, images can take thought beyond itself.

There are two types of images, representational and presentational. Each grows out of the priority granted to thought, on the one hand, or imagination, on the other. When thought is granted priority, images are *representational*; images stand in for thoughts or words. The image "yellow globe," for instance, is an image that might represent or stand in for the word "moon."

When imagination is granted priority, images become *presentational*. According to the poet Ezra Pound, it is possible that the image "presents an emotional complex in an instant of time." When images are presentational, the image takes priority, giving rise to thought. In order for presentational images to function correctly, the context or situation for an image must be clear. When the preacher tells a story about someone being fooled by a prank on April Fools' Day and describes the poor victim as "red-faced," the preacher does not need to say that the person was embarrassed. The image, used in a particular context, has already accomplished the task of presenting this thought to the listener.

Thomas Troeger points out that the best imagery is achieved through "logosomatic language," language in which meaning and embodied experience are caught up together in such a way that what is spoken in the sermon becomes "as vivid as a drawing." This is the reason, he says, children's sermons are so often more powerful than adult sermons.

One of the keys to finding the appropriate image for a thought is to reflect theologically on the thought itself. Often, the thought for which the preacher seeks an image is too general, lacking particularity. If the preacher is searching for an image for "sin," for example, it is important to do enough theological reflection to determine whether sin in this instance is disobedience, idolatry, pride, hiding, structural sin, personal sin, or something else. As the idea becomes more focused and particular, concrete images are more likely to present themselves.

Patricia Wilson-Kastner reminds preachers to be careful to investigate how an image portrays God and God's relationship to human beings. She also urges caution regarding the possibility of unchecked relationships between a chosen image and another that might be unwanted. She encourages imagery that is (1) common and immediately familiar to the listener, (2) multidimensional and able to invoke and sustain a plurality of meanings, and (3) open-ended, in order to provoke active and creative thought.

Images are pervasive to sermons. They are embedded in word pictures, metaphors, examples, *illustrations, turns of phrase, and allusions, and can be reinforced by bodily *postures and tones of voice. David Buttrick calls this pervasive aspect of a sermon the "image grid." I have called it "the cultural code." Patricia Kastner-Wilson uses the literary term "imagery." Sometimes it is called "illustrative development." All are terms denoting the total image field in a sermon.

Thomas Troeger, *Imagining a Sermon* (Nashville: Abingdon Press, 1990); David Buttrick, *Homiletic: Moves and Structures* (Philadelphia: Fortress Press, 1987); Mary Catherine Hilkert, *Naming Grace: Preaching and the Sacramental Imagination* (New York: Continuum, 2003); Ezra Pound, "A Few Don'ts by an Imagiste," *Poetry* (Chicago) 1 (1913): 198–206; John S. McClure, *The Four Codes of Preaching: Rhetorical Strategies* (Minneapolis: Fortress Press, 1991, reprinted, Louisville, KY: Westminster John Knox Press, 2003); Patricia Wilson-Kastner, *Images for Preaching* (Minneapolis: Fortress Press, 1989).

imagination   *The cognitive faculty of forming and projecting *images.*

Preachers who identify with the *New Homiletic have become far more interested in the poetic and artistic aspects of preaching and have found older rhetorical approaches less interesting. As a result, Thomas Troeger asserts that over the last thirty years homiletics has changed from sacred *rhetoric into "imaginative theology."

In the first place, the word "imagination" describes the total generative worldview projected in a preacher's sermons. Many forms of imagination are imputed to preachers. Mary Catherine Hilkert describes at work in most Reformation traditions of preaching a "dialectical imagination" that stresses the otherness of God, the pervasiveness of human sin, the paradox of the crucifixion, the moral ambiguity of human existence, and future forms of eschatology. In the Roman Catholic tradition Hilkert identifies a "sacramental imagination" that emphasizes the presence of God in creation and incarnation, the church as sacrament of salvation, and a more realized form of eschatology. Walter Brueggemann encourages preachers to develop a "prophetic imagination," capable of reconstruing reality in terms defined by the biblical prophets. For Brueggemann, imagination is the power to reframe existence as it is seen by God. Fred Craddock underscores "empathetic imagination," preachers' ability to attend closely to the world around them, to receive the world as others receive it, and to find appropriate ways to reflect this reception of the world in images. Ellen Davis speaks of the preacher's "exegetical imagination" and "interpretative imagination" as a way to describe what happens when preachers enter the biblical world and interpret it for preaching. She also argues for a "critical imagination" as crucial for moral discernment in the reading and interpretation of Scripture.

The second use of the word "imagination" in preaching refers to the cognitive faculty used by preachers to discern and shape particular images for preaching. Some theorists of knowledge have argued that imagination is not so much about fantasy and the creation of imaginative worlds, as it is a means of *knowing* more about reality itself. Ian Barbour, Sallie McFague, and Garrett Green have demonstrated that imagination is a way of using symbols to probe the mysterious depth of reality. Just as scientists cannot find certain subatomic particles but must imagine them in order to make sense of reality, so theologians and preachers posit such things as evil to make sense of certain known and experienced realities.

Creativity theorists and practical theologians such as James E. Loder have pointed out that imagination functions by going outside the box in order to resolve cognitive tension or conflict. Paul Scott Wilson shows how the preacher's imagination works to resolve the tension experienced between polarities of existence and in the tensions that exist in homiletic practice itself. When the preacher experiences cognitive conflict, the preacher's mind begins to scan for resolving images. These images accomplish two things: (1) they hold together the tension, and (2) they suggest a resolution. In the preacher's workshop, there are many great theological fulcrums for this tensional imaginative process: judgment and grace, despair and hope, life and death, evil and goodness, and so forth.

Richard Eslinger describes four steps of homiletic imagination involved in *biblical preaching as the preacher moves from cognitive conflict to sermonic resolution. First, the preacher's imagination *conforms* deeply to a tradition and worldview. Second, preachers exercise *patience* as they attend carefully to the biblical witness, identifying the range of issues or problems raised by the text. Third, preachers begin to think *sermonically* as they wrestle with the tensional convergence of tradition, Scripture, and their own preaching context. Finally, preachers begin to think *paradigmatically* as they undergo paradigm shifts and discover new insights that will shape the thought and imagery of preaching.

Mary Catherine Hilkert, *Naming Grace: Preaching and the Sacramental Imagination* (New York: Continuum International Publishing, 2003); David Buttrick, *Homiletic: Moves and Structures* (Philadelphia: Fortress Press, 1987); Richard L. Eslinger, *Narrative and Imagination: Preaching the Worlds That Shape Us* (Minneapolis: Fortress Press, 1995); Ellen F. Davis, *Imagination Shaped: Old Testament Preaching in the Anglican Tradition* (Valley Forge, PA: Trinity Press International, 1995); Fred B. Craddock, *As One without Authority*, revised and with new sermons (St. Louis: Chalice Press, 2001); James E. Loder, *The Transforming Moment: Understanding Convictional Experiences*, 2nd ed. (Colorado Springs, CO: Helmers & Howard Publishing, 1989); Paul Scott Wilson, *The Practice of Preaching* (Nashville: Abingdon Press, 1995); Thomas H. Troeger, *Imagining a Sermon* (Nashville: Abindgon Press, 1990); Walter Brueggemann, *The Prophetic Imagination*, revised and updated edition (Minneapolis: Augsburg Fortress Press, 2001); Walter Brueggemann, *Cadences of Home: Preaching among Exiles* (Louisville, KY: Westminster John Knox Press, 1997); Ian G. Barbour, *Myths,*

Models, and Paradigms: A Comparative Study in Science and Religion (New York: Harper & Row, 1974); Sallie McFague, *Metaphorical Theology: Models of God in Religious Language* (Minneapolis: Augsburg Fortress Press, 1997); Garrett Green, *Imagining God: Theology and the Religious Imagination*, paperback edition (Grand Rapids: Wm. B. Eerdmans Publishing Co., 1998).

inclusive language   *Sermonic language intentionally designed to welcome and include the wide diversity of people present in and beyond worship.*

Language is a dynamic force, deeply related to history and context and powerfully constitutive of social reality and behavior. The explicit and implicit assumptions carried by language regarding gender roles, race, class, ethnicity, and sexuality should be taken with the utmost seriousness. Many Christian denominations today have embraced inclusive language. These denominations have decided that when words, symbols, or actions exclude cultures, races, or the needs and identities of believers, they are not faithful to the life, death, and resurrection of Jesus Christ. Inclusiveness, therefore, is understood to be a theological act, not an act of political or ideological correctness.

The inclusive language movement emerged out of the women's liberation movement of the late 1960s and early 1970s. Both movements have undergone significant change since that time. In recent years, the word "inclusive" has been challenged for tacitly supporting the idea that there is a *center* that includes a *margin*. Critics of otherness and "othering" in language usage have encouraged a still more critical approach to inclusive language. They encourage a *deconstruction or decentering so that the church becomes a community in which all persons are "others" and no one represents the "same" or the "center."

The use of inclusive language involves the recognition of persons from other races and cultures; persons with *disabilities; women and men; persons of all ages; those who have experienced divorce, sexual or domestic violence, or other forms of violence; gay, lesbian, bisexual, and transgendered persons; and so on. Inclusive preachers make use of language for God that is as broad and diverse as biblical language, so that all persons find themselves included, addressed, challenged, and loved.

The use of inclusive language can be a very subtle matter, and requires ongoing vigilance and sensitization. The way that *illustrations, *images, and *culture are used in sermons is often loaded with gendered, classist, racist, ageist, and ableist assumptions. Inclusive preachers avoid angry gestures in the pulpit that can terrorize women or children who are victims of sexual or domestic violence. They try to avoid uncritically using language about "blindness" to Christ or "deafness" to the Word, placing "black" hats onto villains and "white" hats onto heroes. They work hard to avoid communicating *anti-Judaism.

Because of habits learned through years of socialization, it is inevitable that mistakes will be made. It is important, therefore, to develop a personal and communal attitude of constant *repair* around the issue of inclusive language. Preachers will do well to let listeners know that inclusive language is one of their commitments, and one of the commitments of their denomination, and invite ongoing feedback regarding oversights and ways that this can be done better. It is important that the community joins the preacher in repairing language. It will take hard work to keep accusations, conflict, and defensiveness from developing, and promote a climate of learning instead of reaction. There are many good denominational resources that, along with other resources, can help preachers and congregations along the way.

John S. McClure, *Other-wise Preaching: A Postmodern Ethic for Homiletics* (St. Louis: Chalice Press, 2001); Kathy Black, *A Healing Homiletic: Preaching and Disability* (Nashville: Abingdon Press, 1996); Christine M. Smith, *Preaching as Weeping, Confession, and Resistance: Radical Responses to Radical Evil* (Louisville, KY: Westminster John Knox Press, 1992); Casey Miller and Kate Swift, *The Handbook of Nonsexist Writing: For Writers, Editors and Speakers*, 2nd ed. (Lincoln, NE: iUniverse Press, 2001); Ronald D. Witherup, *A Liturgist's Guide to Inclusive Language* (Collegeville, MN: Liturgical Press, 1997); Nancy Hardesty, *Inclusive Language in the Church* (Louisville, KY: Westminster John Knox Press, 1988); *An Inclusive Language Lectionary* (Louisville, KY: Westminster John Knox Press, 1984–1987); Elaine Ramshaw, *Liturgical Language: Keeping it Metaphoric, Making It Inclusive* (Collegeville, MN: Liturgical Press, 1996).

inductive sermon   *A *form of preaching in which the preacher delays the full statement of the sermon's *theme or *idea.*

In traditional homiletic theory, grounded more narrowly in theories of *rhetoric, inductive logic was held to be far inferior to *deductive logic. The reasons for this can be attributed to the persuasive and legal purposes of rhetoric. Proofs based on appeals to experience were deemed to be subjective and inadequate. One could not "prove" something based on similar or analogous forms of experience.

In the 1970s, Fred Craddock argued for inductive forms of preaching as a way to meet the growing need for more participative and dialogical forms of communication in the pulpit. Craddock envisioned inductive preaching as a more cooperative form of communication, in which preacher and listener could be involved in a shared journey toward insight or meaning.

The inductive sermon moves from the presentation of the particulars of experience toward a general truth. The inductive outline might look like this:

a.
b.
1.
A.
I.

Inductive preachers and their listeners tend to be persons who enjoy more ambiguity and are willing to tolerate some delay in the arrival of final meanings and conclusions. The preacher's subject is detoured through the telling of stories and the creation of images as listeners are invited to participate in a set of shared experiences that lead up to the preacher's point. Inductive sermons are left open-ended and, in many cases, invite the listener to supply conclusions.

Similar to Kenneth Burke's New Rhetoric of *identification, induction is grounded in cooperation rather than persuasion. Inductive preaching is designed to facilitate participation in preaching and to include listeners as active meaning makers. The goal is not to assert something as true, but to help listeners recognize the truth they already know but may have forgotten or lost along the way.

Fred B. Craddock, *As One without Authority*, revised and with new sermons (St. Louis: Chalice Press, 2001); Robin Meyers, *With Ears to Hear: Preaching as Self-Persuasion* (Cleveland: Pilgrim Press, 1993); Lucy Atkinson Rose, *Sharing the Word: Preaching in the Roundtable Church* (Louisville, KY: Westminster John Knox Press, 1997); Ronald J. Allen, ed., *Patterns of Preaching: A Sermon Sampler* (St. Louis: Chalice Press, 1998); Michael Duduit, ed., *Handbook of Contemporary Preaching* (Nashville: Broadman & Holman Publishers, 1993); Richard L. Eslinger, *A New Hearing: Living Options in Homiletical Method* (Nashville: Abingdon Press, 1987).

inflection   *Altering the pitch or emphasis given to a word in order to clarify or embellish its meaning.*

The concept of inflection enters homiletics through the world of music, especially vocal performance. In certain popular traditions of music, especially the blues, the pitch of a note is often bent or pushed in a variety of ways in order to further nuance the sound. The same is true in preaching, where the inflection of a word tells the listener much about its actual meaning. For instance, in the sentence "We all are sinners," the word "all" can be inflected with anger, exasperation, or with questioning in one's voice. The way the word is inflected changes its meaning.

Communication scholars often use the word "paralanguage" to speak of aspects of inflection. Included in this category are such things as emphasis, loudness, and the force that is used to produce sound. In some instances, pause and *rate of *delivery are also classified as forms of inflection.

G. Robert Jacks, *Getting the Word Across: Speech Communication for Pastors and Lay Leaders* (Grand Rapids: Wm. B. Eerdmans Publishing Co., 1987); Joseph A. DeVito, *Human Communication: The Basic Course*, 10th ed. (Boston: Allyn & Bacon, 2005).

introduction   *The beginning of a sermon, in which the sermon's *idea is introduced.*

In recent homiletic theory, introductions are considered less as the initial section preceding the *body of the sermon and more as a part of the overall way in which the preacher establishes the general experience of the sermon that is to follow. According to J. Randall Nichols, introductions are the time when a preacher creates a "communication contract" that establishes the overarching frame, tone, and general expectations of the *listener. The key to a good introduction, therefore, grows less from the sermon's outline or structure, and more from the overall *purpose and quality of *communication the preacher wishes to establish.

Paul Scott Wilson suggests six strategies for creating introductions. First, he suggests telling a story that is the "flip side" of the theme. In other words, if the preacher's *focus sentence is "God wants to forgive us," the preacher might tell a story of a person who is desperate for forgiveness. Second, the preacher might narrate a "not-too-serious" experience of the sermon's general theme. Third, the preacher might start with an imaginative re-creation of the biblical text. Fourth, the preacher might introduce an issue in today's world requiring justice or resolution. A fifth strategy involves briefly renarrating a newspaper story that strongly implicates the sermon's theme. Finally, the preacher might start with a fictional narrative (so long as it is obvious that what is being said is fantasy and not fact). Other strategies abound. In all cases, however, the introduction sets forth the theme, purpose, and promise of the sermon.

J. Randall Nichols, *Building the Word: The Dynamics of Communication and Preaching* (San Francisco: Harper & Row, 1980); Thomas G. Long, "Pawn to King Four: Sermon Introductions and Communicational Design," *Reformed Review* 40, no. 1 (Autumn 1986): 27–35; Paul Scott Wilson, *The Four Pages of the Sermon: A Guide to Biblical Preaching* (Nashville: Abingdon Press, 1999).

itinerant   *A traveling preacher.*

Jesus and the apostle Paul were primarily itinerant preachers who moved from town to town, speaking on hillsides, in the marketplace, in people's homes, and in synagogues. According to John Koenig, in the early church, itinerant charismatic preachers were hosted in house and tenement churches. The *Didache* indicates that these traveling preachers were welcomed, but also tested by the wisdom residing within the community of faith. During the Middle Ages, itinerant preachers preached the Crusades, and many Dominicans and Franciscans were also itinerant preachers. In the North American context, itinerancy is usually associated with the Methodist tradition, especially circuit riders. The circuit rider rode on horseback across a designated circuit engaging in open-air and revival preaching. The Methodist tradition of moving preachers after a three-year residency may be rooted as well in John Wesley's appreciation of itinerancy. It is widely known among Methodists that John Wesley once said that if he preached in a single place for more than a year, he would likely preach himself and his congregation to sleep.

Because they were not allowed to preach from established pulpits, many women became itinerant preachers. In the early to mid-nineteenth century, Jarena Lee, the first female evangelist in the African Methodist Episcopal Church, preached in homes, schools, public meetinghouses, and open-air contexts across the northeastern United States. There were many other women preachers in this same mold, including Harriet Livermore, Nancy Towle, and Mary Stevens Curry.

Today's itinerants are revival preachers, television evangelists, professional homileticians who travel on weekends, and well-known preachers who preach at large conferences. Itinerancy is not a congregation-based practice and requires unique skills. Instead of relating the gospel to the very particular experiences of the local congregation, itinerants draw upon more general forms of human experience in order to achieve some *identification with listeners.

Some argue that it is a good practice within any congregation to regularly hear from itinerant preachers. This permits the church to be constantly instructed by both seasoned pastors who know a congregation's particular concerns and by charismatic individuals from outside who can bring a fresh message that may be needed. In some situations, itinerants can say things that are difficult for people to hear. This makes itinerancy a good form of preaching for both *evangelistic and *prophetic genres of preaching.

Ted A. Campbell, "Itinerant and Open-Air Preaching," in William H. Willimon and Richard Lischer, eds., *Concise Encyclopedia of Preaching* (Louisville, KY: Westminster John Knox Press, 1995); Catherine A. Brekus, *Female Preaching in America: Strangers and Pilgrims 1740–1845* (Chapel Hill: University of North Carolina Press, 1998); Jarena Lee, "My Call to Preach the Gospel," in Richard Lischer, ed., *The Company of Preachers: Wisdom on Preaching, Augustine to the Present* (Grand Rapids: Wm. B. Eerdmans Publishing Co., 2002), 75–82; John

Koenig, *New Testament Hospitality: Partners with Strangers as Promise and Mission* (Philadelphia: Fortress Press, 1995); John S. McClure, *The Roundtable Pulpit: Where Leadership and Preaching Meet* (Nashville: Abingdon Press, 1995).

kerygma* and *didache   *The distinction between proclamation (*kerygma*) and teaching (*didache*) in the New Testament.*

In his landmark work *The Apostolic Preaching and Its Developments*, C. H. Dodd maintained a sharp distinction between preaching and teaching in the New Testament. Looking primarily at the sermons in Acts, Dodd identified the *kerygma* as an evangelical core message focused in the *proclamation of Christ's life, death, resurrection, glorification, and future return. He asserted that it is through the proclamation of this message, as opposed to *didache* or moral instruction, that it "pleased God to save humanity" (1 Cor. 1:21).

Years later, Robert C. Worley produced a book entitled *Preaching and Teaching in the Early Church*, in which he argued that Dodd had far overstated the case. Worley argued that preaching and teaching are more interdependent and complementary. Many others have joined Worley, urging preachers and homileticians not to overly separate the proclamatory and educational functions of preaching. George Sweazey, for instance, insists that the proclamation of the good news is always informative and teaches the meaning of Christian faith. At the same time, when a preacher teaches, there is always some appeal for a commitment to Christ. Others, such as Lucy Rose and Eunjoo Mary Kim, have critiqued an overemphasis on *kerygma* because the word usually implies unchanging truth. This, they contend, is too static, reducing the plurality of the biblical witness to a single christological theme. This can inhibit preaching's responsiveness to contemporary experiences, issues, and concerns.

Homileticians are usually interested in the word *kerygma* because it represents the ongoing need to articulate and preserve the uniqueness of the preaching task. Preachers should be careful, however, not to emphasize the identification of preaching and *kerygma* to the exclusion of other important *purposes for preaching in the church.

C. H. Dodd, *The Apostolic Preaching and Its Developments* (New York: Harper & Row, 1964); Robert C. Worley, *Preaching and Teaching in the Early Church* (Philadelphia: Westminster Press, 1967); George E. Sweazey, *Preaching the Good News* (Englewood Cliffs, NJ: Prentice-Hall, 1976); Eunjoo Mary Kim, *Preaching the Presence of God: A Homiletic from an Asian American Perspective* (Valley Forge, PA: Judson Press, 1999); Lucy Atkinson Rose, *Sharing the Word: Preaching in the Roundtable Church* (Louisville, KY: Westminster John Knox Press, 1997); James W. Thompson, *Preaching Like Paul: Homiletical Wisdom for Today* (Louisville, KY: Westminster John Knox Press, 2000); J. Robert Hjelm, "Didache and Kerygma: A Preaching Option," *Covenant Quarterly*, Aug.

1981–Feb. 1982, 97–111; Herbert H. Farmer, *The Servant of the Word* (New York: Charles Scribner's Sons, 1942); James I. H. McDonald, *Kerygma and Didache: The Articulation and Structure of the Earliest Christian Message* (Cambridge: Cambridge University Press, 1980).

kinesics   *An official term in the communication sciences, indicating body language or any form of bodily motion that communicates.*

Paul Ekman and Wallace B. Friesen classify body language in five different categories. First, body language can be used as an *emblem*. Emblems are signs that take the place of words; for instance, the wiggling fingers on both hands to indicate quotation marks, or the finger motioning "come here." Second, some bodily movements operate as *illustrators*. These movements or postures literally illustrate or show the message. If a preacher says, "In Jerusalem," pointing to the left with one arm, and "In Ephesus," pointing to the right with the other arm, the body is being used as an illustrator. The third use of the body is as an *affect display*. Affect displays are *facial expressions or *postures that convey emotional meaning. Slumping shoulders and a drooping face, for instance, signal weariness. A fourth group is *regulators*. Regulators, more common in dialogical forms of communication, are ways of monitoring, sustaining, or controlling the speech of another person. Nodding one's head and muttering "Mm" or "Yes" are regulators. The *call-and-response dynamics in American folk and black preaching are regulators. Finally, body movements can be *adaptors*. Adaptors are forms of body language performed out of the speaker's sense of need, such as scratching an itch on the head, leaning on the pulpit, or taking off one's glasses.

Paul Ekman, Wallace V. Friesen, and Phoebe Ellsworth, *Emotion in the Human Face: Guidelines for Research and an Integration of Findings* (New York: Pergamon Press, 1972); Joseph A. DeVito, *Human Communication: The Basic Course*, 10th ed. (Boston: Allyn & Bacon, 2005); G. Robert Jacks, *Getting the Word Across: Speech Communication for Pastors and Lay Leaders* (Grand Rapids: Wm. B. Eerdmans Publishing Co., 1987).

language   *The verbal and bodily signs used in preaching.*

Language indicates both the sounds or signals that indicate certain meanings and the system by which signs and signals are related. We both *speak* a language, and we *know* a language. Homileticians encourage preachers to use language that is clear, indigenous, and pleasing to the ear. Henry Mitchell argues that polishing one's language before preaching is the most important element in the final stages of sermon preparation. Preachers should attend carefully to grammar, consistency of tense and person, sentence and paragraph structure, and precision in language. They should ensure proper *pronunciation and word choice, avoiding inappropriate clichés, colloquialisms, and slang. Although most homileticians encourage preachers to expand their vocabularies, reading good novels, theology, history, and so on, they encourage preachers to use words that are common and understood and to avoid exotic or highly technical forms of speech. Most homileticians also encourage preachers to avoid flowery language and to use adjectives and adverbs sparingly. The best language is strong on particularity and active verbs.

There are two major theories of language, which generate very different forms of preaching. Empirical theories of language attempt to bind language to physical and verifiable entities or behavior. In the current generation of homileticians, those with this view associate language closely with the way it is *used*. For them, the meanings of words are learned only as they are used in a language-group. One knows the meaning of biblical words only inasmuch as one practices or performs those words with others, in real life. *Postliberal homileticians such as Charles Campbell and William Willimon have encouraged this way of thinking about language in preaching. They encourage preachers to reperform biblical words and categories, unabashedly using the odd, ancient language of faith. Listeners should not be helped to translate biblical language into modern categories, but encouraged to step into the world of biblical language and *use* it in order to learn and practice biblical faith.

The phenomenological theory of language, on the other hand, gives primacy to metaphor and symbol in understanding the nature and function of language. The purpose of language is not to generate or describe forms of religious practice or use but to disclose the hidden ground from which all of reality, including transcendent reality, proceeds. In this model, language is a means of approaching, or giving back, the transcendent reality that words can only point to or symbolize. Homileticians who hold this theory of language encourage more *inductive, *narrative, or poetic forms of preaching that promote ambiguity and subtlety in order to connote something more than words can actually say. They teach preachers to use *image, *narrative, *dialogue, *metaphor, and other figures of speech to take listeners to the threshold of language, pointing beyond language to an encounter with God.

There are other aspects of language that are significant for homiletics today. First, language can marginalize individuals or groups. Women, persons with disabilities, the elderly, and others have appealed for *inclusive language from the pulpit. Second, some homileticians have begun to take a more *strategic view of language. Nora Tubbs Tisdale, for instance, encourages *congregational study of signs and symbols in order to link preaching to the

strategic development of a "local theology." Finally, some encourage a
*dramatist approach to language, using *performative language to create an
encounter or event, through the immediacy of sign, sound, and *embodiment.

John S. McClure, "Language, theories of," in William H. Willimon and Richard
Lischer, eds., *Concise Encyclopedia of Preaching* (Louisville, KY: Westminster John
Knox Press, 1995), 292–95; Charles L. Campbell, *Preaching Jesus: New Directions
for Homiletics in Hans Frei's Postliberal Theology* (Grand Rapids: Wm. B. Eerdmans
Publishing Co., 1997); John S. McClure, "Preaching and the Redemption of Lan-
guage," in Jana Childers, ed., *Purposes of Preaching* (St. Louis: Chalice Press,
2004), 83–90; Henry H. Mitchell, "Polishing the Sermon," in John S. McClure,
Best Advice for Preaching (Minneapolis: Fortress Press, 1998), 85–98; Leonora
Tubbs Tisdale, *Preaching as Local Theology and Folk Art* (Minneapolis: Fortress
Press, 1997); Jana Childers, *Performing the Word: Preaching as Theatre* (Nashville:
Abingdon Press, 1998); Richard F. Ward, *Speaking from the Heart: Preaching with
Passion* (Eugene OR: Wipf & Stock, 2001).

law and gospel   *A phrase used for the formal dialectic between bad news and
good news in preaching, attributed to the Lutheran tradition of homiletics.*

In an age in which homileticians are increasingly concerned with *anti-
Judaism in preaching, the language of law and gospel has fallen on hard times.
When using this language to think about preaching, it is important not to
think reductively of the Old Testament as law and the New Testament as
gospel. Law and gospel, or what Paul Scott Wilson calls "trouble" and "grace,"
are present throughout the biblical canon.

At the heart of the preaching of law and gospel there resides what Mary
Catherine Hilkert calls the "dialectical *imagination." Dialectic involves a
thesis set into conflict with its antithesis only to be resolved by a unique synthesis. Dialectical imagination, therefore, asserts the work of Jesus Christ as
the synthesis term or resolution within what Richard Lischer calls the "divine
dialectic." This dialectic includes a large set of possibilities for thesis and
antithesis: order-chaos, freedom-bondage, life-death, and so on. No matter
which dialectic is preached, the first aspect of such preaching is to introduce
antithesis: to awaken the listener to his or her true situation. This is the function of law. On one level, this involves what theologian Paul Tillich called
existential awakening or "ontic shock," an awakening to meaninglessness,
guilt, anxiety, and finitude. At a still deeper level, however, this is an awakening to a profound estrangement from God. In the second part of this dialectic, the preacher transitions from the law to the good news of God's grace in
Jesus Christ.

Lischer warns against several "confusions" that should be avoided in the
preaching of law and gospel. First, he warns against the mechanical application of law and gospel through which every sermon, no matter what scriptural

text, bears this structure. He warns, in this regard, against "gospel pragmatism," which simply asks each week "What problem needs solving?" Second, he warns against preaching either grace without judgment (cheap grace), or judgment without grace, which can devolve into the preaching of terror or simply "harangue." Third, he warns against becoming preoccupied with analyzing the bad news, which tends to be far more interesting (and available), thus giving the proclamation of the good news short shrift. Fourth, he warns against turning the gospel into a form of moralism, inviting people to follow Jesus our example. Fifth, he warns against preaching *about* the gospel, describing the good news rather than offering it as an encounter. Finally, he encourages preachers not to preach the gospel in a "law-tone." A preacher's *tone and message need to match.

Herman G. Stuempfle Jr., *Preaching Law and Gospel* (Philadelphia: Fortress Press, 1978); Richard Lischer, *A Theology of Preaching: The Dynamics of the Gospel* (Durham, NC: Labyrinth Press, 1992); Paul Scott Wilson, *The Four Pages of the Sermon: A Guide to Biblical Preaching* (Nashville: Abingdon Press, 1999); Martin Luther, "Proclamation versus Moralism," in Richard Lischer, ed., *The Company of Preachers: Wisdom on Preaching, Augustine to the Present* (Grand Rapids: Wm. B. Eerdmans Publishing Co., 2002), 115–19.

lectio continua   *A set of prescribed readings designed to preach continuously through a book of the Bible. (See *lectionary.)*

lectio selecta   *A set of prescribed biblical readings chosen to conform to the church calendar or other theological pattern. (See *lectionary.)*

lectionary   *Prescribed sequences from Scripture to be read aloud in worship.*

As the ancient Hebrew oral tradition was written down in the sacred writings (Torah, Prophets, and Psalms), time was allotted during worship to read these writings aloud. During the time of Jesus, there were readings in the synagogue. In Luke 4, when Jesus was in the synagogue, the text tells us that Jesus "found the place." This indicates that there might have been some practice of prescribed or continuous reading during worship. By the fourth century we can see clear evidence of lectionaries. The *Apostolic Constitutions* refers to a five-lesson sequence, and the *Homilies of Augustine* indicates that two lessons were read at the mass as a norm, and three at festivals. At this stage, however, the lectionary was primarily a continuous reading through the biblical text, or what is sometimes called *lectio continua*. Between the eighth and seventeenth centuries, a variety of lectionaries were developed. These were mostly selections of readings formulated to coordinate with a variety of church calendars. These are sometimes called eclogadic lectionaries. The word "eclogadic," from the Greek *ecloge*, meaning "choice" or "selection," indicates the assigning of texts to dates for particular purposes. This is also sometimes called *lectio selecta*. At the Council of Trent (1570), the Roman Catholic Church fixed the lectionary. This lectionary survived until Vatican II in the 1960s.

Many of the Reformers, especially Zwingli, preferred *lectio continua*, arguing that eclogadic lectionaries prevented access to the entire Bible. Calvin favored one reading at each service. Focusing attention on the gospel, he would read a chapter or so each Sunday. The Anglican Church introduced a sequential principle, ordering the lectionary in such a way as to cover the whole Bible, or its major parts, over a period of time. This is a form of *lectio selecta*, based primarily on the principle of biblical coverage, rather than on the need to illuminate the church calendar. This became the model for the lectionaries that currently exist.

During the modern period, the focus turned to developing preaching lectionaries. Preaching lectionaries are multiple-year lectionaries designed to help preachers cover the full range of the biblical witness. As a result of Vatican II, in 1969 the Roman Catholic Church published *Ordo Lectionum Missae*, a new lectionary. This lectionary organized the readings with reference to the life, death, and resurrection of Jesus. This christocentric organizing principle underlies all lectionaries since. When fleshed out, this lectionary established a three-year cycle of readings. The Gospels are chosen to be semicontinuous in chapter sequence, with Year A concentrating on Matthew, Year B focusing on Mark, filled out with John, and Year C centered on Luke. During the major church seasons, the book of John is spread out evenly, and on Sundays after Easter readings from the book of Acts are substituted. Old Testament texts are not continuous, and are chosen to reinforce the Gospel, give background to the Gospel, or provide contrast to the Gospel. The Epistle readings are semicontinuous in sections of three to sixteen weeks and are not chosen to relate in content with the Old Testament and Gospel readings. This basic pattern of readings continues in the new lectionaries used today.

During the 1970s, many Protestant denominations adopted the new Roman Catholic lectionary with some modifications. Presbyterians and Lutherans substituted canonical Old Testament passages where Old Testament apocryphal writings existed in the Roman Catholic lectionary. Lutherans and Episcopalians revised the lectionary to include greater diversity from Acts. During the 1980s, as a result of ecumenical consultations including Anglicans, Protestant mainline denominations, and the Roman Catholic Church, a *Common Lectionary* was produced. In 1983, the National Council of Churches published Year A of an inclusive-language lectionary, and Year B and Year C followed shortly. Further revisions have been made since, as feminist critiques and critiques by Old Testament scholars have led to a variety of modifications found in *The Revised Common Lectionary*. The new lectionary includes two tracks of Old Testament readings—one related to the Gospels and one not.

There are several advantages to lectionary preaching, especially for preachers in traditions where *biblical preaching is expected. In the first place, lectionaries encourage preaching that deals more closely with the biblical text. Preachers begin sermon preparation with exegetical study and brainstorming biblical texts. Second, the use of *The Revised Common Lectionary* promotes ecumenical relationships. The same text is preached in many churches each Sunday. In many communities, preachers from multiple traditions gather weekly to discuss lectionary texts and sermon preparation. Third, the repetition of a cycle of readings can promote, over time, a greater knowledge of the Bible in a congregation. Fourth, the lectionary can ensure that a larger range of the biblical witness is heard in the pulpit. It can help preachers avoid the problem of preaching their own idiosyncratic "canon within the canon." Fifth, lectionary preaching can help congregations recognize the relationships that exist between biblical texts. Finally, lectionary preaching can help congregations hear the unique qualities of certain biblical books, especially the Gospels, by spending a year with one Gospel and a particular set of biblical texts.

There are several disadvantages and problems with lectionary preaching. First, starting with texts can lead preachers to preach completely irrelevant sermons. Second, assuming that biblical texts will always contain a word of good news for today can invite preachers to misconstrue the meaning of a text in order to discover some relevant, positive message for today. Third, because of the repetition of readings, there is some temptation for the preacher to preach the same sermon, or a slightly revised sermon, the next time a text rolls around. Fourth, there has been much discussion regarding the christological principle at work in the lectionary, which makes the Gospels the controlling influence for most preaching. This places the Old or First Testament and the Epistles into a clearly subordinate relationship. Much of the richness of the Old Testament and Epistles can be lost. Since the Gospels constitute only about 10 percent of canonical scripture, the amount of Old Testament that can be read in conjunction is small. Finally, several consultations by women have pointed out that many of the great texts about women have been excluded. Some of the concerns among Old Testament scholars and women preachers have been addressed, at least in part, in *The Revised Common Lectionary*.

Andy Langford, "The Revised Common Lectionary 1992: A Revision for the Next Generation," *Quarterly Review* 13 (Summer 1993): 37–48; Marjorie Procter-

Smith, "Beyond the New Common Lectionary: A Constructive Critique," *Quarterly Review* 13 (Summer 1993): 49–58; Marjorie Procter-Smith, "Lectionaries: Principles and Problems," *Studia Liturgica* 22, no. 1 (1992): 84–89; *The Revised Common Lectionary: Consultation on Common Texts* (Nashville: Abingdon Press, 1992); Peter C. Bower, *Handbook for the Revised Common Lectionary* (Louisville, KY: Westminster John Knox Press, 1996); Ronald J. Allen and Clark M. Williamson, *Preaching the Gospels without Blaming the Jews: A Lectionary Commentary* (Louisville, KY: Westminster John Knox Press, 2004); Ernest T. Campbell, "A Lover's Quarrel with Preaching," in Michael Graves, ed., *What's the Matter with Preaching Today?* (Louisville, KY: Westminster John Knox Press, 2004), 51–58.

listener   *One who regularly listens to sermons.*

The word "listener" strongly implies the word "hearing." For this reason, Kathy Black has critiqued the priority of the word in homiletics, because it might exclude the hearing impaired, for whom visual aspects of preaching may be of more importance. The idea of sermon listening designates not only physical hearing, but all aspects of the *reception* of preaching. Listening involves cognition, emotion, memory, imagination, personality, tradition, conventions and expectations, social location, and other factors.

Although a "turn to the listener" has been commonly recognized among homileticans since the time of Fred Craddock's work on inductive preaching, preachers have always taken the listener into careful consideration. Beverly Zink-Sawyer traces this history, highlighting Jesus' use of familiar language and imagery, Augustine's use of rhetoric, Calvin's emphasis on preaching as a corporate act, the Puritan concern for *application, the revivalist preacher's emphasis on *extemporaneous sermons that more actively involve listeners, and the close attention to the stuff of daily life and suffering in the preaching of women such as Phoebe Palmer and Sojourner Truth. In the early twentieth century, concern for the listener is most closely associated with the preaching of Harry Emerson Fosdick, who insisted that each sermon must take into account a felt need of the listener. Fred Craddock's *inductive approach, introduced in the 1970s, provided a form of preaching that, although monologue in presentation, was dialogical in form, increasing the role of the listener in the preaching event.

By the mid-1990s homileticians began to question the assumption common to inductive preaching that preachers could and should attempt to identify with listeners (see *identification). More and more, preachers are aware, not of similarities or points of empathic contact with listeners, but of the *difference* of each listener. This awareness of diversity is intensified by psychological studies that make preachers aware of different personalities, worldviews, and need-based expectations among listeners. Recent homiletic models such as *contextual, *conversational, *collaborative, and *testimonial preaching have moved into this gap, suggesting ways in which listeners themselves can become more active in sermon preparation. It is no longer enough to be "relevant." Preachers must be "real," speaking *from* the actual lived world of listeners. Preachers in these models move beyond empathically assuming relevant points of identification, to asking listeners to disclose real points of identification themselves.

Most recently, empirical studies have been conducted on both sides of the Atlantic studying what, in fact, listeners are doing during sermons. The recent *Listening to Listeners Project resulted in four books that challenge many standard assumptions made by preachers and homileticans. It is increasingly relevant to speak, not only of preaching as a religious practice, but also of sermon listening as an important religious and spiritual practice. In other words, sermon listening seems to fit into a larger set of human practices of listening for truth, meaning, direction, discernment, insight, wisdom, and vocation, many of which listeners would not consider to be explicitly Christian in nature. It is possible, therefore, to study the uniqueness of sermon listening as a practice of discernment or listening in relation to other such practices.

Several cautions are commonly suggested when considering the role of listeners in preaching. First, keep in mind the role of the Holy Spirit in preaching, so that one does not assume that the transaction between preacher and listener is entirely a matter of *communication or *rhetoric. Over and over again, listeners interviewed in the Listening to Listeners Project asserted their own awareness of the active role of God's Spirit when they listened to sermons. Second, preaching should not be given over entirely to meeting people's needs. Karl Barth and other Christian theologians remind us that at times preaching tells us what we *should* need. The collective wisdom of listeners interviewed in the Listening to Listeners Project is also clear on this. Many of them tell us that they rely on the preacher to bring a word from God that may not match their own interests or desires. Third, although it is important to find ways through *feedback to include listeners in the preaching process, and to promote other methods that deepen the listener's participation in preaching, it is also important to keep in mind the preacher's congregation-granted *authority to be the one who brings the word into their midst. Beverly Zink-Sawyer reminds those within the Reformation traditions that preaching celebrates not only the priesthood of all believers, but also the idea that ministers are ordained as ministers of Word and Sacrament.

In the last analysis, the idea of the listener in homiletics must be taken with the utmost seriousness. The practice of sermon listening is a complex phenomenon that has received more attention in recent homiletics than ever before. Preachers today have the potential to be better informed about sermon listening and more responsive to listeners than preachers of any prior generation.

Beverly Zink-Sawyer, "The Word Purely Preached and Heard: The Listeners in the Homiletical Endeavor," *Interpretation* 51, vol. 4 (2004): 342–58; Kathy Black, *A Healing Homiletic: Preaching and Disability* (Nashville: Abingdon Press, 1996); James R. Nieman and Thomas G. Rogers, *Preaching to Every Pew: Cross-Cultural Strategies* (Minneapolis: Augsburg Fortress Press, 2001); John S. McClure, *The Roundtable Pulpit: Where Leadership and Preaching Meet* (Nashville: Abingdon Press, 1995); Lucy Atkinson Rose, *Sharing the Word: Preaching in the Roundtable Church* (Louisville, KY: Westminster John Knox Press, 1997); Leonora Tubbs Tisdale, *Preaching as Local Theology and Folk Art* (Minneapolis: Fortress Press, 1997); Fred Craddock, *As One without Authority*, revised and with new sermons (St. Louis: Chalice Press, 2001); O. Wesley Allen Jr., *The Homiletic of All Believers: A Conversational Approach* (Louisville, KY: Westminster John Knox Press, 2005); John S. McClure, Ronald J. Allen, et al., *Listening to Listeners: Homiletical Case Studies* (St. Louis: Chalice Press, 2004); Ronald J. Allen and Mary Alice Mulligan, *Make the Word Come Alive: Lessons from Laity* (St. Louis: Chalice Press, 2006); Ronald J. Allen, *Hearing the Sermon: Relationship, Content, Feeling* (St. Louis: Chalice Press, 2004); Diane Turner-Sharazz, Dawn Ottoni Wilhelm, Ronald J. Allen, and Mary Alice Mulligan, *Believing in Preaching: What Listeners Hear in Sermons* (St. Louis: Chalice Press, 2005); John S. McClure, *Other-wise Preaching: A Postmodern Ethic for Homiletics* (St. Louis: Chalice Press, 2001); John S. McClure, "The Practice of Sermon Listening," *Congregations* 32, no. 1 (2006): 6–9.

Listening to Listeners Project   *A major empirical study of sermon listeners.*

The Listening to Listeners Project was led by Ronald J. Allen and funded by the Lilly Foundation. Between 2001 and 2002, a research team interviewed 263 sermon listeners in 28 churches of various shapes, sizes, locations, denominations, and racial-ethnic compositions across the midsection of the United States. Interview questions were organized using three classical rhetorical categories, *ethos, *logos, and *pathos, along with the additional category of *embodiment. Results were published in four books and many articles.

John S. McClure, Ronald J. Allen, Dale P. Andrews, L. Susan Bond, Dan P. Moseley, and G. Lee Ramsey Jr., *Listening to Listeners: Homiletical Case Studies* (St. Louis: Chalice Press, 2004); Ronald J. Allen, *Hearing the Sermon: Relationship, Content, Feeling* (St. Louis: Chalice Press, 2004); Diane Turner-Sharraz, Dawn Ottoni Wilhelm, Ronald J. Allen, and Mary Alice Mulligan, *Believing in Preaching: What Listeners Hear in Preaching* (St. Louis: Chalice Press, 2005); Ronald J. Allen and Mary Alice Mulligan, *Make the Word Come Alive: Lessons from Laity* (St. Louis: Chalice Press, 2006); Ronald J. Allen, "Assessing the Authority of a Sermon," *Encounter* 67 (2006): 63–74; Ronald J. Allen, "Is Preaching Caught or Taught? How Practitioners Learn," *Theological Education* 41 (2005): 137–52; Ronald J. Allen, "What Do Lay People Think God Is Doing in the Sermon?"

Encounter 66 (2005): 365–75; Ronald J. Allen, "What Makes Preaching Disciples Preaching?" *Disciples World* 4, no. 2 (2005): 28–39; Ronald J. Allen, "Preaching after a Tragedy: Listening to Congregations after September 11, 2001," *Encounter* 66 (2005): 221–32; Ronald J. Allen, "How Do People Listen to Sermons?" *Preaching* 21, no. 1 (2005): 52–55; Ronald J. Allen, "Preaching to Listeners: What Listeners Most Value in Sermons," *Homiletics* 17, no. 5 (2005): 7; Ronald J. Allen, "Three Settings on Which People Hear Sermons," *Lectionary Homiletics* 16, no. 1 (2004–05): 1–3; John S. McClure, "The Practice of Sermon Listening," *Congregations*, Winter 2006, 6–9; Diane Turner-Sharazz, "The 'So What' Factor in the Sermon: How the Sermon Connects," *Journal of Theology*, 2005, 45–58.

liturgical preaching   *Preaching that takes its content and character from its relationship to the liturgy.*

The relationship between Word and sacrament has a long and complex history. Liturgical theologians point out that, in the early church, there was an essential unity between Word and Table, such that these two were never separated from one another. The "Liturgy of the Word," therefore, always assumed a complementary "Liturgy of the Table." This relationship fell apart during the late Middle Ages and Reformation, but the Roman Catholic Church and many Protestant traditions are attempting to overcome this separation today.

There are three primary models that relate preaching to the liturgy. These models are not mutually exclusive. The first is an *educational* model. This model takes two different shapes. The first, more typically a Roman Catholic and Anglican approach, asserts that the sermon should be designed to support the teaching function of the liturgy. The sermon provides further instruction regarding the church's message and mission as it is presented in the liturgy. The Scripture readings, sermon, church calendar, and liturgical themes constitute a catechism for the community of faith.

In many Reformed, Methodist, and Baptist churches, this educational relationship undergoes a reversal, with the liturgy taking on a supportive role in enabling the teaching function of the sermon. In this model, the entire liturgical process is made subservient to the lesson taught from the pulpit.

A second model is *contextual-revelational.* In this model, the gathering together of Christians for worship provides the proper context within which the revelation of God's Word occurs. Liturgy provides the proper context because of its close connection with the life of the people and consequently its ability to actualize or bring into being what is revealed by the Word of God. This is sometimes called a "revelation and response" model, in which the proclamation of the Word is revelation and liturgy is response. Preaching and liturgy, therefore, constitute a dialogue through which the liturgy fulfills what preaching proclaims. Typically, Protestant and Catholic liturgical scholars accept this model, but with one primary difference. The question upon which differences rest is: "Can we speak of the liturgy as *part* of God's self-revelation?" For the Reformed and Lutheran traditions, the answer to this question is usually no. In the Protestant traditions the liturgy is more *functional* in nature and is judged by its adequacy to actualize God's self-revelation through preaching. For the Roman Catholic, on the other hand, the liturgy is the *divine* liturgy, integral to God's self-revelation.

The third model is *sacramental*. Here preaching is always seen to have its end in one sacrament or another. Just as missionary preaching is confirmed or sealed in the sacrament of baptism, so Lord's Day preaching is confirmed in the sacrament of the Lord's Supper. Before Vatican II, Roman Catholic theologians understood this relationship as preparatory, with preaching paving the way for the conferral of divine grace at the sacrament. Vatican II produced a more complementary model, in which each aspect of worship produces a different, but complementary, form of grace. Reformed theologies have spoken more of a "unified" view. Howard Hageman, for instance, asserts that Word and Table are not in a preparatory or even complementary relationship, but are "different media for the same reality . . . Christ's coming into the midst of His people." The sacramental model for relating preaching and liturgy, whether preparatory, complementary, or unified, calls for the frequent, preferably weekly, celebration of the Lord's Supper in order to be fully actualized.

What then are the main characteristics of liturgical preaching and how is it to be done? First, from the educational perspective, liturgical preaching can draw its content from liturgical sources at the same time that the liturgy can be informed by the educational purposes of the sermon. Preachers can preach the text of the ecumenical common lectionaries and organize their themes around the church calendar and the liturgical ordering of time. At the same time, the liturgy can respond to particular thematic elements or emphases in sermons, further embellishing and deepening the sermon's message.

Each season of the church year promotes certain educational emphases for both liturgy and preaching. Easter conveys a passage from darkness to light, sorrow to joy, life to death. The major themes of the Easter season are the presence of Christ in our midst and the presence of the newly baptized within the community of faith. Ascension Day, which occurs during the season of Easter, celebrates the exaltation of Jesus as Lord of church and world. Pentecost Day, also part of the fifty days of Easter, celebrates themes of the giving of the Holy Spirit and the inauguration of the *kerygma and the church. Post-Pentecost "ordinary time" is bounded on each end by two festivals: Trinity Sunday and Christ the King Sunday. Each of these Sundays presents opportunities to preach church doctrines. The first Sunday of Advent provides the opportunity to preach future eschatology. The second and third Sundays of Advent focus on preparation for the birth and ministry of Jesus. The fourth Sunday of Advent involves more immediate preparation for the birth of Jesus and focuses on Mary. Christmas Eve is an opportunity to preach the full mystery of the incarnation. Epiphany accentuates themes of baptism and the journey of the magi. Post-Epiphany ordinary time ends with the transfiguration, which juxtaposes the glory of Christ with his descent into Jerusalem. Lent is historically a time to preach catechetical and ethical messages. In the early church Lent was a time during which the catechumens or novices in the faith received final preparation and training for baptism at the Easter Vigil. Sermons can support this process of education at the same time that they encourage a time of preparation for Easter through repentance and spiritual reflection. Holy Week begins with Passion/Palm Sunday. This is an opportunity to preach both the entry of Jesus into Jerusalem and the entire passion story. In some churches, the entire drama of the passion is read aloud, enacted, or portrayed in music. Maundy Thursday and Good Friday services offer an opportunity to go more deeply into the passion narrative and explore the atoning work of Christ.

The second way to develop liturgical preaching is to find ways to connect preaching to the Table. This can be done even when the Liturgy of the Table is not celebrated, as is often the case in Protestant denominations. If the Table is not celebrated, elements from the eucharistic service, such as offertory and a prayer of thanksgiving, can follow closely upon the preaching of the Word. References to the Table and to the mystery of meeting Christ there can be a regular part of the sermon.

The third way to promote liturgical preaching is to preach within a defined liturgical space and ritual practice. Preachers can commit to standing at a pulpit or lectern or in some other designated location in proximity to both Scripture and Table. At the same time, preaching can be accompanied by certain ritual processes in which its relationship to Scripture and Table can be accentuated. These elements also reinforce the office of the preacher as a presider or ordained minister of both Word and Sacrament. In some Reformed traditions, the preacher introduces the sermon with a prayer for illumination in which the vocation of the preacher as the one who seeks out God's Word on behalf of the people is emphasized. This prayer can take the form of an epiclesis or invocation of the Holy Spirit as the one who will ensure that preaching becomes God's Word for today. Where the Lord's Supper is not regularly celebrated, the preacher may preach from behind the table in order to ritually express the Word-Table relationship.

Finally, liturgical preaching will be typically christological in nature, drawing closely upon the church year, which is shaped to conform to the life, death, and resurrection of Jesus Christ. Liturgical preaching ultimately gives expression to the mystery of Jesus Christ and represents a prayerful way of reapproaching that mystery.

John Koenig, *God's Word at Mass* (New York: Hawthorn Press, 1967); Howard Hageman, *Pulpit and Table: Some Chapters in the History of Worship in the Reformed Churches* (Richmond: John Knox Press, 1962); Charles L. Rice, "Less Is More: Preaching as a Liturgical Act," *Journal for Preachers* 10, no. 3 (Easter 1983): 14–20; Charles L. Rice, *The Embodied Word: Preaching as Art and Liturgy* (Minneapolis: Fortress Press, 1991); J. Frank Henderson, "The Minister of Liturgical Preaching," *Worship* 56, no. 3 (1982): 214–30; Harry Boonstra, "Preaching and Liturgy: The Dance of Worship," *Perspectives* 7, no. 6 (June 1992): 17–20; Linda L. Clader, "Preaching the Liturgical Narrative: The Easter Vigil and the Language of Myth," *Worship* 72, vol. 2 (March 1998): 147–62; James A. Wallace, *Preaching to the Hungers of the Heart: Preaching on the Feasts and within the Rites* (Collegeville, MN: Liturgical Press, 2002).

logos   *A Greek philosophical word, originally designating the principle of rational order in the universe, and later used to indicate persuasive appeals to rationality, order, and organization in *rhetoric.*

In the Fourth Gospel, the writer identifies the incarnate Jesus with the preexistent Word or *Logos*. Some have related this word to Sophia or Wisdom in Proverbs 8, who is spoken of as a companion, or possible attribute, of God during the event of creation. The character of Wisdom is also sometimes taken to be a figure for the second person of the Trinity. Theologian Marjorie Suchocki identifies the divine *Logos* as God's "whispered Word." This Word is always at work at preconscious levels within God's creation. According to Suchocki, the goal of preaching is to raise this whisper to the level of a shout, which is precisely what happened at the incarnation.

In rhetorical theory, all aspects of *content* and *order* are part of the *logos* of a sermon. The *logos* of preaching, therefore, refers to all aspects of preaching that answer questions such as: What am I going to say? What will my sermon be about? (subject) What will I say about what I'm going to say? (predicate) How will I order the elements of the sermon? What comes first? What follows? How will I begin and end? What explanations, arguments, warrants, or proofs are required in order to convince listeners? What similar lines of reasoning can I use that will be recognized by listeners? How can I appeal to common-sense thinking?

Communication studies indicate that rational clarity is valued more highly than anything else in public speaking. When listeners to sermons appeal to preachers to be clear and make sense, they are stressing the importance of *logos* in preaching.

Marjorie Hewitt Suchocki, *The Whispered Word: A Theology of Preaching* (St. Louis: Chalice Press, 1999); Lucy Lind Hogan and Robert Reid, *Connecting with the Congregation: Rhetoric and the Art of Preaching* (Nashville: Abingdon Press, 1999).

Lowry Loop   *A sermon *form that moves through five stages resembling a *narrative *plot: upsetting equilibrium (Oops!), analyzing the discrepancy (Ugh!), clue to resolution (Aha!), experiencing the gospel (Whee!), and anticipating the consequences (Yeah!) (see plot).*

manuscript   *A written script used to support sermon *delivery.*

Manuscript delivery is located at the opposite end of the spectrum from *extemporaneous delivery. Some homileticians argue that, even if not taken into the pulpit, the production of a full manuscript is an important step in the sermon preparation process. They believe that preachers who produce a full manuscript are more likely to have attended carefully to all of the details of sermon preparation, especially organization and *development.

This form of delivery offers two advantages. If the preacher desires precision of content, manuscript preaching ensures that carefully crafted words will make it from preacher's study into the pulpit. Preachers whose styles tend to be more literary or poetic usually prefer that a precise turn of phrase not get lost. Manuscript preaching can also be helpful for the preacher who suffers performance anxiety. Although it is not necessary to rely on the script for every word, it is comforting to know it is present if needed.

The principle problem with manuscript preaching is that a preacher may in fact *read* the sermon. Nothing distracts more from the sense of a genuine, spirit-led sermon than a preacher whose head is down, moving line by line through the flipping pages of a manuscript. For this reason, manuscript preaching requires extra time for polishing delivery. In some instances, where the preacher is telling a story or providing an illustration from personal experience, it is a good idea to leave a blank space in the manuscript, encouraging freedom from the manuscript and eye contact with listeners. Another strategy involves underlining crucial words or turns of phrase and allowing oneself to speak freely and with less accuracy large portions of the manuscript that do not need careful wording. Some preachers will go the further step, reducing a manuscript to an outline, a method sometimes called "preaching with *notes." If the preacher desires to use precise wording, it is still possible to include key words or turns of phrase in an extended outline.

Some preachers, who have a background in theater or excellent short-term memories, will memorize a manuscript verbatim. For most, however, this kind of memorization is too time-consuming. It can also produce a form of preaching that seems too close to acting.

Thomas G. Long, *The Witness of Preaching*, 2nd ed. (Louisville, KY: Westminster John Knox Press, 2005); James W. Cox, *Preaching: A Comprehensive Approach to the Design and Delivery of Sermons* (San Francisco: Harper & Row, 1985).

memory *The immediate or long-term remembrance of sermons by listeners, and the relationship of preaching as a whole to the church's larger memory of its past.*

For many preachers the goal of preaching is that the sermon be remembered either in the short term or the long term. Homiletican David Buttrick, for instance, places a great deal of emphasis on whether a sermon "forms in consciousness" and can thus be consciously remembered. Preachers who are concerned with sermon recall will typically use more *images, repetition, mnemonic devices, sound bites, acronyms, and carefully structured sermon *moves. They will also be careful not to overload listeners with complex information.

The other way to think about memory in preaching is to attend to the form that memory takes in preaching. This includes all the ways the sermon accesses the deep memory of the church's tradition contained in its core documents, especially the Bible. There is a close relationship between the shape that memory takes in preaching and the form of *hermeneutics involved in the preaching task. The way that the preacher interprets Scripture (and all past events) actually promotes a form of memory within a congregation.

In the first instance, homiletic memory is *kerygmatic* in nature. Here, memory is grounded in oral tradition and the passing on of "family stories." Like the sermons in the book of Acts, the preacher tells the "old, old story" over and over again, accenting certain elements within that story that are crucial for the contemporary community of faith. The cyclical, repetitive nature of the *liturgical year and *lectionary preaching supports this form of memory in the church.

The second form of memory is *mimetic* or imitative in nature. In this model, the preacher sees the past as an *original to be copied*. This form of memory can be traced to the bridge between memory in an oral culture and memory in a manuscript culture, where copying originals became the primary way of preserving the past. In this model, preachers will typically want people to hear, see, or even hold a copy of the original. Is the pulpit Bible large enough for all to see? Are listeners following along in pew Bibles? Do they bring their own Bibles? Preachers in this model will also use forms of dynamic equivalence when they interpret the Bible, identifying characters or concepts in today's world that are analogous to those in the Bible. The goal of mimetic memory is to imitate the past in similar words, postures, patterns of thinking, and emotions. Mimetic forms of preaching express a deep desire for the Christian community to become *like* some model from the past.

The third form of memory is *reconstructive*. This form of homiletic memory is historical in nature and very concerned with accuracy. Preachers are less concerned that listeners imitate the past. Instead, they reconstruct the ancient world so that listeners can live in *accurate continuity* with the past. Preachers in this model are very concerned about the precise historical context of biblical passages. Listeners are treated to special knowledge about "Matthew's community" or "John's theology." The goal is to measure and synchronize the sermon's remembering.

The fourth type of memory in the pulpit, and one that has become increasingly important in the postmodern context, is *counter-memory*. Counter-memory arises out of the Cartesian suspicion of all traditions. It attempts to attend to *others* within the margins of the Christian tradition whose voices may not have had a place at the table as the tradition was defined. Counter-memory also looks at the ways in which the central tradition, with all its forms of memory, has caused suffering. The preacher recalls a history of suffering within the core tradition itself, or what Elaine Ramshaw calls tradition's "dangerous memory."

Most preachers will accentuate one or two of these forms of memory in preaching. It is possible, however, for preachers to support all of these forms of memory, deepening the memory or anamnesis of the congregation.

John S. McClure, "Exiting the House of Tradition: Preaching and Counter-memory," in John S. McClure, *Other-wise Preaching: A Postmodern Ethic for Homiletics* (St. Louis: Chalice Press, 2001), 27–45; David Buttrick, *Homiletic: Moves and Structures* (Philadelphia: Fortress Press, 1987); Fred B. Craddock, "Preaching: An Appeal to Memory," in Mike Graves, ed., *What's the Matter with Preaching Today?* (Louisville, KY: Westminster John Knox Press, 2004), 59–73; Elaine Ramshaw, *Ritual and Pastoral Care* (Minneapolis: Augsburg Fortress Press, 1987).

mentoring   *A one-to-one training relationship between a novice preacher and an expert sustained over an extended period of time.*

Although mentoring and supervision are often confused, mentors, unlike supervisors, are usually self-selected by the novice or learner. The goals of mentoring are many: character development, learning a style and tradition, developing insider knowledge, vocational and personal support, and reaching one's full potential. In their infancy, many seminaries or "schools of the prophets" sent preachers into the field, pairing them with mentors for the purpose of learning pastoral skills, congregational leadership, and a tradition of preaching. In the African American churches, mentoring continues to be an important aspect of homiletic training. Cleo LaRue points out that in the black churches novice preachers are not declared fit to preach by virtue of their seminary certifications, but are required to seek the church's blessing, which can be achieved only through demonstration of proficiency. This proficiency is best achieved through a mentoring relationship.

Mentoring typically offers several benefits. First, mentors are sponsors. They provide fundamental emotional, spiritual, and moral support for novices. At times they provide institutional guidance and protection, as the novice preacher moves through denominational or organizational structures. Second, mentors are counselors. They provide practical wisdom, advice, tips, and personal insights about preaching. Third, mentors are coaches. They teach basic skills and instill the motivation required to build self-confidence in the task of preaching. Fourth, mentors are spiritual guides. They nurture faith and provide a sense of spiritual direction in the process of claiming identity as a preacher. Finally, mentors provide living models of preaching, demonstrating in practice all the essential elements required to be faithful to a particular tradition of preaching.

Cleophus J. LaRue, "Two Ships Passing in the Night," in Mike Graves, ed., *What's the Matter with Preaching Today?* (Louisville, KY: Westminster John Knox Press, 2004), 127–44; Cleophus J. LaRue, *The Heart of Black Preaching* (Louisville, KY: Westminster John Knox Press, 1999); E. K. Bailey and Warren W. P. Wiersbe, *Preaching in Black and White* (Grand Rapids: Zondervan Press, 2003); Henry Mitchell, *Black Preaching: The Recovery of a Powerful Art* (Nashville: Abingdon Press, 1990); Wayne McDill, *The Twelve Essential Skills for Great Preaching* (Nashville: Broadman & Holman, 1998); John H. Westerhoff, *Spiritual Life: The Foundation for Preaching and Teaching* (Louisville, KY: Westminster John Knox Press, 1994); Dave Stone, *Refining Your Style: Learning from Respected Communicators* (Loveland, CO: Group Publishing, 2004).

metaphor   *The creation or extension of meaning through the juxtaposition of terms (faith and mustard seed, Jesus and good shepherd, etc.).*

David Buttrick argues that all of preaching is, to some extent, "metaphor-making," as preachers uncover unique ways to juxtapose God's grace and human life. These juxtapositions are fresh in each generation, evoking new meanings, forms of thought, and ways of living.

Preachers use metaphors as figures of speech in preaching in order to illustrate sermons. Tom Long identifies a "metaphor-type" of *illustration in which the preacher places an experience and a concept next to one another without explanation. This juxtaposition encourages the listener's imagination to draw out connections and meanings. Unlike analogies, which are rooted in simile or *likeness*, metaphors push further into the mystery of God's presence in the world by inviting listeners to consider forms of real *presence*. Preachers who use metaphors are not simply looking for analogies, they are looking for juxtapositions in which a concept and an image (faith and mustard seed) share what Philip Wheelwright calls the same "tenor," or intuitive core. In other words, as a concept is juxtaposed with an image from experience, there is something in the image that is, at its core, the precise thing being communicated.

Thomas G. Long, *The Witness of Preaching*, 2nd ed. (Louisville, KY: Westminster John Knox Press, 2005); David Buttrick, *Homiletic: Moves and Structures* (Philadelphia: Fortress Press, 1987); Philip Wheelright, *Metaphor and Reality* (Bloomington: Indiana University Press, 1962); John S. McClure, *The Four Codes of Preaching: Rhetorical Strategies* (Minneapolis: Fortress Press, 1991; reprinted, Louisville, KY: Westminster John Knox Press, 2003); Janet Martin Soskice, *Metaphors and Religious Language* (Oxford: Clarendon Press, 1985).

metonymy   *Linking ideas, images, or words together in a linear progression of thought.*

Whereas *metaphor, the opposite of metonymy, functions through the juxtaposition of likes and unlikes, metonymy links words and thoughts together in a linear fashion through some form of sequential internal logic. Paul Scott Wilson observes that this often involves a chaining together of images, words, or phrases that occur and recur throughout the sermon. He identifies three key forms of metonymy in sermons. The first type is metonymy between *sentences* through which each new sentence picks up a thread of thought that has been woven into the previous sentences. This is the internal connection between sentences. The second type is metonymy between *paragraphs*. Wilson points out that the preacher must attend to "carrying forward one developing line of thought," providing "sufficient links" between what has been said in one paragraph and the next. The third type is metonymy as *history and tradition*. In this model, according to Wilson, "a specific event in history is chosen to represent an entire century, or a quotation to represent a particular community, or traditions are identified to link people today with those in the past." Preachers are also using metonymy when they provide *examples* of larger ideas. Wilson points out that this is what Tom Long has in mind when he discusses the sermon example or ""*synecdoche-style" *illustration.

Wilson points out that metonymy can, of course, lead us astray, as in the case of free association. By attempting to connect things together in ways that are too idiosyncratic or obscure, preachers can lose listeners along the way. And metonymy can break down when preachers put in too many logical steps, providing an overabundance of links, so that a sermon becomes bogged down and loses logical energy.

On the whole, metonymy is that deep element within preaching, operating beneath, around, and through such things as links, repetition, internal connections, examples, and *transitions, ensuring that the listener is able to make linear progress through the sermon. It includes all necessary clues that help listeners move from start to finish with the preacher.

Paul Scott Wilson, *The Practice of Preaching* (Nashville: Abingdon Press, 1995).

modes   *A term coined by David Buttrick to indicate the homiletic impact of three models of *hermeneutics.*

Buttrick identifies three modes: the mode of immediacy, the mode of reflection, and the mode of praxis. The first two modes are text-centered. The third is life-situation centered.

The mode of *immediacy* is most appropriate to the preaching of biblical narratives. The preacher moves in and out of the biblical narrative, allowing the plot line of the story and the performative intentions of the text's language to guide the process of sermon brainstorming and organization. Listeners are invited to identify with (not psychologize) characters in the biblical text and enter into the way that narrative plots intend toward certain meanings. In this mode, the goal is not to find some analogous situation in contemporary life for the text to address. This is not a process of translating an original meaning into today's idiom. Instead, the language of the text creates in the preacher and listener's consciousness a "distinctively shaped field of meaning." The preacher preaches this *pattern* of meaning, rather than a theme or idea. Buttrick's mode of immediacy is designed to supercede older *expository models of preaching. He opts for a more sophisticated, literary, and symbolic *hermeneutic of the Bible.

In the mode of *reflection*, the preacher reflects on the way the text's literary elements and language intend a field of theological meaning, so that the sermon becomes a more reflective thinking out of this pattern of meaning. Instead of preaching the text's literary intentions, the preacher explores the theological field of meaning contained within that intention. This amounts to a theological hermeneutic for preaching.

In the *praxis* mode, the preacher begins, not with a biblical hermeneutic, but with a contextual hermeneutic. The preacher begins by interpreting lived experience or situations. These situations should not be superficial in nature but should raise larger questions of human existence and history. Preachers think through these situations in human categories and then in categories dictated by the gospel and Christian theology. The preacher then reframes the situation in light of the Christian revelation. Buttrick argues that the key to this mode is to engage in a *theological analysis of the situation*. This analysis may or may not lead the preacher to a biblical text to preach. It is enough to work with a theological *idea that is derived from the larger biblical witness.

David Buttrick, *Homiletic: Moves and Structures* (Philadelphia: Fortress Press, 1987).

move   *A term created by David Buttrick to describe each unit of thought within a sermon.*

Eschewing the traditional language of sermon *points, often associated with more *deductive forms of sacred *rhetoric, Buttrick strove to help preachers think about preaching as an event that expresses a more *conversational form of logic. Buttrick observed that, within conversations, interlocutors sequence together any number of movements of thought, discovering and creating connections and coherence along the way. According to Buttrick, when these "moves" or "modules of language" are given adequate expression, they "form in consciousness" so that a common understanding is achieved.

Buttrick emphasizes that when using this kind of conversational logic with large groups such as congregations, preachers must slow the speed of movement and remove rapid shifts in subject matter. According to Buttrick, a sermon move needs to take about four minutes, and sermons should contain between four and six moves, given the time constraints in most congregations.

Each move has a beginning, middle, and end. Typically, at the beginning, the preacher creates a "move statement" that connects with what has gone before and focuses the congregation's consciousness. The goal is to establish both the perspective and mood of the move. Then the move is further developed by way of *image, *illustration, analogy, and so on. Move *development will also take into account potential oppositions to what is being said. Preachers need to create *contrapuntals to deal with these. Finally, each move will have a brief section of closure in which the preacher ensures that a unified understanding has been achieved.

David Buttrick, *Homiletic: Moves and Structures* (Philadelphia: Fortress Press, 1987); Ronald J. Allen, *Interpreting the Gospel: An Introduction to Preaching* (St. Louis: Chalice Press, 1998); Paul Scott Wilson, *Preaching and Homiletical Theory* (St. Louis: Chalice Press, 2004); Henry Mitchell, *Celebration and Experience in Preaching* (Nashville: Abingdon Press, 1990).

multicultural preaching *Preaching that embraces and welcomes cultural diversity within the congregation.*

The increasingly multicultural context in North America poses a range of issues for preachers. Although some resources for the planning of worship and for church leadership currently exist, there is very little written regarding multicultural preaching. Recently James R. Nieman and Thomas G. Rogers have published a book based upon interviews with practicing preachers who have some experience with multicultural congregations. Their book provides several helpful insights.

In the first place, Nieman and Rogers assert that it is crucial for the congregation as a whole to adopt both a theology and an ethic that support and encourage the welcoming of persons from other cultures. Congregations must assess whether, in fact, they are truly open to others and decide consciously to pursue the presence of a wide range of persons in their midst. Unless the congregation has a core commitment to embracing cultural diversity, multicultural preaching will have no real effect.

Second, preachers must assess their listeners. This process should take place regularly. Some of Nieman's and Rogers's interview questions could be revised for this process: (1) Describe the congregation's cultural diversity and your place in that mix. What would an outsider coming in to preach need to know in order to preach effectively in this context? (2) What expectations about preaching already affect what you do? (3) What gets in the way of good preaching here? What seems to work well? Less well? (4) What cultural mores or conventions are present that might affect how you preach? (5) What themes are most important for this congregation to hear at this time?

Third, it is important to study the social and cultural context and its demographics. Sermons can be written to respond to the issues and problems of living together as a diverse community beyond the congregation. Nieman and Rogers highlight typical issues caused by class distinctions, such as wealth and security, and issues caused by cultural displacement or "placelessness," such as a sense of danger, grief, and loss, as well as the need for spiritual place, sanctuary, and hope.

Fourth, preachers can be careful about the ways they teach the faith to persons from other cultures. Nieman and Rogers encourage respect for the traditional religious backgrounds of listeners, coupled with the clear articulation of the basic, distinctive elements of Christian faith. They also encourage preachers to teach the core ideas and values of Christian faith on a fairly regular basis.

Fifth, preachers can use multicultural illustrations and images, working to locate the good news in varied cultural experiences. Preachers will need to get to know well persons from cultures other than their own, in order to learn best how to identify and celebrate the ways that God's grace is experienced in their lives.

Sixth, preachers can consider *conversational or *collaborative forms of preaching that can build relationships around the pulpit itself. Preachers can establish presermon round-table discussions that are intentionally multicultural. This provides a regular context for listening to the ways persons from other cultures relate biblical ideas to their lives. This process should provide ample time for storytelling so that the preacher can hear the ways the gospel is relevant for diverse forms of experience.

Seventh, preachers can allow time in worship for *testimony. According to Lucy Rose, testimony is an important way of including marginal voices within a congregation. Testimony allows congregations to hear the different and often unique ways the gospel is received and understood. Testimony also allows diverse persons to gain a foothold in the church's practice of *proclamation.

Finally, preachers can pay special attention to the ways in which ritual process, liturgical symbols, vestments, artifacts, and music respond to cultural diversity. The context for preaching can be intentionally multicultural and express, in a natural and indigenous way, the cultural diversity present and hoped for in worship.

James R. Nieman and Thomas G. Rogers, *Preaching to Every Pew: Cross-Cultural Strategies* (Minneapolis: Augsburg Fortress Press, 2001); Justo L. González and Pablo Jiménez, *Púlpito: An Introduction to Hispanic Preaching* (Nashville: Abingdon Press, 2005); Eunjoo Mary Kim, *Preaching and the Presence of God: A Homiletic from an Asian American Perspective* (Valley Forge, PA: Judson Press, 1999); Jung Young Lee, *Korean Preaching: An Interpretation* (Nashville: Abingdon Press, 1997); Charles R. Foster, *Embracing Diversity: Leadership in Multicultural Congregations* (Herndon, VA: Alban Institute, 1997); Lillian Daniel, *Telling It Like It Is: Reclaiming the Practice of Testimony* (Herndon, VA: Alban Institute, 2005); Thomas G. Long, *Testimony: Talking Ourselves into Being Christian* (San Francisco: Jossey-Bass, 2004); Eric H. F. Law, *The Bush Was Blazing but Not Consumed: Developing a Multicultural Community through Dialogue and Liturgy* (St. Louis: Chalice Press, 1996); Kathy Black, *Worship across Cultures: A Handbook* (Nashville: Abingdon Press, 1998); Brian K. Blount and Leonora Tubbs Tisdale, eds., *Making Room at the Table: An Invitation to Multi-cultural Worship* (Louisville, KY: Westminster John Knox Press, 2000).

mythic communication   *Any form of communication designed to establish, legitimize, or maintain a worldview.*

When developing his theology of story, theologian John Dominic Crossan argued that mythic and *parabolic communication represent polar opposites. Mythic forms of communication are those which take irreconcilable opposites, such as human/superhuman, mortal/immortal, male/female, legitimate/illegitimate, and good/evil, and produce a narrative *mediation* or resolution through which these terms can be rhetorically or poetically reconciled. He goes on to argue that the major forms of narrative are all based on the relative success or lack of success of this kind of narrative mediation.

In the *Four Codes of Preaching*, I use Crossan's theory to identify a range of mythic worldviews that can be promoted in preaching. Each of these worldviews is defined by the extent and quality of the mediation of irreconcilable opposites by the preacher. If this mediation is very weak or does not appear at all, the preacher is promoting a *tensive* theological worldview. If mediation is strong, incomplete, and must continue, an *oppositional* worldview is supported. If mediation is successful, restoring order, an *equilibrist* worldview is promoted. If mediation is superabundantly successful, leading to untold blessings, a victorious or *permutational* worldview is supported.

These mythic worldviews do not rely on a specific theological content. They are defined by the way any theology is expressed, rather than by the preacher's theological persuasion. Any of these mythic worldviews—tensive, oppositional, equilibrist, or permutational—can be found among preachers whose theological content is conservative evangelical, liberal, liberationist, feminist, and so forth.

James Hopewell, in his book *Congregation: Stories and Structures*, offers a more content-driven approach to congregational worldview. He identifies a similar range of congregational worldviews, based on Jungian archetypes. He calls these worldviews empirical, canonical, gnostic, and charismatic. W. Paul Jones, in his book *Theological Worlds*, creates yet another useful typology.

John Dominic Crossan, *The Dark Interval: Towards a Theology of Story* (Sonoma, CA: Polebridge Press, 1988); John S. McClure, "The Theosymbolic Code," in *The Four Codes of Preaching: Rhetorical Strategies* (Minneapolis: Fortress Press, 1991; reprinted, Louisville, KY: Westminster John Knox Press, 2003), 93–135; John S. McClure, "The Narrative Function of Preaching," *Liturgy* 8, no. 2 (Fall 1989): 47–51; James Hopewell, *Congregation: Stories and Structures* (Minneapolis: Augsburg Fortress Press, 1987); W. Paul Jones, *Theological Worlds: Understanding the Alternative Rhythms of Christian Belief* (Nashville: Abingdon Press,

1989); Herbert Anderson and Edward Foley, *Mighty Stories, Dangerous Rituals: Weaving Together the Human and the Divine* (San Francisco: Jossey-Bass, 2001); L. Susan Bond, "Taming the Parable: The Problem of Parable as Substitute Myth," *Homiletic* 25, no. 1 (Summer 2000): 1–12.

narrative preaching   *Preaching in which some aspect of narrative exerts a controlling influence on the sermon.*

In 1980 three books appeared using narrative as a starting point from which to understand the nature, purpose, and method of preaching: *The Homiletical Plot: The Sermon as Narrative Art Form*, by Eugene Lowry; *Preaching the Story*, by Edmund Steimle, Morris Niedenthal, and Charles Rice; and *Telling the Story: Variety and Imagination in Preaching*, by Robert A. Jensen. At the same time, Fred Craddock's *inductive method of preaching came to fruition, a method incorporating storytelling as a way to promote *identification between preacher and listener. Since that time, many homileticians have supported the relationship between narrative and preaching. Although the lines are not always drawn in a clear fashion, there are four broad avenues to narrative preaching: narrative hermeneutics, narrative development, narrative enculturation, and narrative worldview.

The first avenue, narrative *hermeneutics*, leads to preaching in which narrative is at the center of the practice of interpreting the Bible. In one approach, the narrative form of the biblical text is used to guide the preacher in forming the sermon. Both Tom Long and David Buttrick have supported *text-to-sermon approaches that encourage preachers to key the development of the sermon to the literary elements of the Bible. Both homileticans focus the preacher's attention on narrative *plot, *metaphor, *image, and symbol. In a different approach, relying on the preacher's ability to correlate contemporary experience and biblical narratives, Charles Rice invites the preacher to discover how the contemporary human story can be imaginatively discovered in the metaphors and images of biblical narrative. In another approach, Henry Mitchell points out that many preachers in the African American tradition of preaching identify creatively with characters in biblical narratives, inviting listeners to step into the biblical story and find themselves there. Charles L. Campbell encourages a similar practice as a way of inviting listeners to relocate themselves within the alternative world of biblical narratives. Mitchell and Campbell shift the emphasis away from biblical symbols, metaphors, images, and plot, to identification with biblical *characters* as the key to hermeneutics for preaching.

The second avenue toward narrative preaching leads to sermons that involve some form of narrative *development*. Preachers take from narrative the form of logic for the sermon. Sermons are plotted instead of outlined, organized to resemble a story that moves from disequilibrium to restored equilibrium. This is not the same as making the sermon follow the plot of the biblical text. The preacher shapes the sermon to match a predetermined narrative genre: movies, sitcoms, parables, and such. Eugene Lowry, in *The Homiletical Plot*, is the homiletician who has encouraged this most strongly.

Another way to use narrative for the development of sermons is to make the sermon into a story itself. Robert A. Jensen, in *Telling the Story*, encourages preachers to preach story sermons. According to Roger Standing, story sermons can be told in the third person, where the preacher is the narrator, or in the first person, where the preacher is a character in the story. In some cases, this model is merged with narrative hermeneutics and the preacher renarrates a biblical story, stepping into the role of a biblical character. This form of preaching is much debated among homileticians, because preachers tend to read thoughts or feelings into biblical characters, psychologizing or spiritualizing them beyond recognition.

A third avenue to narrative preaching leads to various forms of narrative *enculturation*. Preachers use elements of narrative such as metaphor, *synecdoche, or image, to *illustrate where the sermon's *ideas are found within contemporary human culture and experience. In some cases, this means beginning the sermon with a current story that expresses a felt need or raises an existential question. In other cases the preacher searches for contemporary stories or images that will either illustrate or *be* an idea or block of thought within the sermon. *Collaborative preachers take the time to ask others how they would relate the biblical narrative to their life stories. A sermon prepared in conversation with the homeless, for instance, will yield different stories, images, and metaphors for illustration than a sermon prepared alone in the pastor's study.

The fourth avenue toward narrative preaching leads to sermons that promote a narrative *worldview*. In this approach, narrative categories, such as *mythic communication, *parabolic communication, narrative character, signs or symbols, are used to help preachers understand how it is that preaching supports and promotes a particular metanarrative or worldview in a congregation. There are two ways in which this is envisioned by homileticians.

The first way argues for the predominance of the *biblical* narrative as worldview in preaching. *Postliberal homiletician Charles L. Campbell has argued against models of narrative enculturation on the grounds that enculturation squeezes Jesus into a box defined by modern human experience and culture. This concedes the biblical worldview to an Enlightenment worldview. Campbell is deeply concerned about the loss of biblical language and categories of thought that occurs when biblical ideas are translated into experiential terms. He argues that the preacher's job is to render the biblical narrative in such a way that listeners will abandon all other narratives and permit their language, identity, and culture to be taken over by the biblical narrative itself. This is accomplished, in large part, by encouraging listeners to identify with biblical characters. In this model, the biblical narrative literally consumes all other narratives.

The second way to narrative worldview is a *practical theological* model. In this model the theological interpretation of narrative biblical categories by congregations and preachers is most important. Here there are two types: congregation-centered and sermon-centered. In the congregation-centered model, espoused by Leonora Tubbs Tisdale, the preacher uses *semiotic tools to exegete the local theology or faith story within a congregation. The preacher asks how, over time, a congregation has learned to interpret categories found in the biblical narrative, such as sin, evil, church, table, Jesus, faith, God, hope. Then the preacher brings a normative *theological* interpretation to this task and makes strategic practical theological decisions regarding what and how to preach, based on gaps, inconsistencies, or problems discovered.

In the second type of practical theological model, I encourage preachers to do a narrative theological analysis of their own sermons in order to determine the theology they preach. Strategic practical theological changes can then be made on the basis of this analysis of the theological worldview latent within sermons. I provide a narrative *structure as a way of organizing this task, based on the work of structuralist literary critic A. J. Gremais. Gremais identified six "actants" or structural constants in any narrative: Giver, Receiver, Opponent, Object, Subject, and Helper.

In the Christian theological narrative, the *Giver* corresponds to God. How is God and God's activity represented in a preacher's sermons? The *Receiver* is the ultimate beneficiary of the narrative and corresponds with the image of the human condition and creation as they are depicted in a preacher's sermons. What is the human condition in the world, according to the preacher? The *Opponent* is the villain or false hero in the preacher's sermons who creates the human condition of the Receiver. This corresponds to all ways in which the preacher typically speaks of sin and evil. The *Object* is the desired end of the faith story told by the preacher: images of redemption and eschatological finality as they are presented in sermons. The *Subject* is the hero or protagonist in a preacher's faith story, questing on behalf of the Receiver to secure the desired Object. The Subject corresponds to ways in which the preacher imagines the Christian community or the individual discovering and expressing faith and mission. This actant includes doctrinal categories of calling, conversion, faith, justification, sanctification, salvation, mission, and perseverance. The *Helper* represents all helping agents in the life of faith, those things that help the hero/Subject in the quest for the desired Object. This includes the ways in which the preacher speaks about Christ, Holy Spirit, the church, sacraments, Bible, and ministry.

Preachers can easily use this narrative grid to analyze a past year or so of preaching in order to determine missing elements, inconsistencies, issues, and problems and to develop practical theological strategies for future preaching. It is also a helpful tool for thinking about *theology and preaching in general. I also encourage preachers to determine whether their preaching typically supports a mythic or parabolic theological worldview.

These two practical theological models would benefit by being put together. Tisdale's model ensures that decisions regarding changes in worldview are grounded in real issues existing in local contexts. My model encourages a close analysis of the operative theology already at work in the preacher's preaching and helps the preacher locate points of friction, or connection, in order to be more intentional and strategic in making changes to preached theology. In both models, it is the lived, operative *theologies* of congregation and preacher that guide the preacher's strategic interest in the way that preaching narrates or "stories" a worldview for the listener.

The category of narrative is not without its detractors. Richard Lischer has argued that, in fact, the gospel narrative contains eschatological elements such as resurrection that are disruptive of narrative and cannot be storied. Lischer has also argued that story is a very modest resource for ethical and social change. Based on more recent developments in social movement theory, Brooks Berndt argues that narrative can in fact become a vital tool for social and ethical change. On another front, David Lose has argued that the all-encompassing narrative claims for the Bible, as set forth by postliberal scholars, violate the incarnational aspect of the gospel. James W. Thompson critiques narrative preachers for the tendency to avoid other genres of biblical literature, especially nonnarrative literature that promotes more "reflective" forms of preaching.

Although these debates are likely to continue, it is clear that the study of the relationship between narrative and preaching leads directly to the center of contemporary homiletics. The garden of narrative has been tremendously fertile for homiletics over the past thirty years, and homileticians will likely continue to gather fruit there in the years to come.

Eugene L. Lowry, *The Homiletical Plot: The Sermon as Narrative Art Form*, expanded edition (Louisville, KY: Westminster John Knox Press, 2001); Edmund Steimle, Morris Niedenthal, and Charles Rice, *Preaching the Story*, reissue (Eugene OR: Wipf & Stock, 2003); Robert A. Jensen, *Telling the Story: Variety and Imagination in Preaching* (Minneapolis: Augsburg Publishing House, 1980); Fred B. Craddock, *As One without Authority*, revised and with new sermons (St. Louis: Chalice Press, 2001); John S. McClure, "Narrative and Preaching: Sorting It All Out," *Journal for Preachers* 15, no. 1: 24–29; John S. McClure, "The Narrative Function of Preaching," *Liturgy* 8, no. 2 (Fall 1989): 47–51; Thomas G. Long, *Preaching and the Literary Forms of the Bible* (Philadelphia: Fortress Press, 1989);

David Buttrick, "Interpretation and Preaching," *Interpretation* 25, no. 1 (Jan. 1981): 46–58; Wayne Bradley Robinson, ed., *Journeys toward Narrative Preaching* (New York: Pilgrim Press, 1990); Henry H. Mitchell, "Preaching on the Patriarchs," in James W. Cox, ed., *Biblical Preaching: An Expositor's Treasury* (Philadelphia: Westminster Press, 1988), 36–52; Joel B. Green and Michael Pasquarello III, eds., *Narrative Reading, Narrative Preaching: Reuniting New Testament Interpretation and Proclamation* (Grand Rapids: Baker Academic, 2003); Henry H. Mitchell, *The Recovery of Preaching* (San Francisco: Harper & Row, 1977); Charles Rice, "Shaping Sermons by the Interplay of Text and Metaphor," in Don Wardlaw, ed., *Preaching Biblically: Sermons in the Shape of Scripture* (Philadelphia: Westminster Press, 1985), 101–20; Charles L. Campbell, *Preaching Jesus: New Directions for Homiletics in Hans Frei's Postliberal Theology* (Grand Rapids: Wm. B. Eerdmans Publishing Co., 1997); Roger Standing, *Finding the Plot: Preaching in a Narrative Style* (Carlisle, UK: Paternoster Press, 2004); David M. Brown, *Dramatic Narrative in Preaching* (Valley Forge, PA: Judson Press, 1981); Leonora Tubbs Tisdale, *Preaching as Local Theology and Folk Art* (Minneapolis: Fortress Press, 1997); Richard Lischer, "The Limits of Story," *Interpretation* 38, no. 1: 26–38; Brooks Berndt, "The Politics of Narrative," *Homiletic* 29, no. 2: 1–11; Thomas G. Long, "What Happened to Narrative Preaching?" *Journal for Preachers* 28, no. 4: 9–14; David J. Lose, "Narrative and Proclamation in a Postliberal Homiletic," *Homiletic* 23, no. 1: 1–14; David J. Lose, *Confessing Jesus Christ: Preaching in a Postmodern World* (Grand Rapids: Wm. B. Eerdmans Publishing Co., 2003); James W. Thompson, *Preaching Like Paul: Homiletical Wisdom for Today* (Louisville, KY: Westminster John Knox Press, 2001).

New Homiletic   *A homiletic movement dating from the late 1960s through mid-1980s that turned away from rational-cognitive models of homiletics and pursued homiletic models grounded in *dialogue, *narrative, *induction, and *imagination.*

The term "New Homiletic" is attributed to David James Randolph, who in 1969 associated a new group of homileticians with the New Hermeneutic of Gerhard Ebeling and Ernst Fuchs. The New Hermeneutic, rooted in the work of Martin Heidegger, stressed a *performative understanding of language and contended that language and human communication generate "word-events." Preaching, in this perspective, would not be a matter of rational argument and persuasion, but an *event* through which the words of preaching provide for an experiential encounter with God. Homileticians representing the New Homiletic include Fred Craddock, who appeals for inductive forms of preaching; Charles Rice, who encouraged the use of literary imagination in the pulpit; Henry Mitchell, who stressed Afro-centric ideas of the experiential and celebrative power of human speech; Eugene Lowry, who encouraged a paradigm shift from rational outline to experiential plot; and the early work of Paul Scott Wilson, who encouraged preachers to make better use of *poetics in preaching.

For New Homiletic preachers, God's truth resides not in well-warranted and proven propositions, but in the ways in which symbols, *images, narratives, myths, parables, and *metaphors yield real knowledge of the experience of God. Sermons are not written to represent the world of faith in ideas and propositions, but to disclose hidden or forgotten meanings through the use of symbols, metaphors, and images.

New Homiletic preachers assume that there are common and essential forms of human experience, and they explore that experience as a repository for grace. They work hard to discover qualities of God's relationship to the world through the exploration and correlation of biblical and life symbols and by creating new metaphoric juxtapositions and reversals in sermons. They encourage imagination and the search for insight into the nature of ultimate reality by journeying outside the lines of formal logic.

In many respects, the New Homiletic represents the fruition of liberal theology and the idea that the Word of God exists as a response to the deepest problems and questions of human existence. This has led, in recent years, to a strong *postliberal and neo-Barthian critique among those who worry that the New Homiletic could reduce theology to anthropology, limiting God to One who responds to human needs.

The fundamental difference, however, between the New Homiletics and postliberal homiletics lies in views of human *language. For the New Homiletician, language expresses depth experience. It is appropriate, therefore, to assume some correlation between what is expressed (language or secondary experience) and what one encounters in life (primary experience). New Homileticians assume that the language they are speaking on Sunday morning is deeply interconnected with reality in all of its aspects. Postliberals, on the other hand, view language as nonfoundational in nature. It is not rooted or grounded in some form of primary experience external to language itself. For the postliberal preacher, language actually precedes "reality" and in fact gives reality to us. This means that the language of faith, for instance, can give to us *experiences for which there is no common reference point in experience at all*.

What both models bear in common is a performative view of language. What language performs for the New Homiletician is the manifestation of God in the world, using distinctively Christian categories. What language performs for the postliberal is the biblical text and the intrusive and alternative world that it brings into being, for which there is no corresponding manifestation in the world. The battle between these two ways of thinking is not likely to subside soon, and it may be that both sides are overdrawing the priority of either "experience" or "language" in their debate.

David James Randolph, *The Renewal of Preaching* (Philadelphia: Fortress Press, 1969); Fred B. Craddock, *As One without Authority*, revised and with new sermons (St. Louis: Chalice Press, 2001); Charles Rice, "Shaping Sermons by the Interplay of Text and Metaphor," in Don M. Wardlaw, ed., *Preaching Biblically:*

Sermons in the Shape of Scripture (Philadelphia: Westminster Press, 1983), 101–20; Edmund A. Steimle, Morris J. Niedenthal, and Charles Rice, *Preaching the Story* (Philadelphia: Fortress Press, 1980); Eugene L. Lowry, *The Homiletical Plot: The Sermon as Narrative Art Form*, expanded edition (Louisville, KY: Westminster John Knox Press, 2001); Charles L. Campbell, *Preaching Jesus: New Directions for Homiletics in Hans Frei's Postliberal Theology* (Grand Rapids: Wm. B. Eerdmans Publishing Co., 1997); Henry Mitchell, *The Recovery of Preaching* (San Francisco: Harper & Row, 1977); Eugene Lowry, *The Sermon: Dancing the Edges of Mystery* (Nashville: Abindgon Press, 1997); John E. Smith, *Experience and God* (Bronx, NY: Fordham University Press, 1995); Richard L. Eslinger, *A New Hearing: Living Options in Homiletical Method* (Nashville: Abingdon Press, 1987); John S. McClure, review of *Preaching Jesus*, by Charles L. Campbell, *Journal for Preachers* 21, no. 2 (1998): 36.

Nommo   *An Afrocentric term, taken from African mythology and folklore, designating the powers of the spoken word to create and generate reality.*

Afrocentric scholar Molefi Kete Asante identifies several unique elements within the idea of Nommo that prove helpful for understanding some of the unique characteristics of African American preaching. First, while Aristotelian rhetoric emphasizes the persuasive product of discourse, Nommo stresses the creative genius and power of the artist. This means that the spoken word is not so much an object as a powerful creative *attitude*. This attitude is deeply social in nature. It creates community in the midst of chaos. Second, Nommo is a collective activity. According to Asante, the distinction between speaker and audience largely disappears in African discourse. The performance of Nommo is a mutually empowering occurrence. Third, Nommo is concerned with restoring stability in the midst of conflict. The way this restoration is accomplished includes, and goes beyond, the way that *imagination resolves cognitive conflict. Nommo restores harmony through *tone*, *volume*, and *rhythm*. Vocal delivery, then, is focused on the search for new levels of harmony. Fourth, Nommo is about *naming*. It brings with it powers of incantation and conjuring, which in fact *produce what is named*. Fifth, Nommo is largely transrational in nature. It seeks a wholistic experience that does not rely on logic or syllogistic reasoning. Finally, Nommo resists chaos and oppression and creates celebration and liberation. It opens discourse and creates new spaces in which freedom of expression can flourish.

Molefi Kete Asante, *The Afrocentric Idea*, revised and expanded edition (Philadelphia: Temple University Press, 1998); Dale P. Andrews, *Practical Theology for Black Churches: Bridging Black Theology and African American Folk Religion* (Louisville, KY: Westminster John Knox Press, 2002); Henry H. Mitchell, *The Recovery of Preaching* (San Francisco: Harper & Row, 1977); L. Susan Bond, *Contemporary African American Preaching: Diversity in Theory and Style* (St. Louis: Chalice Press, 2003); Theophus H. Smith, *Conjuring Culture: Biblical Formations of Black America* (New York: Oxford University Press, 1994).

notes, preaching with *A method of *delivery making use of an outline or abbreviated notes.*

Often attributed to the great revivalist preacher Charles G. Finney, who used sermon "skeletons" in the pulpit, preaching with notes occupies the middle ground between *extemporaneous and *manuscript types of delivery. Preachers who preach from notes usually preach from some sort of outline, either culled from a complete manuscript or produced as the final written element in sermon preparation. It may contain key words, sentences, or phrases that lead into each section of the sermon. Outlines can be printed on small cards, or typed in bold-faced print on a single sheet of paper. Other supportive notes or documents may also be taken into the pulpit, such as exact quotations and newspaper clippings to be read.

Clyde Fant describes another method of preaching with notes called the "oral manuscript." In this model, preachers prepare sermons entirely in the oral domain and then jot down key lead-in sentences that will introduce each block of thought. Because the entire sermon preparation is done orally, the preacher avoids the problem of producing a written manuscript that must be reduced to an outline, and the accompanying sense that this manuscript must be remembered verbatim in the pulpit.

The advantage of preaching from notes is the increased ability to connect with one's listeners. Having some reference point in the pulpit also tends to relax both preacher and listener, decreasing the worry that the preacher will become lost. For those who do not feel self-confident enough to preach extemporaneously, but who prefer more contact with listeners than a manuscript permits, preaching from notes presents a good alternative.

James Cox, *Preaching: A Comprehensive Approach to the Design and Delivery of Sermons* (San Francisco: Harper & Row, 1985); Thomas G. Long, *The Witness of Preaching*, 2nd ed. (Louisville, KY: Westminster John Knox Press, 2005); Ronald J. Allen, *Interpreting the Gospel: An Introduction to Preaching* (St. Louis: Chalice Press, 1998); Clyde E. Fant, *Preaching for Today* (New York: Harper & Row, 1975).

occasional preaching *All forms of preaching that occur in response to occasions outside the normal weekly Lord's Day service.*

Preachers are called upon to preach at a variety of occasions: ecumenical Thanksgiving services, *weddings, *funerals, ordinations, commencements, church festivals, and conferences. In most of these situations, the preacher must engage in some form of *topical or *contextual preaching in what David Buttrick calls the *mode of praxis. The preacher starts with the situation at hand and then develops a theological perspective by asking the question, "What is God doing here?" From that point, the preacher can move toward identifying an appropriate biblical text, allowing the exegesis of the text to flesh out the theological theme. It is not necessary, however, to always focus on a specific text. In some cases, it is appropriate to preach a theological idea that is at work throughout Scripture.

Thomas G. Long and Neely Dixon McCarter, *Preaching in and out of Season* (Louisville, KY: Westminster John Knox Press, 1990); Scott M. Gibson, *Preaching for Special Services* (Grand Rapids: Baker Publishing Group, 2001); James A. Wallace, *Preaching to the Hungers of the Heart: Preaching on the Feasts and within the Rites* (Collegeville, MN: Liturgical Press, 2002); Ronald J. Allen, *Preaching the Topical Sermon* (Louisville, KY: Westminster John Knox Press, 1992); William D. Watley, *Sermons on Special Days: Preaching through the Year in the Black Church* (Valley Forge, PA: Judson Press, 1987).

oral   *Referring to the physical production of sound or speech.*

The word "oral" is paired with the word "*aural" to indicate the entire complex of speaking and hearing in preaching. The idea of preaching as an oral-aural event is focused on the acoustical aspects of preaching. The word "oral" indicates all of the vocal elements of preaching, inasmuch as they are used to generate and deepen meaning and facilitate communication. Most ancient cultures relied on the oral transmission of tradition through stories, myths, and legends. Most of the Bible was originally produced orally.

Folk traditions of preaching rely primarily on passing along the content of a tradition orally. Within oral traditions of preaching, the education and training of the preacher tends to occur by means of *mentoring, where oral styles of communication are learned by imitation. The idea of orality assumes that preaching is both communal and deeply participatory in nature. In some traditions, especially in African American churches, this oral/aural participation becomes stylized in the dynamics of *call and response.

Walter J. Ong, *The Presence of the Word: Some Prolegomena for Cultural and Religious History* (New Haven, CT: Yale University Press, 1967); Henry Mitchell, *The Recovery of Preaching* (San Francisco: Harper & Row, 1977); Paul Scott Wilson, *The Practice of Preaching* (Nashville: Abingdon Press, 1995); Tex Sample, *Ministry in an Oral Culture: Living with Will Rogers, Uncle Remus, and Minnie Pearl* (Louisville, KY: Westminster John Knox Press, 1994).

orator   *A preacher who delivers an eloquent and persuasive sermon.*

The idea of the orator is most often associated with the rhetoric of Cicero. Cicero presents the orator as the absolute master of all language and communication, known for wielding tremendous power within Roman society and politics. When attached to the preacher, the word "orator" usually refers to a preacher who is eloquent and skilled in the rhetorical arts. Reference is also made to the preacher's persuasive power and ability to attract large audiences. The orator-preacher usually has a significant public ministry.

The idea of the preacher as orator is often disputed. P. T. Forsyth argued that preaching is completely distinct from oratory, taking its cue, not from Greek *rhetoric, but from the Hebrew *prophets. He distinguishes between the *inspiration* of the orator and the *revelation* brought by the prophets and preachers.

Cicero, *On the Ideal Orator*, translated and with introduction, notes, and appendixes, glossary, and indexes, by James M. May and Jacob Wisse (New York: Oxford University Press, 2001); Halvord R. Ryan, *Harry Emerson Fosdick: Persuasive Preacher*, Great American Orators (Westport, CT: Greenwood Press, 1989); David B. Cheeseborough, *Philips Brooks: Pulpit Eloquence*, Great American Orators (Westport, CT: Greenwood Press, 2001); P. T. Forsyth, *Positive Preaching and the Modern Mind* (New York: A. C. Armstrong, 1907).

parabolic communication *A form of communication designed to introduce contradiction and unexpected irresolution, where reconciliation and order are assumed.*

According to John Dominic Crossan, parable is the polar opposite of myth and functions as an agent of *deconstruction, interruption, and change (see *mythic communication). Many parables take what *listeners expect to hear and reverse it. For instance, in the New Testament story of the Pharisee and the publican, we assume that the original listener expected the Pharisee's prayer to be accepted by God and the publican's to be rejected. In the story, however, the opposite occurs, opening the listener to new meanings.

Parabolic preaching encourages an *iconoclastic* worldview in congregations. Listeners learn to expect and enjoy the introduction of contradictions or unexpected tensions where none previously existed. In this way of thinking, God cannot be "storied" and remains elusive and surprising, able to change and bring about change at any time.

John Dominic Crossan, *The Dark Interval: Towards a Theology of Story* (Sonoma, CA: Polebridge Press, 1988); John S. McClure, "The Theosymbolic Code," in *The Four Codes of Preaching: Rhetorical Strategies* (Minneapolis: Fortress Press, 1991; reprinted, Louisville, KY: Westminster John Knox Press, 2003); Herb Anderson and Edward Foley, *Mighty Stories, Dangerous Rituals: Weaving Together the Human and the Divine* (San Francisco: Jossey-Bass, 2001); L. Susan Bond, "Taming the Parable: The Problem of Parable as Substitute Myth," *Homiletic 25*, no. 1 (Summer 2000): 1–12.

pastoral preaching   *Preaching that promotes care within the church and encourages a mission of care in the world.*

Harry Emerson Fosdick is often quoted as saying that preaching is "counseling on a group scale." Although pastoral preaching need not be viewed as an act of counseling, the idea that preaching is a part of the church's ministry of the cure of souls has a long and venerable history. Pastoral theologian Seward Hiltner asserted that preaching can have a central role in the larger shepherding ministry within a congregation. G. Lee Ramsey, following Hiltner, asserts that pastoral care is a theological perspective that should be operative in all preaching, whether in the foreground or not. The preacher's theological understanding of what it means to shepherd and offer care is deeply embedded in the way that the human condition is articulated in preaching and the ways that the church is understood to respond to that condition. Over time, pastoral preaching creates what Ramsey calls "the caring community," a larger communal sanctuary or safe holding environment for the deepest issues within the congregation and the world.

Beyond this pastoral dimension that should be a part of all sermons, it is often the case that pastoral preaching deliberately addresses deeply personal concerns. In this sense, preaching actually becomes a form of group counseling. According to J. Randall Nichols, there is a role for pastoral sermons that address specific human needs. Nichols asserts that such sermons will have both a pastoral (shepherding, caregiving) *strategy*, and a pastoral *subject* (suffering, pain, sexual and domestic violence, depression, divorce, loss, and so forth).

Nichols identifies several key objectives for all preaching that has pastoral intention and content. First, it should help people discover God's grace and purpose for their lives. This does not mean the preacher is an answer person or the holder of the keys. The pastoral preacher helps the listener find his or her own way. Second, pastoral preachers are not to help listeners escape into a mythological fantasy world in order to deal with problems or issues. Instead, pastoral preaching helps listeners learn to live in the real world with a greater sense of competence. Third, pastoral preaching helps people take responsibility for their feelings and actions. It does not promote a victim mentality. Although listeners may indeed have been the victims of terrible things, the ultimate goal is to move beyond victimization to empowerment and responsible action. Fourth, pastoral preaching should help individuals and congregations learn how to go through life transitions. Transition is a fundamental experience in life, whether associated with death, divorce, empty nest, or aging. Preachers need to help congregations think through what it means to grieve and find new ways to move forward in life. This is especially true in *funeral preaching. Fifth, pastoral preaching should help people move beyond concern with their own issues or problems to a place where they can bond with others in common mission. The goal of pastoral preaching is not self-fulfillment but fullness of life lived in community. Sixth, pastoral preaching frees people to feel. This does not mean emoting; rather the goal is to help people accept that they do, in fact, have real feelings, and take responsibility for them in the healthiest way possible. Seventh, pastoral preaching helps people make sense out of their lives. This does not mean explaining things away. It means working with people to find a way through that has both theological and emotional integrity. Finally, using Paul Tillich's language for justification by faith, Nichols asserts that pastoral preaching is about helping people "accept acceptance." Accepting the fact that God really does love and care is sometimes one of the most difficult but important breakthroughs for the living of full and healthy lives.

Although much has been made of the distinctions between pastoral and prophetic preaching, Nichols identifies at least one aspect of both that places them on common ground. This is the business of helping people *reframe* their lives in a way that provides a fresh, transforming, and restorative theological vision for living. Walter Brueggemann, making use of Freud's theory of psychoanalysis and dream interpretation, speaks similarly of prophetic preaching as "re-imagination." According to Brueggemann, prophetic preaching "re-scripts" reality, encouraging human transformation "through the playful entertainment of another scripting of reality." For the prophetic preacher, this script is defined by the biblical vision for justice. For the pastoral preacher, the new script is defined by the biblical vision of care and human restoration.

Harry Emerson Fosdick, "Personal Counseling and Preaching," *Pastoral Psychology* 3, no. 22 (Mar. 1952): 11–15; Edmund Holt Linn, *Preaching as Counseling: The Unique Method of Harry Emerson Fosdick* (Valley Forge, PA: Judson Press, 1966); Seward Hiltner, *Preface to Pastoral Theology* (Nashville: Abingdon Press, 1979); G. Lee Ramsey, *Care-full Preaching: From Sermon to Caring Community* (St. Louis: Chalice Press, 2000); J. Randall Nichols, *The Restoring Word: Preaching as Pastoral Communication* (San Francisco: Harper & Row, 1987); Edward P. Wimberly, *Moving from Shame to Self-worth: Preaching and Pastoral Care* (Nashville: Abingdon Press, 1999); Walter Brueggemann, *Cadences of Home: Preaching among Exiles* (Louisville, KY: Westminster John Knox Press, 1997).

pathos   *Persuasive appeals to *listeners' emotions.*

Pathos is one of the three means of persuasion identified by Aristotle (see *ethos and *logos). The question guiding homiletic *pathos* is, "Why should my listeners care?" The preacher searches for ways to engage the worldview and emotions of the congregation in order to persuade them that what is being said is true and should be taken seriously. Preachers use *empathy and *identification to enter the lives of the congregation in search of ways to connect the message with things that truly matter to listeners.

The idea of *pathos* can be abused in preaching. Preachers can use manipulative means such as sentimental illustrations to toy with the emotions of listeners. In some instances, preachers will find heart-rending stories and build entire sermons around them. One of the most striking findings of the *Listening to Listeners Project was the keen awareness among sermon listeners of this kind of manipulation. Some listeners identified this as a sign of lack of preparation on the preacher's part. Others felt it showed that the preacher underestimated their intelligence. Most felt manipulated and distracted.

The goal of sermon *pathos* is not to manipulate or break down the defenses of the listener. Rather, the goal is an open, empathic correlation of the sermon's message with important concerns in the lives of listeners, so that they will personally invest in what is being said.

Lucy Lind Hogan and Robert Reid, *Connecting with the Congregation: Rhetoric and the Art of Preaching* (Nashville: Abingdon Press, 1999); André Resner Jr., *Preacher and Cross: Person and Message in Theology and Rhetoric* (Grand Rapids: Wm. B. Eerdmans Publishing Co., 1999).

performance   *The public presentation of a sermon, usually associated with preaching as *drama.*

performative language   *Language in preaching that serves to create an effect or bring something into being.*

The idea of performative language comes from *speech act theory, a theory of language which asserts that the purpose of language is not to *mean* but to *do.* Preaching is performative inasmuch as it attempts to bring about a real, immediate, "in the moment," encounter, rather than promoting reflection on whether an assertion is true, false, reasonable, or helpful.

Several homileticians, in very different ways, have incorporated the idea of performative language into their homiletic theories. David Buttrick's *mode of immediacy is grounded in the theory of performative language. He argues that sermons can adopt the performative intentions of biblical language, *doing* what the biblical language seeks to do. Homileticians interested in preaching as *drama, such as Jana Childers and Richard Ward, are also concerned with the performative qualities of language. They broaden the definition to include nonverbals, or *kinesics. *Postliberal homileticians emphasize the *constructive* function of language through which the performance of a system of language (biblical language, for instance) works like a grammar to call into being actual forms of reality and practice. For the postliberal preacher, biblical language constitutes a new reality through its performative power in the pulpit. In the African American tradition, the performative aspects of language can be traced, in part, to the Afrocentric idea of *Nommo, through which speech is said to name reality in such a way as to conjure it or to invoke it. In this instance, performative language creates empowerment and community in the midst of oppression and chaos.

David Buttrick, *Homiletic: Moves and Structures* (Philadelphia: Fortress Press, 1987); Stanley P. Saunders and Charles L. Campbell, *The Word on the Street: Performing the Scriptures in the Urban Context* (Grand Rapids: Wm. B. Eerdmans Publishing Co., 2000); Charles L. Campbell, *The Word before the Powers: An Ethic of Preaching* (Louisville, KY: Westminster John Knox Press, 2002); Jana Childers, *Performing the Word: Preaching as Theatre* (Nashville: Abingdon Press, 1998); Richard F. Ward, *Speaking from the Heart: Preaching with Passion* (Eugene, OR: Wipf & Stock, 2001); Molefi Kete Asante, *The Afrocentric Idea*, revised and expanded edition (Philadelphia: Temple University Press, 1998); Theophus H. Smith, *Conjuring Culture: Biblical Formations of Black America* (New York: Oxford University Press, 1994); Henry H. Mitchell, *The Recovery of Preaching* (San Francisco: Harper & Row, 1977).

personality   *The psychology of the preacher in the event of preaching.*

It is important to distinguish personality, a psychological term, from the word *character, an ethical term, **ethos*, a rhetorical term, and *authenticity, a philosophical term. These terms are related, however, inasmuch as they refer to qualities of the preacher that are important for *communication. When the well-known nineteenth-century preacher Phillips Brooks defined preaching as the bringing of "truth through personality," he was, in fact, referring precisely to this larger configuration of qualities brought into the pulpit in the person of the preacher. Craig Loscalzo points out that Brooks meant to call attention to the human and incarnational aspect of preaching, the fact that God chooses to communicate through earthen vessels and clay pots.

As modern psychology blossomed in the twentieth century, homiletic literature demonstrated an increased concern for the personality of the preacher in mostly psychological terms. In the 1950s and 1960s, the journal *Pastoral Psychology* published regular articles on this subject. Psychologists worried about authoritarian pathologies in the pulpit and about preachers who were manipulative, angry, aggressive, or hostile. By the mid-1970s, in some denominations, psychological testing became standard ordination procedure for preachers in training.

J. Randall Nichols urges preachers to become aware of how personal

struggles and issues of faith are, in fact, subtexts in the pulpit. He urges homileticians not just to help preachers to write sermons, but to be involved in "the training of the personality of the preacher." When one considers personality and preaching, it is important to focus attention on vocational identity, mental health, and spiritual formation. James Cox, adapting an image by H. H. Rowley, points out that the word of God comes through the personality of the preacher "like the rays of light that pass through colored glass. It is the same light, yet it is wholly modified by what it passes through." Walter Burghardt goes still further: "Ultimately, I am the word, the word that is heard."

Phillips Brooks, *Eight Lectures on Preaching* (London: SPCK Press, 1959); Rufus Bowman, "Personality and Preaching," *Pastoral Psychology* 5, no. 48 (Nov. 1954): 8–12; Earl Furgeson, "Preaching and Personality," *Pastoral Psychology* 10, no. 7 (Oct. 1959): 9–14; Craig Loscalzo, *Preaching Sermons That Connect: Effective Communication through Identification* (Downers Grove, IL: InterVarsity Press, 1992); J. Randall Nichols, *Building the Word: The Dynamics of Communication in Preaching* (San Francisco: Harper & Row, 1980); James W. Cox, *Preaching* (San Francisco: Harper & Row, 1985); Walter J. Burghardt, SJ, *Preaching: The Art and the Craft* (New York: Paulist Press, 1987); Hans Van Der Geest, *Presence in the Pulpit: The Impact of Personality in Preaching* (Atlanta: John Knox Press, 1981); André Resner Jr., *Preacher and Cross: Person and Message in Theology and Rhetoric* (Grand Rapids: Wm. B. Eerdmans Publishing Co., 1999).

pitch   *The relative highness or lowness of the preacher's voice.*

Pitch is an important aspect of *articulation. Pitch is also helpful for making a sermon *audible. Words and sentences that vary in pitch are easier to hear and follow. Varying one's pitch in a natural way is also a crucial element for maintaining the listener's attention and interest.

It is important to use pitch in a *meaningful* way, that is, as a tool for interpreting meaning. For instance, a rising pitch at the end of a sentence usually indicates a question. Pitch helps the preacher communicate the precise meaning of words or sentences.

Problems with pitch can be identified by listening to oneself on audio or video equipment. It is usually easy to hear repetitious or predictable patterns. Altering predictable pitch patterns takes practice and periodic audio or video evaluation.

G. Robert Jacks, *Getting the Word Across: Speech Communication for Pastors and Lay Leaders* (Grand Rapids: Wm. B. Eerdmans Publishing Co., 1987); Joseph A. DeVito, *Human Communication: The Basic Course*, 10th ed. (Boston: Allyn & Bacon, 2005).

plagiarism   *Intentionally presenting someone else's ideas, language, stories, or sermon as one's own.*

Using another preacher's materials as one's own has a long history in the church. Raymond Bailey points out that Augustine proposed that those better at delivering sermons than composing them should preach the wisdom of others. Augustine added, however, that this should be done "without deception." In an age of lectionary resources and Internet sermon stores, the speed with which a preacher can "cut and paste" another's thoughts into a sermon has increased dramatically.

There are several typical types of sermon plagiarism. In some cases, entire sermons are presented as the preacher's own work. In other instances, sentences, turns of phrase, or quips are used in passing. Another common form of plagiarism involves taking someone else's story, or even personal experience, and passing it off as one's own. Finally, there is the practice of taking basic themes, approaches to a subject, or outline, and using them as one's own. Richard Lischer points out that, in some African American preaching traditions, this last approach is common. He traces the ways that Martin Luther King Jr. reappropriated the sermon approaches and outlines of great preachers and reworked them in new contexts. He also points out that, in many cases, a stylized approach to certain kinds of subjects is present within the African American community or its folklore. This style or attitude is often used by the preacher to great effect, with no expectation of attribution.

There are some who argue for forms of soft plagiarism in preaching. After all, is anything really original? William Willimon, for instance, argues that we are all products of traditions. He goes on to argue that, to some extent, treating ideas as property is more a capitalist than Christian concept. Others argue that attribution in preaching can become boring and distracting and that most people would rather not hear it. Some argue that learning by imitating others' ideas and storytelling is important. Although all of these arguments make some sense, it is important to draw the line somewhere.

The essential problem is not copying or borrowing, but passing someone else's thoughts or words off as one's own. This constitutes a serious breach of *ethics and presents the danger, in Carter Shelley's words, of "undermining the preacher's credibility." There is also an issue of personal integrity and spiritual formation. Eugene Lowry points out that, in essence, pulpit plagiarism betrays the trust placed in the preacher by the congregation. Shelley also points to a loss of immediacy, relevance, and authenticity when plagiarism is common. Typically, copied material pulls the preacher out of the present situation and into some other world. Finally, there is the problem of dependence on others. Shelley points out that a constant practice of using the material of others stunts and distorts the preacher's own personal development and can lead to a loss of *voice in preaching.

Homileticians offer several guidelines for practice. First, they advise never telling another person's story as one's own, which represents the pinnacle of falseness in the pulpit. Second, without getting into name-dropping, preachers can offer brief thanks for all sources. If sermons will be published and made available in the narthex or online, it is crucial to ensure that these attributions are included as footnotes in the typed sermon. Third, preachers should limit the preaching of others' sermons to special occasions or absolute crisis situations. When this occurs, preachers should acknowledge publicly that this is being done. Finally, Laurie Tiberi presents a good general rule: "When in doubt, attribute."

Raymond H. Bailey, "Ethics in Preaching," *Review and Expositor* 86 (1989): 533–37; Eugene L. Lowry, "Preaching or Reciting: Theft in the Pulpit," *Christian Ministry*, Mar.–Apr. 1991, 9–12; William H. Willimon, "Borrowed Thoughts on Sermonic Borrowing," *Christian Ministry*, Jan.–Feb. 1997, 14–16; Laurie Tiberi, "Borrowing Is OK: Lying Is Not," *Christian Ministry*, Jan.–Feb. 1997, 17–18; Richard Lischer, "How the Preacher King Borrowed Sermons," *Christian Ministry*, Jan.–Feb. 1997, 19–21; Carter Shelley, "Preaching and Plagiarism: A Guide for Introduction to Preaching Students," *Homiletic* 27, no. 2: 1–13; Hunter Beckelhymer, "No Posturing in Borrowed Plumes," *Christian Century* 91, no. 5 (Feb. 1974): 138–42; Johnston McKay, "And Finally . . . No Copyright on Sermons," *Expository Times* 115, no. 3 (Dec. 2003): 108.

planning   *The discipline of looking ahead and organizing preaching goals.*

Planning is an essential aspect of the successful preaching ministry. Preachers must always look ahead, anticipating those aspects of church and community life that should influence sermon preparation. First, this means paying careful attention to the *liturgical calendar*, which includes the major seasons of the liturgical year: Easter, Pentecost, Advent, Christmas, Epiphany, Transfiguration, and Lent. Second, it means attending to the *ecclesiastical calendar*, which varies from denomination to denomination. This may include such things as World Communion Sunday, Race Relations Sunday, and Ecumenical Relations Sunday. Third, preachers must attend to the *local church calendar*, which includes such things as baptisms, confirmations, commissioning of church officers, and stewardship Sunday. Finally, there is the *civic calendar*, which includes public holidays such as Thanksgiving, the birthday of Martin Luther King Jr., and, for better or worse, special cultural celebrations such as Mother's Day and Super Bowl Sunday. All of these calendars will have some impact on sermon planning.

Another aspect of sermon planning, increasingly popular today, is the planning of sermon series. Preachers can decide to preach through a portion of

Scripture or preach several teaching series addressing personal, ecclesial, or social issues. Series planning can dovetail with the liturgical calendar. Lent, for instance, is a good time to pursue topics related to catechizing or teaching faith, especially in churches committed to a liturgical evangelism process that culminates in Easter baptisms or celebrations of membership (see *evangelistic preaching).

In multiple-staff congregations, sermon planning involves administrative coordination, especially with church musicians. This may mean that preachers need to select preaching texts and broad topics well ahead of time. Choirs generally need to begin rehearsing anthems eight to ten weeks in advance.

Tom Long identifies several goals for sermon planning that are useful to remember. First, preachers should be flexible. Always allow room for the unexpected to occur. When unscheduled events of significance occur, especially crisis events, it is *always* important for the preacher to revise the preaching plan. Second, preachers should strive for variety, ensuring their preaching covers a range of themes cutting across the many calendars that must be kept. Third, sermon planning should try to achieve some breadth. Preaching cannot all be focused on personal issues, social issues, or favorite portions of Scripture. Fourth, preachers should seek depth. In some cases, a single sermon is not enough to cover an important topic. Returning to a theme can help the preacher keep from skimming the surface of an important topic. Finally, preachers should always be prepared to respond to the immediate needs of the congregation. A sermon plan should be sensitized by the emerging issues within a congregation.

Many preachers take an annual or semiannual retreat to plan sermons. Once a basic outline for six months or a year has been established, the preacher can take the time to do some initial spadework with the biblical texts, in order to supply helpful information to musicians or others involved with worship planning.

Thomas G. Long and Neely Dixon McCarter, *Preaching in and out of Season* (Louisville, KY: Westminster John Knox Press, 1990); Thomas G. Long, "Patterns in Sermons," in John S. McClure, ed., *Best Advice for Preaching* (Minneapolis: Fortress Press, 1998), 35–49; Ronald J. Allen, *Preaching the Topical Sermon* (Louisville, KY: Westminster John Knox Press, 1992).

plot   *A literary term used to describe the organization of a sermon to follow the linear pattern of a story.*

In the late 1970s and early 1980s homileticians became very interested in the relationship between preaching and *narrative. In 1980 Eugene L. Lowry published a very popular little book entitled *The Homiletical Plot: The Sermon as Narrative Art Form*. In this book, he created what is now commonly known as the *Lowry Loop to describe the way a simple narrative plot functions in a sermon. The first part of the loop involves *upsetting the equilibrium*. An enigma is presented that energizes the sermon's forward movement: something is wrong that needs fixing, something is out of balance that needs restoration, something is missing that needs finding, something is confusing that needs clarification, and so forth. This problem is deepened in the second, downward part of the loop, called *analyzing the discrepancy*. Like a good plotline, the sermon goes deeper into the problem at hand, complicating the issue and creating a heightened concern among listeners. At this point, the sermon reaches the bottom of the loop, in which the preacher *discloses the clue to resolution*. This is the decisive turning point in the plot. The gospel brings a reversal or "Aha" that begins to move the loop upward toward resolution. From here the sermon moves upward in the fourth part of the loop, *experiencing the gospel*. The preacher fleshes out the good news of the gospel and its meaning. Finally, at the end of the loop, the sermon helps the congregation *anticipate the consequences*. The preacher unpacks fully the implications of the sermon's message for the living of life. In order to help preachers remember each aspect of the loop, Lowry created a little memory device for each part of the loop: Oops! Ugh! Aha! Whee! Yeah!

It is important to distinguish between "problem-solution" sermons and plotted sermons. In a problem-solution sermon, the preacher rationally *explains* a problem or issue and then asserts the gospel as a logical answer. Problem-solution preaching, therefore, is nondialogical. The problem is introduced arbitrarily by the speaker and then resolved. David Buttrick points out that plots are far more interactive in development. Plotted problems have to be negotiated between preacher and listener. They are developed inductively, as enigmatic or troublesome experiences, throwing both preacher and listener into the midst of shared problems. Buttrick also argues that plotting accentuates point of view in preaching. Is the preacher "in the sermon" scrapping around with a problem alongside listeners? Or does the preacher adopt a "third-person-omniscient" point of view in which preacher and listener are overhearing or observing others dealing with a problem?

The other way plot enters the sermon is by way of the biblical text. Many preachers have become interested in adopting the shape of the biblical narrative as the *form of their sermons. David Buttrick especially has encouraged this approach in his arguments for the *mode of immediacy in preaching.

In the last analysis, the idea of plot may be the single most influential aspect of the narrative and preaching movement. It remains a useful tool for organizing and enlivening sermon messages.

Eugene L. Lowry, *The Homiletical Plot: The Sermon as Narrative Art Form*, expanded edition (Louisville, KY: Westminster John Knox Press, 2001); David

Buttrick, *Homiletic: Moves and Structures* (Philadelphia: Fortress Press, 1987); Richard L. Eslinger, *A New Hearing: Living Options in Homiletical Method* (Nashville: Abingdon Press, 1987); Thomas G. Long, *Preaching and the Literary Forms of the Bible* (Philadelphia: Fortress Press, 1989); Don M. Wardlaw, ed., *Preaching Biblically: Sermons in the Shape of Scripture* (Philadelphia: Westminster Press, 1983); Paul Scott Wilson, *The Practice of Preaching* (Nashville: Abingdon Press, 1995).

pluralism *Multiple and sometimes competing views of God and ultimate reality.*

In today's world, diversity comes in the shape not only of *multiculturalism, but of different religious or secular claims regarding ultimate reality. Preachers must decide how they will deal with these claims.

It is not appropriate to equate pluralism with relativism, the idea that, since there are so many religions and religious philosophies, "anything goes." Pluralism encourages some form of *conversation, *dialogue, debate, or argument about these matters in an attempt to sort out basic categories, differences, and similarities. Faced with religious and theological pluralism, preachers typically adopt one of five stances.

First, some preachers will preach a *radical exclusivism*. Although they may accept basic forms of legal and social tolerance, they nonetheless reject other belief systems entirely and assert the uniqueness and singularity of the Christian revelation as they understand it. A second model is *radical inclusivism*. This way of thinking moves to the other extreme and asserts that the differences between belief systems are peripheral to their essential truths, which are at bottom very similar. Within a broad range of the world's dominant belief systems, inclusivists identify similar ethical ideals such as justice, peace, and compassion. In *hierarchical pluralism*, a third option, a belief system is distinguished from others as a higher and more complete truth. Although all religions or belief systems contain some element of truth, there is an ascending ladder of religions, with a particular understanding of Christianity as the pinnacle. A fourth option is *radical pluralism*, which views different religious worldviews as completely incompatible language games. Each is operating through its own very particular history, culture, language, and set of practices. It is a mistake to think that the essence of a belief system lies under its particulars. Learning a religious worldview is like learning a language, and the truths rendered by different languages are totally distinct. Finally, there is *dynamic pluralism*. This model, like radical pluralism, asserts that religious worldviews are like distinct language games. Dynamic pluralism, however, has a more fluid vision of the ways cultures and languages are interrelated. Dynamic pluralists do not accept the idea that worldviews, languages, and religious practices can be altogether pure. At the same time, they assert that the rules of one language game can be influenced, and perhaps even transformed, by the rules of another game. The Christian, for instance, might learn something helpful about prayer in its relation to human suffering by studying forms of Buddhist contemplation. A liberal Christian might learn something fruitful about forms of worship from a fundamentalist.

Pluralism is here to stay, and, as should now be obvious, there is a pluralism of ways to respond to pluralism! Preachers will need to decide, in conversation with others, how to situate themselves and their preaching in the midst of this diverse and complicated world.

Burton Z Cooper and John S. McClure, *Claiming Theology in the Pulpit* (Louisville, KY: Westminster John Knox Press, 2003); Chris Altrock, *Preaching to Pluralists: How to Proclaim Christ in a Postmodern Age* (St. Louis: Chalice Press, 2004); James R. Nieman and Thomas G. Rogers, *Preaching to Every Pew: Cross-Cultural Strategies* (Minneapolis: Augsburg Fortress Press, 2001); Thomas H. Troeger, *The Parable of Ten Preachers* (Nashville: Abingdon Press, 1992).

poetics   *A broad category that includes all of the* literary *elements relevant to the practice of preaching.*

Included in the poetics of preaching are elements such as allegory, analogy, *narrative, narrative character, comparison, description, *image, *metaphor, simile, *metonymy, *parable, *plot, sequence, and *synecdoche.

Paul Scott Wilson, *The Practice of Preaching* (Nashville: Abingdon Press, 1995); Thomas H. Troeger, "The Poetics of the Pulpit for Post-Modern Times," in Richard L. Eslinger, ed. *Intersections: Post-Critical Studies in Preaching* (Grand Rapids: Wm. B. Eerdmans, 1994), 42–64.

point   *An older term designating the core of an assertion made in preaching.*

In some quarters today, it is still common parlance to speak about sermon points, or preachers making points. The word "point" implies sharpness, force, emphasis, and assertiveness. It is, therefore, a term more appropriate to sermon *forms in which *deductive assertions or arguments are being made. There is some likelihood that this word also implies its *kinesics or body language counterpoint: the *gesture of pointing at one's audience. It also indicates outlining, in which there are points and subpoints. This language has recently found its way in computer terminology, with the popularity of PowerPoint presentation software.

It should be noted that this language has been largely discarded in homiletics today, in the wake of *inductive and *narrative preaching. It is more typical today to hear preachers speak of *moves, movements of thought, thought blocks, or sequences. "Point" is still a useful word, however, especially when preachers are using more *deductive forms of preaching. This language can also help the preacher identify in a very specific way exact thoughts, assertions, or ideas within a sermon.

H. Grady Davis, *Design for Preaching* (Philadelphia: Fortress Press, 1958); Joseph M. Webb, *Preaching without Notes* (Nashville: Abingdon Press, 2001); Mark Galli and Craig Brian Larson, *Preaching That Connects: Using Journalistic Techniques to Add Impact* (Grand Rapids: Zondervan Press, 1994); Wayne McDill, *The Twelve Essential Skills for Great Preaching* (Nashville: Broadman & Holman, 1998).

postliberal preaching   *Preaching people* into *the biblical story.*

Postliberalism is *post*liberal in the sense that it is largely a reaction to liberalism in theology and preaching. Liberal theologians typically assume that there is a point of contact between revelation and human experience and seek to find existential or philosophical correlations between biblical categories of thought and human reason or experience. Just as Karl Barth denied this point of contact, postliberal theologians assert the uniqueness, strangeness, or oddness of biblical faith, asserting that it cannot be correlated or translated into modern philosophical or existential categories. Key postliberal scholars, such as the biblical theologian Hans Frei and systematic theologian George Lindbeck, have claimed strongly the absolute primacy of *language, including religious practices, for creating and sustaining Christian faith.

Postliberal preaching is predicated on the presupposition that language precedes and constructs experience and reality. In this sense, it is a strongly linguistic homiletic. The goal of preaching is to relanguage people's lives. Postliberal preaching is also grounded in a *narrative worldview. Instead of translating biblical categories into common experiential categories (the liberal option), the goal is to somehow translate, or convert, human experience into categories provided by the biblical narrative. Postliberal homileticians such as Charles L. Campbell are very critical of *inductive preaching and narrative enculturation in preaching, which place the accent on translating biblical language into categories and stories derived from human experience. Instead of preaching narratives that attempt to *experientialize biblical texts*, postliberal preachers focus on using the biblical text to *textualize human experience*.

The primary criticism of this model is its tendency, in some versions, toward forms of sectarianism that isolate preaching from any integral relationship with the public square. Since all language is constructed in and by language games or practices, preachers may settle for forms of exclusive, hierarchic, or radical *pluralism, in which there is no room for dialogue across language games or worldviews. This can support isolationist thinking or

all-encompassing, hegemonic biblical theologies that are immune from critiques issuing from other narratives that testify about real human experiences
of suffering.

Postliberal homileticians and others are addressing these issues in a variety
of ways. Charles L. Campbell and Stanley P. Saunders encourage preachers to
improvise the Scriptures in social contexts in which human suffering is greatest. This is not done to persuade or transform either the suffering listeners or
their persecutors. Instead, the preacher places the biblical narratives, especially biblical characters, into solidarity with those who are suffering and proclaims a biblical message of resistance and hope. David Lose urges postliberal
preachers toward dynamic forms of pluralism, by asserting the permeability of
the boundaries of so-called language games and appealing for a mutually cor-
recting conversation across confessional stances.

Charles L. Campbell, *Preaching Jesus: New Directions for Homiletics in Hans Frei's
Postliberal Theology* (Grand Rapids: Wm. B. Eerdmans Publishing Co., 1997);
Mark Ellingsen, *The Integrity of Biblical Narrative: Story in Theology and Procla-
mation* (Minneapolis: Fortress Press, 1990); George Lindbeck, *The Nature of
Doctrine: Religion and Theology in a Postliberal Age* (Philadelphia: Westminster
Press, 1984); William H. Willimon and Stanley Hauerwas, *Preaching to
Strangers: Evangelism in Today's World* (Louisville, KY: Westminster John Knox
Press, 1992); William H. Willimon, *Peculiar Speech: Preaching to the Baptized*
(Grand Rapids: Wm. B. Eerdmans Publishing Co., 1992); William Willimon,
The Intrusive Word: Preaching to the Unbaptized (Grand Rapids: Wm. B. Eerd-
mans Publishing Co., 1994); Stanley P. Saunders and Charles L. Campbell, *The
Word on the Street: Performing the Scriptures in the Urban Context* (Grand Rapids:
Wm. B. Eerdmans Publishing Co., 2000); Charles L. Campbell, *The Word before
the Powers: An Ethic of Preaching* (Louisville, KY: Westminster John Knox Press,
2002); David J. Lose, *Confessing Jesus Christ: Preaching in a Postmodern World*
(Grand Rapids: Wm. B. Eerdmans Publishing Co., 2003).

postmodern preaching   *Preaching that responds to the postmodern situation.*

Although postmodernism can be construed in a wide variety of ways, the word
generally refers to a situation influenced by a *deconstructive* critique through
which all larger metanarratives (worldviews) are decentered, brought down to
size, and placed alongside other narratives, little and big, in a competing marketplace of ideas and systems of meaning. As post*modern*, the modern Enlightenment metanarrative has been the first to undergo critique and decentering.
No one has escaped, however, and Christianity, capitalism, consumerism, and
other metanarratives have also undergone similar downsizing and been placed
alongside all other possible worldviews. Postmodernism asserts that there is

no common human vantage point from which to objectively or redemptively view reality, whether it be reason, human experience, biblical revelation, systems of exchange or value, or any other system. This means, ultimately, that there are no center and no margins. We live in a context of radical difference, in which everyone is "other" and no one is "same."

Since the Enlightenment metanarrative grounded in reason and common human experience formed the backbone of the liberal *New Homiletic, and the biblical metanarrative as normative constitutes the center of *postliberal preaching, this is a significant metacritique for many homileticians and preachers today. Is it possible to preach in a truly decentered way?

Several responses to the decentering of liberal assumptions regarding common human experience have been forthcoming. In one model, homileticians pursue forms of preaching that will welcome a broad range of other narratives, with all their differences, into homiletic practice. This is typically accomplished through *collaborative or *conversational models of preaching. These are homiletics of welcome, through which a multitude of others are seated at the homiletic table, contributing to both brainstorming sermons and providing *feedback. The concern to welcome *difference* in preaching has also issued in a number of homiletic textbooks embracing *multicultural perspectives, the perspective of victims of domestic violence, victims of racism, classism, ageism, ableism, and so on. Another model, suggested by David Lose, asserts the importance of the preacher's confessional stance within a broad homiletic conversation. In still another model, Anna Carter Florence and others have begun to argue that a reinvestigation of *testimony will be the best way of encouraging a decentered homiletic.

In response to the decentering of narratives, including the biblical narrative, postliberal homiletician Charles Campbell has stressed the ways in which preaching constitutes a local improvisation or local performance of the biblical text. This leads to multiple forms of communal and individual practice that could not easily have been predicted, based on the biblical narrative in and of itself. Although listeners are invited into the biblical metanarrative, they are not expected to become clones of biblical characters. Each local improvisation of the language of the biblical text will yield a different local narrative and form of practice.

One problem posed by postmodern decentering is the linking together of radical individualism with the politics of identity, which may encourage people simply to go separate ways rather than learn to work together. This could lead to a dissipation of the kinds of solidarities among different people required to bring about real social change. How can preachers create a sense of common purpose and support strong forms of social solidarity with persons who are defined mostly by difference? In most cases, these solidarities, or what Mary Fulkerson and Anna Carter Florence call "affinities," will emerge only by placing oneself into real proximity with others in face-to-face situations, so that vulnerability and common responsibility for one another can emerge. Again, collaborative and conversational approaches to preaching are sugges-tive, since they rely on building some form of real relational network around the pulpit.

There are, of course, many reactionary ways to preach in a postmodern context. Some preachers see nothing but relativism, chaos, and nihilism in the pluralism and openness fostered by postmodernity, and find in this an oppor-tunity to reassert a timeless evangelical message. Chris Altrock, for instance, encourages preachers to use postmodern technologies and careful communi-cation strategies to target and evangelize cultural postmoderns who are anx-ious about truth and seek to belong somewhere in a pluralist, multicultural, and decentered world.

Cultural postmoderns express a relative distaste for ecclesiastical institu-tions and denominations. They are not likely to identify themselves as Pres-byterian, Lutheran, Methodist, and so on. This is to be expected in a decentered society. The catchphrase for this phenomenon is, "They like Jesus, but not the church." This is sometimes called a "post-Christendom" context for preaching. So-called postmoderns place a very high premium on *authen-ticity, *relationships, and the creation of small groups, communities of inter-est, and networks of friends. Such community building is crucial in an age in which larger institutions have lost their power as carriers of group identity. For this reason, small groups are increasingly important in many churches. Preachers, therefore, might follow suit, considering ways to build a commu-nity of learning and proclamation around the pulpit. Again, collaborative, con-versational, and *testimonial models are suggestive.

Ronald J. Allen, Barbara Shires Blaisdale, and Scott Black Johnston, *Theology for Preaching: Authority, Truth, and Knowledge in a Postmodern Ethos* (Nashville: Abingdon Press, 1997); John S. McClure, *Other-wise Preaching: A Postmodern Ethic for Homiletics* (St. Louis: Chalice Press, 2001); John S. McClure, *The Roundtable Pulpit: Where Leadership and Preaching Meet* (Nashville: Abingdon Press, 1995); Lucy Atkinson Rose, *Sharing the Word: Preaching in the Roundtable Church* (Louisville, KY: Westminster John Knox Press, 1997); Kathy Black, *A Healing Homiletic: Preaching and Disability* (Nashville: Abingdon Press, 1996); Christine Smith, *Preaching as Weeping, Confession, and Resistance: Radical Responses to Radical Evil* (Louisville, KY: Westminster John Knox Press, 1992); John S. McClure and Nancy Ramsay, eds., *Telling the Truth: Preaching about Sex-ual and Domestic Violence* (Cleveland: United Church Press, 1999); Chris Altrock, *Preaching to Pluralists: How to Proclaim Christ in a Postmodern Age* (St. Louis: Chalice Press, 2004); David J. Lose, *Confessing Jesus Christ: Preaching in a Postmodern World* (Grand Rapids: Wm. B. Eerdmans Publishing Co., 2003);

Jeffrey Francis Bullock, *Preaching with a Cupped Ear: Hans Georg Gadamer's Philosophical Hermeneutics as Postmodern Wor(l)d*, Berkeley Insights in Linguistics and Semiotics (New York: Peter Lang, 1999); Walter Brueggemann, *Cadences of Home: Preaching among Exiles* (Louisville, KY: Westminster John Knox Press, 1997).

posture   *The position or stance of the preacher's body during preaching.*

Posture is a powerful communicator. Intentionally or not, posture can communicate whether preachers are tired, defensive, angry, relaxed, awkward, frustrated, and so forth. Good, upright posture is a key element in healthy vocalizing, *articulation, and *projection. In order for sound to be adequately formed and projected, the diaphragm must be unrestricted. Postures that are too relaxed or slouching can constrict breathing and promote a loss of breath control. The best default posture is one in which the preacher is standing with weight on both feet, leaning forward slightly, as if about to move forward. Posture will need to change and vary in order to assist in the communication of emotion or thought.

G. Robert Jacks, *Getting the Word Across: Speech Communication for Pastors and Lay Leaders* (Grand Rapids: Wm. B. Eerdmans Publishing Co., 1987); Anita Taylor, Teresa Rosegrant, Arthur Meyer, and B. Thomas Samples, *Communicating*, 4th ed. (Englewood Cliffs, NJ: Prentice Hall, 1986).

proclamation   *The announcement of good news.*

The word "proclamation" is closely associated with the image of the preacher as *herald, announcing the *kerygma, and the image of the preacher as *evangelist, proclaiming the good news. Richard Jensen, making use of Gerhard Ebeling's "event-theology" of the Word of God, asserts that proclamation is an event. It is an announcement that interrupts human existence with a saving Word.

Sometimes proclamation is set over against teaching or exhortation (see *kerygma* and *didache*). Gerhard Forde associates the term closely with the word "sacrament" in order to distinguish it from teaching. In this respect, proclamation is not an act of explaining or saying something *about* God's Word; it is the living presence of that Word within the gathered community. Forde goes further and asserts that proclamation, therefore, depends on the essential unity of Word and sacrament in worship.

Some have argued that this term, on its own, fails to do justice to either the teaching purpose within all forms of preaching, or the experiential and incarnational aspects of preaching, through which the preacher becomes a *witness, or someone who has "been there." These elements are not necessarily excluded by the term "proclamation." In recent years, the term has been used by homileticans to include all *genres and *purposes of preaching.

Gerhard Forde, *Theology Is for Proclamation* (Minneapolis: Fortress Press, 1990); Henry Grady Davis, *Design for Preaching* (Philadelphia: Fortress Press, 1958); Richard A. Jensen, *Telling the Story: Variety and Imagination in Preaching* (Minneapolis: Augsburg Publishing House, 1980); Thomas G. Long, *The Witness of Preaching*, 2nd ed. (Louisville, KY: Westminster John Knox Press, 2005); James Cox, *Preaching* (San Francisco: Harper & Row, 1985); D. W. Cleverley Ford, *The Ministry of the Word* (Grand Rapids: Wm. B. Eerdmans Publishing Co., 1979).

projection   *Control of the volume, enunciation, and range of the voice to become more *audible.*

Preachers need to speak with sufficient volume and clarity to be heard by all. The goal of projection is to get the voice above ambient room noise. This noise varies widely from sanctuary to sanctuary. The general goal, with or without a public address system, is for the preacher's voice to be audible from the rear of the sanctuary, without straining the voice or pinching throat muscles. From the location of preaching, the preacher should be able to hear the voice bounce back from the farthest wall.

G. Robert Jacks, *Getting the Word Across: Speech Communication for Pastors and Lay Leaders* (Grand Rapids: Wm. B. Eerdmans Publishing Co., 1987).

pronunciation   *Using the voice to speak a word correctly.*

In order for pronunciation to be correct, two things must occur. Initially, the preacher must decide how a word should be pronounced. Although there are regional, local, and ethnic variations, most dictionaries will provide an accepted pronunciation. Some Bibles use diacritical marks to help with pronunciation. Concordances often provide correct pronunciation, and a variety of helpful resources is also available. Once the preacher has decided on a correct pronunciation, the word must be practiced until the preacher is comfortable saying it aloud.

Henry H. Mitchell, *Black Preaching: The Recovery of a Powerful Art* (Nashville: Abingdon Press, 1990); W. Murray Severance and Terry Eddinger, *That's Easy for You to Say: Your Quick Guide to Pronouncing Bible Names*, book and CD-ROM edition (Nashville: Broadman & Holman, 1997); William O. Walker, *The HarperCollins Bible Pronunciation Guide* (San Francisco: HarperSanFrancisco, 1994).

prophetic preaching *An imaginative reappropriation of traditional narratives and symbols for the purpose of critiquing a dangerous and unjust present situation and providing an alternative vision of God's future.*

According to Walter Brueggemann, the prophetic *imagination is inspired by the absolute freedom of God to create something new and redemptive in the face of the status quo or "imperial reality." The prophet knows that God is free to bring about an alternative reality, and sets out to preach the community of faith toward this vision.

In the African American tradition, prophetic preaching identifies the biblical narrative as the listener's own story, a story that moves from suffering and lament to liberation and hope. The black tradition of social prophecy also links prophetic preaching to a practical theology of enlistment, pastoral care, and community organization for social action. This tradition had a powerful impact on the civil rights movement and inspired the social movement preaching of William Sloane Coffin, who left Riverside Church in New York to lead the nuclear disarmament movement in the 1980s and 1990s.

Prophetic preaching is often done in a *topical way, reacting to social issues and crises. It can also be an ongoing aspect of one's preaching ministry as a whole, emanating from the preacher's appropriation of the full biblical witness. In either case, Dawn Ottoni Wilhelm observes three key characteristics of all prophetic preaching. First, it voices God's passion for those who suffer. Second, it proclaims a vision of hope, a clear alternative for the future. Brueggemann calls this a "battle for language," in which the preacher asserts an alternative "script" to the one usually assumed by the listener. Third, prophetic preaching points the way forward, providing practical wisdom about how, in fact, the community can proceed.

There are several things for prophetic preachers to remember. First, prophetic preachers are not only *against* something, they are also *for* some alternative. Prophetic preaching is not just critique; in fact, critique may not be the best way to lead a congregation against social injustice. According to Walter Brueggemann, lamentation and grieving may be better forms of social criticism than ideological critique, because they move the listener closer to their own pain in a world of suffering. Then, when preaching new vision, Brueggemann encourages preachers to move from lament to doxology in order to energize the new vision.

Second, as much as possible, prophetic preachers should find ways to connect with the church's existing sense of mission. Most congregations already have ministries through which they are helping to alleviate some aspect of the pain of the world. Preachers can use this as an opening to explore larger systemic dimensions of injustice or oppression.

Third, prophetic preachers need to attend very carefully to the analysis of social reality. It is important to read, study, and engage in critical conversation with those who are experts about what is happening in the world. At the end of the day, however, preachers are theologians, not political theorists, political philosophers, sociologists, or historians. The goal is not political harangue or a learned lecture on social policy, but the articulation of God's redemptive plan.

Fourth, prophetic preaching, especially among listeners resistive to theologies of justice, should be closely linked to *pastoral preaching and to the caring ministry of the church. Listeners are more willing to hear difficult words about justice when they know the preacher cares about them. Prophetic preaching also shares with pastoral preaching the concern to reframe or rescript human life in redemptive ways and to encourage personal and social responsibility. Many, if not all, of the deepest pastoral issues in a congregation are closely connected with structural, social, or systemic issues.

Finally, prophetic preachers should practice what they preach. Prophetic preachers should preach to themselves. Consistency of witness goes a long way toward encouraging others that new ideas can lead to new forms of action. When listeners hear that the preacher is also in need of, and undergoing, prophetic transformation, they are more likely to come along for the journey.

Walter Brueggemann, *The Prophetic Imagination*, revised and updated edition (Minneapolis: Augsburg Fortress Press, 2001); Henry H. Mitchell, *Black Preaching: The Recovery of a Powerful Art* (Nashville: Abingdon Press, 1990); Dawn Ottoni Wilhelm, "God's Word in the World: Prophetic Preaching and the Gospel of Jesus Christ," in David B. Greiser and Michael A. King, eds., *Anabaptist Preaching: A Conversation between Pulpit, Pew, and Bible* (Telford, PA: Cascadia Publishing House, 2003), 76–93; Walter J. Burghardt, SJ, *Preaching the Just Word* (New Haven, CT: Yale University Press, 1996); J. Philip Wogaman, *Speaking the Truth in Love: Prophetic Preaching to a Broken World* (Louisville, KY: Westminster John Knox Press, 1998); Thomas G. Long, "Preaching in the Prophets," in Michael Duduit, ed., *Handbook of Contemporary Preaching* (Nashville: Broadman & Holman Publishers, 1993), 306–9; Linda L. Clader, *Voicing the Vision: Imagination and Prophetic Preaching* (Harrisburg, PA: Morehouse Publishing Co., 2004).

purposes   *The functions of preaching in the church and world.*

The New Testament provides several words for preaching, each of which expresses a different purpose. *Keryssein* indicates public proclamation of the *kerygma* by a *herald or messenger. *Euangelizein* indicates that the messenger brings a specific content: the good news or *euangelion*. *Didaskein* and *didache* point to the public teaching purpose of preaching. *Martyrein* or *testimony usually indicates the truth-telling purpose of preaching on behalf of a community. The word *homilein* refers to the *conversational dimension of preaching through which preaching achieves communal and liturgical purposes. *Thera-

pein points to the shepherding or *pastoral care-giving purpose of preaching. *Prophetein* indicates preaching's *prophetic purpose.

Beyond these classical purposes for preaching, there exists a range of purposes that emerges each week from particular biblical texts interpreted in different situations. Tom Long suggests that every sermon should have a *focus statement that indicates the sermon's unique purpose.

The results of the *Listening to Listeners Project indicate an enormous range of *individual* purposes for sermons. During sermons, listeners are cutting and pasting words, images, and thoughts into their own lives in ways preachers cannot control. Listeners are voracious meaning makers and will find purposes for sermons that cannot be anticipated. In the last analysis, therefore, the purpose of the sermon rests in the capable hands of the Holy Spirit.

O. C. Edwards, *A History of Preaching* (Nashville: Abingdon Press, 2004); Dietrich Bonhoeffer, "The Proclaimed Word," in Richard Lischer, ed., *The Company of Preachers: Wisdom on Preaching from Augustine to the Present* (Grand Rapids: Wm. B. Eerdmans Publishing Co., 2002), 31–37; H. Grady Davis, *Design for Preaching* (Philadelphia: Fortress Press, 1958); Thomas G. Long, *The Witness of Preaching*, 2nd ed. (Louisville, KY: Westminster John Knox Press, 2005); John S. McClure, "The Practice of Sermon Listening," *Congregations*, Winter 2006, 6–9; Diane Turner-Sharazz, Dawn Ottoni Wilhelm, Ronald J. Allen, and Mary Alice Mulligan, *Believing in Preaching: What Listeners Hear in Sermons* (St. Louis: Chalice Press, 2005).

rate   *The speed at which the preacher speaks.*

Rate is another important element of *articulation. Several common problems are associated with rate. The first is speaking too fast. Listeners require enough time to turn sounds into words, words into units of meaning (phrases, sentences), units of meaning into thoughts and feelings, and thoughts and feelings into memories, knowledge, and plans for action. Although this large number of cognitive and emotional processes can occur at a remarkable rate of speed, it is important for preachers to speak slowly enough for all these functions to take place. The second problem is speaking too slowly. When this occurs, the listener's mind will wander or listeners will complete dangling thoughts in ways that may not match the preacher's intentions. Communication theorists encourage approximately 140–160 words per minute. Finally, it is important to vary one's speaking rate in order to avoid monotony. Too much variation will appear unnatural. The goal is to vary the rate of speech in a way that adds natural emphasis and conversational variety.

G. Robert Jacks, *Getting the Word Across: Speech Communication for Pastors and Lay Leaders* (Grand Rapids: Wm. B. Eerdmans Publishing Co., 1987); Gordon I.

Zimmerman, James L. Owen, and David R. Seibert, *Speech Communication: A Contemporary Introduction*, 3rd ed. (New York: West Publishing Co., 1986).

relationship   *The rapport between preacher and *listener.*

In a recent empirical study of listeners, the *Listening to Listeners Project, one of the most striking findings was the importance to listeners of a meaningful relationship with the preacher. Lucy Lind Hogan and Robert Reid refer to this as "external *ethos." Listeners testify that where there is a good relationship they are more willing to pay attention. They also say that a good relationship with the preacher helps them to understand better, invest more in what is said, and feel predisposed to respond to the message.

Ronald J. Allen and Mary Alice Mulligan, *Make the Word Come Alive: Lessons from Laity* (St. Louis: Chalice Press, 2006); Ronald J. Allen, *Hearing the Sermon: Relationship, Content, Feeling* (St. Louis: Chalice Press, 2004); Diane Turner-Sharazz, Dawn Ottoni Wilhelm, Ronald J. Allen, and Mary Alice Mulligan, *Believing in Preaching: What Listeners Hear in Sermons* (St. Louis: Chalice Press, 2005); Lucy Lind Hogan and Robert Reid, *Connecting with the Congregation: Rhetoric and the Art of Preaching* (Nashville: Abingdon Press, 1999).

resources   *Ongoing sources of support for the preacher's ministry.*

Preachers require two basic kinds of resources: resources for personal nurture and resources for sermon preparation. There are several good resources for personal nurture and formation. First, preachers can join or create a small group of preachers for the purpose of study or sermon feedback. This can be a good place to discuss issues or problems related to preaching and to become part of a larger learning community. Second, preachers can take part in a variety of continuing education events. Although preaching conferences can be helpful, the best continuing education comes not from the advice and modeling of great preachers, as inspiring as this can be. Preachers learn more when they are involved in small groups where the focus is narrow and there is ample time for feedback and dialogue. Third, preachers need a life apart from the church. Learning to enjoy life fully will keep the preacher refreshed and in touch with what is going on in the world. Preachers can also develop the habit of reading for enjoyment. Fiction, historical novels, newspapers, and magazines help stimulate the preacher's imagination and cultural awareness.

In order to adequately support the sermon preparation process, preachers will need several resources on their bookshelf. If the preacher knows biblical languages, the first shelf should hold good Hebrew and Greek lexicons and perhaps Hebrew and Greek grammars. Next to these books, the preacher should have several good Bible translations. Alongside these can sit a good concordance, wordbook, and Gospel parallel, along with Bible atlases and dictionaries.

On the next shelf go the preacher's commentaries. Here, the key is diversity. Preachers should look for commentaries that represent a range of types of biblical criticism, theology, social locations, and cultures. Commentaries should include feminist perspectives and those who have addressed violence or the so-called texts of terror in the Bible. There should also be resources that address *anti-Judaism, handicappism, racism, and interpretations of human sexuality. Sometimes it is helpful to have a good one-volume commentary of the whole Bible for quick reference. Lectionary commentaries can also be helpful. The best ones are new each year, providing fresh perspectives.

On the next shelf go theological and historical books. Once again, a range is best. Perspectives on church history, from the origins of the church to the present, are a crucial resource. There should also be voices from the margins. It is wise to include liberationist, feminist, and womanist theologians, as well as theologians from other cultures. Theologians who address cultural and social change are also helpful.

Next, the bookshelf should have a homiletics section. The homiletics library should include several basic texts on the theory and practice of preaching and a variety of books that will help the preacher stay abreast of new developments in homiletics. This shelf can include theological, biblical, and homiletic journals that contain articles and bibliography designed to keep the preacher up to date regarding new developments in theology, biblical studies, and homiletics. Journal articles and book reviews are the best way for preachers to discover new books to read.

Finally, the preacher's bookshelf can include a section for literature. This might include fiction, historical novels, poetry, plays, and magazines that include literature, outstanding editorial commentary, and longer journalistic articles.

Thomas E. Ridenhour, "Essential Resources for Preaching," in John S. McClure, ed., *Best Advice for Preaching* (Minneapolis: Fortress Press, 1998), 151–70; Barbara Brown Taylor, *The Preaching Life* (Cambridge: Cowley Publications, 1993).

rhetoric   *The skill of using language and speech effectively or persuasively.*

Aristotle in *The Rhetoric* called rhetoric "the faculty of discovering in the particular case what are the available means of persuasion." He identified three principle means of persuasion: *ethos*, appeals to the speaker's character; *logos*, appeals to reason; and *pathos*, appeals to listeners' emotions. Cicero in *De Inventione* identified five principles of rhetoric: invention (arriving at something

to say), arrangement (organizing the message), *style (language choice),
*memory (ways to commmit the speech to memory), and *delivery.

Over the years homiletics has maintained an on-and-off relationship with the
discipline of rhetoric. Theologians of *proclamation harbor well-warranted fears
that rhetoric will usurp the function of God's Spirit in preaching. Many, especially *feminist theologians, find the emphasis on persuasion in the field of rhetoric to be potentially unethical, manipulative, and overly hierarchal in nature.

Both John Chrysostom and Augustine were trained as rhetoricians, as were
many well-known theologians and preachers over the centuries. John Broadus
was probably the best-known American homiletician to understand preaching
as "sacred rhetoric." In recent years, the *dramatist rhetoric of Kenneth Burke
has had some influence on homiletics. Burke, by means of his theory of *identification, attempted to modify the persuasive element within classical rhetoric, asserting that the primary goal of rhetoric was not persuasion but
cooperation between speaker and listener.

The word "rhetoric "has broadened in meaning to include all of the symbolic and socially constructive uses of language in preaching. Burke's work, in
particular, has fostered this broader understanding of rhetoric. The field of
*semiotics has also contributed to this shift in understanding.

Although arguments about the differences between rhetoric and *proclamation are likely to continue, it is clear that the discipline of rhetoric has
remained a useful conversation partner for homiletics, increasing our understanding of nearly every aspect of the homiletic process.

Lucy Lind Hogan and Robert Reid, *Connecting with the Congregation: Rhetoric and
the Art of Preaching* (Nashville: Abingdon Press, 1999); James Kay, "Reorienta-
tion: Homiletics as Theologically Authorized Rhetoric," *Princeton Seminary Bul-
letin* 24, no. 1 (2003): 16–17, 20–22; Thomas G. Long, "And How Shall They
Hear? The Listener in Contemporary Preaching," in Gail R. O'Day and
Thomas G. Long, *Listening to the Word: Studies in Honor of Fred B. Craddock*
(Nashville: Abingdon Press, 1993), 167–88; André Resner Jr., *Preacher and Cross:
Person and Message in Theology and Rhetoric* (Grand Rapids: Wm. B. Eerdmans
Publishing Co., 1999).

self-disclosure   *References in the sermon to the preacher's life.*

Because of the current interest in *authenticity, *character, *personality, and
*relationship in preaching, interest in self-disclosure among preachers has
risen to a new level. In self-disclosing *illustrations, preachers use stories or
vignettes in which they are central players.

Homileticians are deeply divided on this issue. On one extreme, John R.
Claypool appeals for the confessional use of the preacher's life story, especially
when the preacher has experienced suffering. Such stories encourage others to

bring the fullness of their experience into the preaching moment. On the other extreme, David Buttrick discourages any self-disclosure in preaching, on the grounds that personal illustrations always "split consciousness." The listener's consciousness will split and focus on the person of the preacher instead of the message. Tom Long points out that *listeners can tell when the preacher *intends* to split consciousness. This observation is borne out by the *Listening to Listeners Project, in which interviewed listeners demonstrated remarkable skills for discerning when preachers are intentionally talking about themselves and when they are using their own lives to help listeners better understand the gospel.

Many preachers today, especially those in larger congregations, use self-disclosure to promote the perceived authenticity of the preacher. These preachers argue that preaching is the only time most listeners will have the chance to get to know them. Years ago, Myron Chartier anticipated this interest in self-disclosure in the pulpit. According to Chartier, modest forms of self-disclosure can signify a healthy personality in the pulpit and promote vital forms of solidarity and relationship between the preacher and congregation.

Chartier outlined several guidelines for appropriate self-disclosure. First, preachers should be consistent, practicing self-disclosure in all areas of life and ministry. If the pulpit is the only place where people are permitted to see into the preacher's life, self-disclosure will be perceived as manipulative. Second, self-disclosure should always be in service to the sermon's message. Even when the primary goal is to promote authentic relationship, the illustration should be message-focused. Preachers should never simply tell stories about themselves in the pulpit. Third, self-disclosure should be other-centered, rather than self-centered. In other words, it should be genuinely designed to encourage the congregation's self-exploration, instead of the preacher's personal catharsis. Fourth, preachers should anticipate the impact of self-disclosure. Premature self-disclosure, too much depth, and too much confession of personal sin can amount to homiletic voyeurism. According to Chartier, preachers should "assess the timing, depth, and emotional tone" of self-disclosure so that listeners will not be overwhelmed or shocked by what is said. Fifth, Chartier encourages a "balanced self-picture," incorporating both strengths and weaknesses, past and present. This will discourage both a totally negative view of human experience and an idealization of the preacher's experience as one like us in every way, but without sin. Finally, Chartier warns self-disclosing preachers that they should expect self-revealing responses from listeners. Sharing oneself encourages others to do the same. Preachers should also be ready for listeners to assume counseling, parental, or even antagonistic roles in relation to what has been disclosed. Many people enjoy meddling in the lives of others and will use this as a chance to try to be caretakers or play games with the preacher.

When it comes to self-disclosure, the majority of homileticians occupy a middle ground, encouraging moderation. J. Randall Nichols draws a helpful distinction between *self-display* and self-disclosure. Talking *about* one's self and one's feelings is very different from telling a story or providing an image in which the preacher is simply an observer, narrator, or reporter. When a preacher uses self-disclosure, the general rule is for the preacher to stay behind the lens of the camera or in the peripheral vision as much as possible. The closer the preacher moves to the camera lens, the more self-disclosure is preacher-focused. In short, self-disclosure should be done modestly, seeing the gospel through the lens of the preacher's life, rather than focusing on the preacher's life itself.

John R. Claypool, *The Preaching Event*, Lyman Beecher Lectures, revised edition (Harrisburg, PA: Morehouse Publishing Co., 2000); David Buttrick, *Homiletic: Moves and Structures* (Philadelphia: Fortress Press, 1987); Thomas G. Long, *The Witness of Preaching*, 2nd ed. (Louisville, KY: Westminster John Knox Press, 2005); Myron R. Chartier, *Preaching as Communication: An Interpersonal Perspective* (Nashville: Abingdon Press, 1981); Richard Thulin, *The "I" of the Sermon* (Eugene OR: Wipf & Stock, 2004); Fred B. Craddock, *As One without Authority*, revised and with new sermons (St. Louis: Chalice Press, 2004); J. Randall Nichols, *The Restoring Word: Preaching as Pastoral Communication* (San Francisco: Harper & Row, 1987).

semiotics   *The study of signs.*

The discipline of semiotics emerged in the 1970s in response to groundbreaking work by structural linguists and literary critics. Semiotics expanded structural linguistic and literary theory into a larger theory of signs that could be used in the analysis of culture.

A "sign" is anything that stands for something else. It can be a word, sound, image, gesture, object, or artifact. Semioticians tend to ask one question: "How is meaning being made through the use of signs?" They are especially interested in how meaning is constructed through *systems of signs*, or *texts*. In large part, this attention to language and speech as texts is what distinguishes semiotics from other academic disciplines such as *rhetoric, *communication theory, content analysis, or discourse analysis. Semioticians look at texts as "structured wholes," seeking to discover *genres, *forms, figures of speech, linguistic conventions, and *codes. They search for meanings that are latent, connotative, or grounded in cultural expectations.

Semiotics has had two effects on recent homiletics. First, I have used semiotics to analyze some of the expected conventions or codes that accompany preaching as a genre of communication. Second, semiotics has found its way into homiletics through the field of *congregational studies. Leonora Tubbs

Tisdale has shown preachers how to exegete local congregations as texts. She encourages the preacher to study the signs, symbols, archival materials, architecture, visual arts, and rituals within the congregation in the way that a cultural anthropologist or ethnographer might study a foreign culture. This can help the preacher work as someone more deeply embedded in a congregation's cultural ethos and narrative. In both models, preachers are encouraged to analyze the systems of signs that exist in sermons and in congregations and then to consider how these sign systems influence both preaching and listening.

John S. McClure, *The Four Codes of Preaching: Rhetorical Strategies* (Minneapolis: Fortress Press, 1991; reprinted, Louisville, KY: Westminster John Knox Press, 2003); Leonora Tubbs Tisdale, *Preaching as Local Theology and Folk Art* (Minneapolis: Fortress Press, 1997); Daniel Chandler, *Semiotics: The Basics* (London: Routledge, 2002).

sermon   *The written text or oral event of preaching.*

The word "sermon" comes from the Latin *sermo*, "speech" or "conversation." The deeper origin of this word is the Latin *serere*, "to link together." The sermon links together four *authorities or authors for Christian faith: Scripture, experience, theological tradition, and human reason. The multiple *genres and *forms of the sermon emerge from the different ways these authorities are linked. For instance, if the authority of the Bible leads the way, the *biblical genre emerges. This could take an *expository form or perhaps a form that follows the biblical *plot. If experience takes a leading role, a *topical genre or an *inductive form might emerge. The way that reason is used may shape preaching into a variety of forms: *deductive, *inductive, plot, or a stock form (problem-solution, if . . . then, etc.). The role of reason also encourages different genres, such as *evangelistic preaching that uses apologetic methods, or *doctrinal preaching that explains aspects of Christian theology. Theological tradition exerts its influence in a *theology of preaching that encourages different genres and forms of preaching.

John S. McClure, *The Four Codes of Preaching: Rhetorical Strategies* (Minneapolis: Fortress Press, 1991; reprinted, Louisville, KY: Westminster John Knox Press, 2003).

speech act theory   *The theory of language as a form of action.*

Speech act theory is associated with linguist J. L. Austin and his student John R. Searle. In his early work, Austin drew a distinction between promissory language or "performatives," and referential language or "constatives." He asserted that performatives are forms of speech that actively oblige the speaker or promise something. Constatives simply refer to the occurrence of present or past actions. Austin later abandoned this distinction, concluding that every utterance is, in fact, performative in nature.

Austin's idea of performative language has been important to describe the way that preaching creates an event that joins preacher and listener together in a cooperative *relationship to *do* something. Perhaps the most important contribution of the work of Austin and Searle is that it calls attention to the *use* value of ordinary words as things that are intended to do things in the world. If Austin and Searle are correct, sermon listeners are more concerned with what a sermon *does* than what a sermon *means*. They are listening for what preaching promises or obligates them to do, rather than exploring the kinds of deep and complex meanings seminary-educated preachers enjoy exploring with their peers.

James L. Austin, *How to Do Things with Words* (Oxford: Oxford University Press, 1962); John R. Searle, *Speech Acts: An Essay in the Philosophy of Language* (Cambridge: Cambridge University Press, 1969).

strategic preaching   *Preaching as a long-term process designed intentionally to change a communicative or symbolic situation.*

Most preachers view preaching as a short-term, tactical practice of transmitting information. *Communication theorists, however, have drawn attention to the inadequacies of the sender-message-receiver or "transmission" model of communication, inherited largely from classical *rhetoric. A whole host of other elements is at work in any communication situation: conventions of listening, worldviews, local history, felt needs, language repertoire, physical setting, and so on. J. Randall Nichols calls this the larger "communicative field" for preaching. Strategic preachers strive to change some of these elements over time, in order to optimize the transformative influence of preaching. If the preacher is concerned only with getting together this Sunday's sermon and does not attend consciously to the relationship between this Sunday's sermon and the larger communicative field, it is likely that preaching will have only a modest impact on the larger worldview of the congregation.

Recent *semiotic approaches to preaching have attempted to take into account the ways preaching has the potential to reshape the signs, symbols, theological worldviews, and conventions of listening within congregations. According to Randall Nichols, the strategic preacher is aware that "messages create communities," or "publics." This is a very complex process and should not be overstated. It is probably too bold to say that sermons actually *construct* the way that a *listener is situated within a communicative field. Listeners are participants in multiple subcultures and negotiate messages from the pulpit at the intersection of many overlapping discourses. Over the long term, however, preaching can provide new categories of thought and encourage new forms of speaking and practice. Preached messages push, pull, nudge, encourage, and cajole listeners. If these messages are consistent and strategic, they can, over time, shift the *position* that listeners occupy within this complex communicative field, opening up new possibilities for thought and action.

Strategic homiletics, therefore, encourages preachers to decide what they are pursuing over the long haul through their preaching. To help them make this decision, preachers can engage in *congregational study, and ask practical theological questions about what and how to preach more strategically based on theological gaps, inconsistencies, or issues within the congregation.

It is important to remember several things about the larger communicative field in this process. First, preachers must be aware of the importance of *relationships*. Nichols encourages preachers to remember that the sermon occurs in the middle of myriad relationships that exist before, during, and after the sermon. How a sermon is processed is largely dependent on the quality of relationships within which it is received.

Second, Nichols encourages preachers to remember that the communicative field for preaching brings with it the expectation that preachers will talk about extraordinary matters of ultimate concern. People show up in church on Sundays because they are asking ultimate questions. They feel, for a variety of reasons, that it is important to connect with forms of language and thinking that will help them to think about issues of ultimate concern. Preachers, therefore, enter the communicative field at a *theological* point, contributing unique insights that could come from no other vantage point.

Third, strategic preachers should remember the power of *assumptions*, their own and their listeners'. A large part of what is being negotiated over time is the set of core assumptions operating within the communicative field. Initially, there will be some give and take if this negotiation is to succeed.

Fourth, Nichols points out that preaching stands at the *intersection between the past and the future*. The congregational, cultural, and individual past cannot be pushed aside, but must be respected and moved through on the way forward. This suggests that some form of congregational study might help preachers understand fully the context in which they preach.

Finally, the strategic preacher takes the time to become aware of the *homiletic* conventions already existing within the congregation. The kind of preaching a congregation is used to hearing exerts a tremendous influence on what they are able to hear. It is wise for the preacher to examine the ways previous favorite preachers used the Bible (*hermeneutics), *illustrations, *ideas, and *theology. The strategic preacher will show some respect for what has gone before, moving *through* the congregation's expectations about preaching, God, and life, on the way to something new.

J. Randall Nichols, *The Restoring Word: Preaching as Pastoral Communication* (San Francisco: Harper & Row, 1987); John S. McClure, *The Four Codes of Preaching: Rhetorical Strategies* (Minneapolis: Fortress Press, 1991; reprinted, Louisville, KY: Westminster John Knox Press, 2003); Leonora Tubbs Tisdale, *Preaching as Local Theology and Folk Art* (Minneapolis: Fortress Press, 1997).

structuralism   *A literary method that looks for meaning not in words themselves but in the relationships between and among them.*

Grounded in the linguistics of Ferdinand de Saussure, the cultural anthropology of Claude Lévi-Strauss, and the literary criticism of Vladimir Propp, structuralism looks at relationships between words, signs, and sentences as *structures, or *systems of transformation.* Homileticians such as Thomas G. Long and David Buttrick have used structuralism for analyzing the essential shape and *performative intention of various types of biblical literature. They encourage preachers to structure sermons based on this analysis. John Dominic Crossan also used structuralism in his important work on myth and parable, which has encouraged homileticians and liturgical scholars to develop ideas of *mythic or *parabolic communication.

Poststructuralism amounts to a radicalizing of structuralism. Inspired by the later work of literary and cultural critic Roland Barthes, poststructuralists posited that there is in fact nothing outside of words and the systems of transformations (structures) through which words are structured into texts. Even the idea of something outside the text is, in fact, posited by texts. Theologian Graham Ward calls this "speculative structuralism," a way of thinking that eventually led to theories of *deconstruction.

John S. McClure, *The Four Codes of Preaching: Rhetorical Strategies* (Minneapolis: Fortress Press, 1991; reprinted, Louisville, KY: Westminster John Knox Press, 2003); Robert Scholes, *Structuralism in Literature: An Introduction* (New Haven, CT: Yale University Press, 1975); David Buttrick, *Homiletic: Moves and Structures* (Philadelphia: Fortress Press, 1987); Thomas G. Long, *Preaching and the Literary Forms of the Bible* (Philadelphia: Fortress Press, 1989); Don M. Wardlaw, *Preaching Biblically: Creating Sermons in the Shape of Scripture* (Philadelphia: Westminster Press, 1983); Graham Ward, *Theology and Contemporary Critical Theory*, 2nd ed. (New York: St. Martin's Press, 2000).

structure *The arrangement of the parts of a sermon to form an integrated whole.*

Some homileticians prefer the word "structure" to the word *"form" as a way of expressing the arrangement of sermon parts. David Buttrick in particular encourages the use of this word, identifying it closely with the natural way that human consciousness produces the order and flow of thought. Buttrick also insists that sermon structure should emerge as a contemporary "re-plotting" of a field of understanding evoked by the biblical passage preached. This idea is echoed among many contemporary homileticians for whom preaching in the shape of Scripture is the key to sermon structure.

The idea of structure has received further nuance by structural literary critics. For structural critics, a structure is *a system of transformation.* Within *narrative theory *genres of narrative structure are determined by the relative success or failure of narrative transformation or mediation within a narrative. Distinctions between preaching as *mythic communication or *parabolic communication hinge upon this understanding of structure.

David Buttrick, *Homiletic: Moves and Structures* (Minneapolis: Fortress Press, 1987); John Dominic Crossan, *The Dark Interval: Towards a Theology of Story* (Sonoma, CA: Polebridge Press, 1988); John S. McClure, "The Theosymbolic Code," in *The Four Codes of Preaching: Rhetorical Strategies* (Minneapolis: Fortress Press, 1991; reprinted, Louisville, KY: Westminster John Knox Press, 2003), 93–135; John S. McClure, "The Narrative Function of Preaching," *Liturgy* 8, no. 2 (Fall 1989): 47–51; James Hopewell, *Congregation: Stories and Structures* (Minneapolis: Augsburg Fortress Press, 1987); L. Susan Bond, "Taming the Parable: The Problem of Parable as Substitute Myth," *Homiletic* 25, no. 1 (Summer 2000): 1–12.

style *A preacher's particular way of preaching.*

We live in a culture obsessed with style. With the proliferation of styles of music, art, media, hair, clothing, furniture, and so on, preachers also come under some scrutiny regarding whether they have developed a unique and attractive style.

The word "style" is very broad and is often used to encompass elements that are more appropriately referred to as *genres, *forms, or *purposes of preaching. The philosopher Alfred North Whitehead once defined style as "the fashioning of power." Style is the way that each preacher fashions or configures his or her powers of *communication. Styles are not necessarily individual or unique. They may be taken from a stylized tradition or represent a configuration of imitated or adapted models of communication. It is appropriate to speak of a preacher's unique personal style, but other homiletic words such as *voice and *authenticity have arisen recently to claim much of the conversation about distinctive style in homiletics.

The powers that influence homiletic style can come from many quarters. In some instances, homileticians speak of traditions of style such as hortatory style, *dialogue style, pedagogical style, *evangelistic style, and so on. At other times, the focus is on verbal elements of style such as plain style, witty style, ambiguous style, poetic style, conversational style, literary style, and journalistic style. Sometimes the accent is on the mood or *tone the preacher uses, as in energetic style, dynamic style, reserved style, hesitant style, and relational style. At other times, the focus is on the *personality of the preacher, as in natural style, personal style, introverted style, shy style, overbearing style, and angry style. In some instances, style is a function of perceived influences on the preacher, as in radio preacher style, revival style, big steeple style, *orator style, university style, and street style.

Some homileticians are rather deterministic about style. James Cox, for instance, says that "our style is what we are, be that good or bad." He admits that this style can be improved but does not think that it can be essentially altered. Others are more optimistic and encourage preachers to work at shaping and constructing a coherent personal style. David Buttrick considers the preoccupation with developing distinctive or unique styles an overemphasis on individual identity that disregards the larger social and communal dimensions of preaching. He argues that preachers may be better off learning to change styles in order to meet the needs of congregations and contexts for preaching.

In *The Four Codes of Preaching* I argue that there are strong stylistic expectations within congregations. These expectations focus on both content and *delivery. Congregations grow accustomed to certain styles of using Scripture, *illustrations, *ideas, theology, *imagination, humor, culture, media, body language, and so on. Preachers have to "negotiate a hearing" for their style of communicating in relation to these expectations.

In the last analysis, preachers can be glad that there are so many rich *resources for style in preaching. There are inner resources of faith, imagination, self-awareness, and embodied energy, and outer resources from cultures, traditions, and congregations. In the service of style, these resources become *powers* for communication that can be fashioned so that, in the words of Elizabeth Achtemeier, the preacher's style is "joyful, appropriate to the context of worship, full of conviction, and characterized by elegance of language."

James T. Maguire, "A Scale on Preaching Style: Hortatory vs. Interactive Preaching," *Review of Religious Research* 22, no. 1 (Sept. 1981): 60–65; Bryan Chapell, *Christ-Centered Preaching: Redeeming the Expository Sermon* (Grand Rapids: Baker Books, 1994); David Buttrick, *Homiletic: Moves and Structures* (Philadelphia: Fortress Press, 1987); James Cox, *Preaching: A Comprehensive*

Approach to the Design and Delivery of Sermons (San Francisco: Harper & Row, 1985); Mark Barger Elliott, *Creative Styles of Preaching* (Louisville, KY: Westminster John Knox Press, 2000); Elizabeth Achtemeier, *Creative Preaching: Finding the Right Words* (Nashville: Abingdon Press, 1980); Alfred North Whitehead, *Adventures of Ideas* (New York: Free Press, 1967).

synecdoche   *Part of something used to represent the whole.*

This word has been adopted into homiletics from the field of *poetics and refers to words or phrases that designate a part or aspect of an entity to stand for the thing in its entirety. For instance White House might be used to represent the whole presidency, or waves might be used to represent the whole sea. Tom Long draws a line connecting synecdoche with the preacher's use of *examples.* According to Long, when the preacher uses an example, listeners are given a partial representation of an entire phenomenon, a "vicarious experience, of the reality being presented."

Thomas G. Long, *The Witness of Preaching*, 2nd ed. (Louisville, KY: Westminster John Knox Press, 2005); Paul Scott Wilson, *The Practice of Preaching* (Nashville: Abingdon Press, 1995).

teaching sermon   *A *genre of sermon focused on teaching the Bible or Christian doctrine.*

New Testament scholars have highlighted the close relationship between preaching and teaching (see *kerygma and didache). There is always an element of teaching in any sermon. The teaching sermon, however, is designed from the beginning with the purpose of biblical or theological teaching in mind. Although both *expository and *doctrinal preaching carry with them certain inherited models of teaching, preachers may find it helpful to think broadly about the ways in which sermons can teach. Not all teaching implies either close textual exposition or the explanation of historically rooted concepts or doctrine.

Ronald Allen offers a variety of helpful suggestions for the teaching sermon. First, there are a variety of ways to teach. Allen points out that a teacher may be an "information giver, questions asker, mentor, gadfly, guide, mediator, antiexample, poet." Second, teachers are not merely conduits for information. They are stimulators of learning, and people learn in a variety of different ways. Preachers should be open to a range of teaching-learning models and prepare sermons that will meet the various ways people learn. Third, Allen warns against manipulative teaching, teaching that exposes listeners to only one way of thinking or intentionally keeps listeners in the dark by avoiding alternatives altogether. Fourth, teaching sermons should be pared down to essentials and not try to cover too much. Allen discourages preachers from cramming an entire curriculum of learning into one sermon. Fifth, teaching sermons should not avoid asking tough questions. This may also mean leaving the answers open-ended, relying on the spiritual wisdom of listeners to move the learning conversation forward. Finally, the teaching sermon needs to be congregation specific. Preachers should decide what aspects of the Bible and theology need covering in a particular context, based on the larger curriculum in the congregation's education program and on the needs and issues that are most pressing.

Ronald J. Allen, *The Teaching Sermon* (Nashville: Abingdon Press, 1995); Ronald J. Allen, *Preaching Is Believing: The Sermon as Theological Reflection* (Louisville, KY: Westminster John Knox Press, 2002); Ronald J. Allen, ed., *Patterns of Preaching: A Sermon Sampler* (St. Louis: Chalice Press, 1998).

testimony   *Truth telling by a *witness to the power of the gospel.*

The idea of preaching as testimony has been revived in recent homiletics. Thomas G. Long, in *The Witness of Preaching*, disassociated testimony from manipulative ideas of evangelism in which it had been reduced to a display of personal faith, unmoored from its relationship to the larger community of testimony. In his more recent work, Long expands his thoughts about testimony to include the everyday testimony of ordinary believers within the community of faith as they "talk themselves into being Christian."

Long and other scholars of testimony find support for their views in the writing of philosopher Paul Ricoeur, who argued in favor of the epistemological importance of testimony for the determination of truth. "Testimony" is a legal term, and indicates a forensic-fiduciary form of reason and truth. In a situation where there is no objective truth, we must rely on the good faith testimonies of many witnesses in order to determine the truth. These witnesses have a fiduciary agreement with the community to tell the truth. Testimonial, then, is not simply a matter of individual stories of conversion or personal blessing, as important as those stories might be. The witness is not testifying on his or her own behalf exclusively but is deeply responsible to and for the whole community.

Walter Brueggemann has developed an Old Testament theology based on a dialectical rhythm between the community of faith's "core testimony" and a range of "counter-testimonies" that function to keep the core testimony true and responsive to God's ongoing revelation (see *witness). Some *feminist homileticians have been drawn to the idea of preaching as counter-testimony. Lucy Rose speaks of personal testimony as a way for marginalized persons to gain a foothold in the conversation about what should be proclaimed in preaching. The witness speaks on behalf of others of similar experience and represents, in many cases, those who otherwise would have no *voice.

Anna Carter Florence has advanced Rose's argument significantly in her recent work on preaching as testimony. As Florence studied the history of women's preaching, she discovered that testifying resides at the heart of this largely hidden tradition. For centuries women have been offering their voices of Christian testimony, even though this testimony was not permitted within the official courts of the church, where the key decisions regarding Christian truth were being made. According to Florence, as women narrated their experiences of God, they sought confirmation for those experiences in the biblical Word, rather than submitting their testimonies to the institutional courts of the church. Inspired by the work of Rebecca Chopp, Florence shows how marginalized women found in the Scriptures an experience of the Word of God as an "open sign." According to Florence, it is this open sign to which women have sealed their narrated and confessed testimonies over the years. In this way, Florence shows how testimony can, in fact, "graf(ph)t" new meanings onto the church/court, within, and in spite of its own dialectical system of testimony and counter-testimony. The hybrid word "graf(ph)t" indicates both a new reading (graph) and a splicing (grafting) of that reading onto the old to create a new growth.

Thomas G. Long, *The Witness of Preaching*, 2nd ed. (Louisville, KY: Westminster John Knox Press, 2005); Thomas G. Long, *Testimony: Talking Ourselves into Being Christian* (San Francisco: Jossey-Bass, 2004); Walter Brueggemann, *Theology of the Old Testament: Testimony, Dispute, Advocacy* (Minneapolis: Fortress Press, 1997); Rebecca Chopp, *The Power to Speak: Feminism, Language, God* (Eugene, OR: Wipf & Stock, 2002); Anna Carter Florence, "Preaching to the Exiles Who Live at Home: Youth, Testimony, and a Homiletic of 'True Speech,' " *Journal for Preachers*, Advent 2000, 23–29; Anna Carter Florence, *Preaching as Testimony* (Louisville, KY: Westminster John Knox Press, forthcoming); Cheryl Bridges-Johns, "Epiphanies of Fire: Para-modernist Preaching in a Postmodern World," paper given at the annual meeting of the Academy of Homiletics, 1996; John S. McClure, *Other-wise Preaching: A Postmodern Ethic for Homiletics* (St. Louis: Chalice Press, 2001); John S. McClure, "From Resistance to Jubilee: Prophetic Preaching and the Testimony of Love," Yale Institute of Sacred Music *Colloquium: Music, Worship, Arts*, vol. 2 (Autumn 2005): 77–85.

text-to-sermon method *The preacher's method of bringing a biblical text into conversation with theology and contemporary life, with the goal of arriving at a sermon *idea.*

Two primary and interlocking elements are involved in all text-to-sermon methods: *study and brainstorming*. The disciplines involved in brainstorming and those belonging to exegetical study are quite different and must be placed into some meaningful interaction in any text-to-sermon method. Homileticians disagree on which should be the cart and which the horse in this process. Should the preacher start by creatively living with the text, brainstorming its relationship with ordinary life, or should the preacher begin in scholarly exegetical study? Those who favor brainstorming, living with the text first, are usually driven by the desire to energize the role of *context and *imagination in preaching. They wish to discourage any process that will lead to premature closure regarding the meaning of the text. Those who support immediate exegetical study are concerned to maximize the role of reason and tradition in preaching. They want to ensure that preachers understand exactly what text they are, in fact, living with. Ronald J. Allen uses the helpful image of a *conversation as a way of leveling the influence of all dialogue partners in this process, from the ordinary to the most scholarly. Preachers can see themselves hosting a conversation about a text that includes a wide range of voices.

Exegetical methods for the scholarly study of biblical texts change constantly. Several exegetical procedures, however, are basic for every preacher. First, the preacher must establish the boundaries of the text. How much of the biblical passage will be included in the sermon? Second, the preacher must do basic textual study, looking for problems with the *language of the text. A good way to spot textual problems quickly is to look at the differences between two or three good Bible translations. Preachers can also look at one good textual commentary. Third, preachers should do grammatical study, investigating key words or phrases. At this point it is helpful to consult Bible dictionaries, encyclopedias, wordbooks, lexicons, and concordances, pursuing the meaning of words which are crucial for understanding the text. Fourth, the preacher should study the text in its larger context in Scripture. What comes before and after this passage? How does this passage relate to the larger outline of this book of the Bible? The quickest way into issues of context is to consult introductory sections to commentaries. It is also important to read the larger context for the passage, asking how the passage functions. Fifth, the preacher should do historical study, determining the likely historical, authorial, or audience situation out of which the text arises and to which it speaks. The easiest way to do this is to consult Old Testament and New Testament introductions. Good critical commentaries will also contain this information. Sixth, the preacher will want to determine the literary or rhetorical genre of the text, along with any tradition of writings to which it is related. Form and tradition criticism are especially important for preachers who desire to adopt the *performative function of the text as the key to sermon *structure, or to preach in what David Buttrick calls the *mode of immediacy. Seventh, the preacher will want to reflect theologically on the passage, identifying key theological words or *themes. Simply determining theological ideas, however, is not enough. The preacher must be aware of his or her operative theology and ask how this theology can help to interpret these ideas in the sermon (see *theology and preaching). Eighth, the preacher will want to look at the text for any *anti-Jewish, racist, patriarchal, or violent elements that should be treated with care. Finally, the preacher will look at commentaries from a range of perspectives: feminist, global, conservative, liberal, and so forth (see *resources for preaching).

Over the years, homileticians and preachers have suggested many helpful practices for brainstorming the relationship between a text and the current situation. Some encourage speaking the text out loud several times, giving weight to different words each time, in order to experience a variety of possible meanings. Pamela Moeller encourages a *kinesics approach, inviting preachers to embody the text in dramatic movements, or enact the text in a dramatic form. Getting the human body involved tends to bring the human senses into interaction with the text and suggest new meanings.

Another common practice is to role-play biblical characters. When doing this, preachers should be careful not to presume that one can *identify with these distant characters beyond a certain point. Before role-playing, the preacher should do some exegetical work in order to know something about the world of the biblical character. This can help preachers avoid psychologizing characters, reducing them to pale reflections of contemporary thoughts and emotions. Instead of role-playing, some homileticians suggest holding a mock *conversation* with a biblical character. This allows the characters to resist our tendencies to remake them after our own likeness.

Many preachers appreciate the communal brainstorming that can occur in a lectionary study group where a group of preachers discusses the weekly text. Others argue that this practice is too in-house and clerical in nature and encourage sermon round tables involving laity from inside and beyond the church. In another common practice, preachers write the text on a sheet of paper so that it can be pulled out during the week for reflection in a variety of situations. They can take the text to other social locations, engaging others in conversation about the text at coffeehouses, homeless shelters, ballparks, malls, and so on. Most preachers will want to develop some combination of these brainstorming practices as a part of their regular text-to-sermon method.

At the end of the text-to-sermon process, depending on one's homiletic model, preachers will arrive at some sense of their message, and its *purpose. This can be stated in what Tom Long calls a *focus statement and a function statement. By the end of the text-to-sermon process, the sermon's central idea and purpose should be clarified.

Fred B. Craddock, *Preaching* (Nashville: Abingdon Press, 1985); Thomas G. Long, *The Witness of Preaching*, 2nd ed. (Louisville, KY: Westminster John Knox

Press, 2005); Ronald J. Allen, *Interpreting the Gospel: An Introduction to Preaching* (St. Louis: Chalice Press, 1998); Paul Scott Wilson, *The Practice of Preaching* (Nashville: Abingdon Press, 1995); Pamela Moeller, *A Kinesthetic Homiletic: Embodying Gospel in Preaching* (Minneapolis: Augsburg Fortress Press, 1993); Henry H. Mitchell, *Black Preaching: The Recovery of a Powerful Art* (Nashville: Abingdon Press, 1990); John S. McClure, *The Roundtable Pulpit: Where Leadership and Preaching Meet* (Nashville: Abingdon Press, 1995); John S. McClure, "Collaborative Preaching from the Margins," *Journal for Preachers* 22 (Pentecost 1996): 12–14; John S. McClure, *Other-wise Preaching: A Postmodern Ethic for Homiletics* (St. Louis: Chalice Press, 2001); Anna Carter Florence, *Preaching as Testimony* (Louisville, KY: Westminster John Knox Press, forthcoming).

theme   *The controlling *idea of a sermon.*

theology and preaching   *The way that a preacher's operative theology functions in preaching.*

Every preacher has an operative or functional theology. This theology represents the preacher's individual take on the Christian tradition as it shows up in preaching. Preachers develop this theology over time through the way they integrate ideas from the Christian tradition with their life and ministry. An operative theology is not a complete systematic theology. It contains certain emphases and certain gaps. It is a "canon within the canon" of the larger theological tradition. Knowing this theology can help preachers determine their strengths and weaknesses and become more *strategic as practical theologians in the pulpit.

As preachers discover this theology, it is crucial that they take time to find themselves within the church's larger theological tradition and contemporary theological constructions. This will help them discover good theologians who speak their language and can help them deepen their commitments and broaden their expressive powers. It will also help them become aware of new possibilities for the development of their theological positions.

In *Claiming Theology in the Pulpit*, theologian Burton Z Cooper and I have developed a theological profile designed to help preachers discover where they stand on a range of key theological issues, including the ways the Bible, tradition, experience, and reason are granted authority, theistic worldview (how God relates to the world), theodicy, atonement, Christ and culture, the relationship between Christianity and other religions, the relationship between Christianity and Judaism, and eschatology. Preachers will find it far easier to interpret biblical texts and to illustrate sermons if they are more deeply aware of the theological perspective they bring to both text and life.

Another aspect of theology and preaching relates preaching to congregational or local theology. Leonora Tubbs Tisdale shows preachers how they can conduct a thorough *congregational study in order to gain a better picture of the congregation's operative theology. Preachers can then be more strategic in addressing problems, gaps, limits, or inconsistencies within congregational theology.

In recent years, homileticians have become aware of the dynamic way that theology is being developed minute by minute in the interactive life of congregations. Theology is not just *semiotic in nature, residing latently in a congregation's ways of using signs and symbols. It is also *dialogic in nature, developing as living human beings talk with one another as believers and decide on the mission of the church. This raises the question, How can preaching locate itself with *immediacy* at the center of this living dialogue in which theological meaning is being created? *Collaborative, *conversational, and *testimonial models of preaching have sought to position preaching in the middle of this more immediate process in which members of a congregation are cocreating their operative theologies. In these models, while the sermon remains a single-party communication event, it is embedded within an interactive, multiparty communication process in which a group of ordinary people are discerning, articulating, and practicing theology.

Burton Z Cooper and John S. McClure, *Claiming Theology in the Pulpit* (Louisville, KY: Westminster John Knox Press, 2003); John S. McClure, *The Four Codes of Preaching: Rhetorical Strategies* (Minneapolis: Fortress Press, 1991; reprinted, Louisville, KY: Westminster John Knox Press, 2003); John S. McClure, "Preaching Theology," *Quarterly Review* 24, no. 3 (Fall 2004): 249–61; Leonora Tubbs Tisdale, *Preaching as Local Theology and Folk Art* (Minneapolis: Fortress Press, 1997); Ronald J. Allen, *Preaching Is Believing: The Sermon as Theological Reflection* (Louisville, KY: Westminster John Knox Press, 2002); Barbara Brown Taylor, *Speaking of Sin: The Lost Language of Salvation* (Cambridge: Cowley Publications, 2000); Lucy Rose, *Sharing the Word: Preaching in the Roundtable Church* (Louisville, KY: Westminster John Knox Press, 1997); John S. McClure, *The Roundtable Pulpit: Where Leadership and Preaching Meet* (Nashville: Abingdon, 1995); O. Wesley Allen, Jr., *The Homiletic of All Believers* (Louisville, KY: Westminster John Knox Press, 2005); Thomas G. Long, *Testimony: Talking Ourselves into Being Christian* (San Francisco: Jossey-Bass, 2004).

theology of preaching *The preacher's understanding of the kind of theological event or transaction with God taking place during preaching.*

Theologies of preaching ask questions such as, What is God doing during the sermon? What is the nature of the *Word of God in preaching? It is important for preachers to consider how they understand preaching as God's Word.

Recently, the homiletic conversation about the theology of preaching has revolved around the type of theological *imagination developed by the preacher. Mary Catherine Hilkert speaks of two basic forms of theological imagination in preaching: a *dialectical* imagination, which locates God's redemptive work more narrowly in the actions of God in and through Jesus Christ, and a *sacramental* imagination, which locates God's Word more widely within the whole of God's creation. This dichotomy is helpful, but it paints in rather broad strokes and can obscure a more detailed range of current theologies of preaching.

First, there is the *existential* theology of preaching, in which preaching supplies a divine Word that answers a crisis or conflict at the heart of human existence. Theologians such as Paul Tillich encouraged this way of thinking about preaching. Human beings are finite, attempting to secure themselves in the world via any number of self-securing idolatries in order to deflect, if only for a while, the deep sense that life is ultimately meaningless and ruled by despair and death. What sermon listeners need, therefore, is a Word of redemption and meaning from outside this situation that will answer their deepest questions about life and death. Preaching brings this Word. The ancient biblical model for this theology of preaching is found in the oracular prophets. Oracle is a form of *prophetic or redemptive speech occurring at the center of some process of human inquiry (in Hebrew, *darash YHWH*, or inquiring of God). There are many instances of oracle throughout the biblical witness, including the interpretation of dreams (Joseph and Daniel), divination, interpretation of lots cast or the oracle of the ephod, Saul and the woman of Endor, and those instances in which Jesus answers an existential question in a way that opens up a new set of redemptive possibilities (the healing of the paralytic, Zacchaeus, Nicodemus, the Syrophoenecian Woman, the woman at the well, the woman with the flow of blood, and so on).

Directly counterposed to this theological model is a *transcendent* theology of preaching. In the transcendent approach, the preacher announces a Word from God that is in no way an answer to human existential questions. To make the Word of God into a response to questions is to severely limit the Word of God. The preacher with a transcendent theology of preaching believes that we do not know the right questions until we have heard the Word. The Word of God has absolute priority. Since we cannot look within our own experience or even within history to find this Word, we have to rely utterly upon the biblical testimony. We find this divine Word in the Bible and in the Christ witnessed to in Scripture. Theologians such as Karl Barth have encouraged this way of thinking about preaching.

This transcendent model and the existential model are typically in great tension with each other. In today's homiletic context, this tension takes the shape of the debate between the liberal *New Homiletic and *postliberal homiletics. The ancient biblical model for this theology of preaching is the kerygmatic preaching of the apostles in the book of Acts. Instead of relating the gospel to immediate human needs, these preachers simply repeated again and again the divine *kerygma*, the story of Jesus Christ.

A third model is the *ethical-political* theology of preaching. These preachers proclaim God's Word as an alternate vision to injustice, inequities of power, suffering, and oppression. Evil and sin are structural in nature and can take the form of principalities and powers that put a stranglehold on all of human life, especially those who are most powerless. God's Word, for this preacher, is a Word of lamentation, resistance, compassion, divine justice, and hope.

Today, ethical-political theologies of preaching take their primary impetus from liberation theology, black theology, womanist theology, and *feminist theology. Ancient biblical models for ethical-political preaching stretch from the prophetic preaching of the Hebrew prophets to Jesus' proclamation of the kingdom of God. In all these forms of preaching, the preacher resists imperial power and sets forth an alternative vision for the world. Two other important biblical models for ethical-political preaching are the concepts of *testimony and the image of the preacher as *fool for Christ. In both of these models the preacher takes an unpopular stand at the expense of ridicule or even death.

A fourth model is the *organic-aesthetic* theology of preaching. In this model, God's Word is available all of the time at a barely whispered level, deep within the organic interconnectedness of all living things. God's Word is the creative *Logos*, which is ordering all of reality from the molecular to the cosmic level with ever-increasing organic complexity and aesthetic design. According to theologian Marjorie Suchocki, the preacher seeks out the "whispered word of God" within the world and draws it up from the level of a whisper to the level of an assertion or proposition. Preachers develop a special sacramental listening or clairvoyance that enables them to hear this Word. Somehow, they know listeners' lives more deeply than *listeners know themselves and are able to help them raise the preconscious Word of God in their lives into consciousness. The best biblical images of this kind of preaching are found in the Gospels, when Jesus is in conversation with disciples and the crowd, using metaphor, story, and parable to take the ordinary bits and pieces of people's lives and transform them into the very stuff of God's revelation. The stories of the rich young ruler, Simon, and Mary and Martha are good examples. People are invited to discover the Word of God as it emerges in the give and take of storytelling and dialogue. In all of these situations, the preacher is helping people take materials that are of a lower form, the created processes of life, and transform them into sacramental vehicles for the revelation of God's Word.

Although there are other theological models afoot in homiletics today, most homileticians and preachers operate roughly within one of these frames of reference, or in a way that strings together two or three of these models. It is easy to see how the preacher's theology of preaching shapes his or her preaching.

Burton Z Cooper and John S. McClure, *Claiming Theology in the Pulpit* (Louisville, KY: Westminster John Knox Press, 2003); Mary Catherine Hilkert, *Naming Grace: Preaching and the Sacramental Imagination* (New York: Continuum, 2003); Karl Barth, *Homiletics* (Louisville, KY: Westminster John Knox Press, 1991); Charles L. Campbell, *Preaching Jesus: New Directions for Homiletics in Hans Frei's Postliberal Theology* (Grand Rapids: Wm. B. Eerdmans Publishing Co., 1997); Christine M. Smith, *Preaching as Weeping, Confession, and Resistance: Radical Responses to Radical Evil* (Louisville, KY: Westminster John Knox Press, 1992); Olin P. Moyd, *The Sacred Art: Preaching and Theology in the African American Tradition* (Valley Forge, PA: Judson Press, 1995); Dale P. Andrews, *Practical Theology for Black Churches: Bridging Black Theology and African American Folk Religion* (Louisville, KY: Westminster John Knox Press, 2002); L. Susan Bond, *Trouble with Jesus: Women, Christology, and Preaching* (St. Louis: Chalice Press, 1999); Kathy Black, *A Healing Homiletic: Preaching and Disability* (Nashville: Abingdon Press, 1996); John S. McClure and Nancy J. Ramsay, eds., *Telling the Truth: Preaching about Sexual and Domestic Violence* (Cleveland: United Church Press, 1999); Walter Brueggemann, *The Prophetic Imagination*, revised and updated edition (Minneapolis: Augsburg Fortress Press, 2001); Marjorie Hewitt Suchocki, *The Whispered Word: A Theology of Preaching* (St. Louis: Chalice Press, 1999); Richard Lischer, *A Theology of Preaching: The Dynamics of the Gospel*, revised edition (Durham, NC: The Labyrinth Press, 1992).

title   *A published name for a sermon designed to indicate the sermon's theme and to arouse interest.*

David Buttrick attributes the use of sermon titles to the triumph of the *topical sermon in North America. However, not every titled sermon is topical. Many *biblical preachers will decide on a title to put in the bulletin, in a newsletter, on a marquee, or in the newspaper. In some African American preaching traditions, a sermon title provides a powerful springboard into the sermon's message and may become a repeated refrain throughout the sermon. In the words of Gardner Taylor, "the title ought to attempt to be the sermon concealed, as the sermon ought to be the title revealed."

It is sometimes argued that sermon titles focus attention on the preacher, artistry, creativity, and relevance, at the expense of biblical content and the work of the Holy Spirit in preaching. Large sermon marquees and alluring sermon titles in newspapers tend to focus on the *personality of the preacher and membership needs of the church and detract from the sermon's integrity. These critiques are well taken and encourage modesty and simplicity when using titles.

There is a range of advice regarding sermon titles, some pieces more helpful than others. First, preachers should be guided by one simple goal: to help the listener know what the sermon is about. The goal of a sermon title is to state in a short but memorable way the sermon's core *idea. If the preacher has prepared a *focus statement, it may be of some help in arriving at a title that conveys the sermon's central idea.

Second, if there is a single biblical text, the preacher can look for ways to relate the sermon title to the text. Perhaps a word, phrase, or key concept within the biblical text can be used in the title. Calvin Miller argues that text-based sermon titles should be "user-friendly." He recalls a sermon on Galatians 4:4 entitled "In the Fullness of Time," preferring it to the more obscure "In Plentitudo Temporis."

Third, sermon titles should capture interest. Homiletician Donald Macleod is reputed to have said that a sermon title should "stop a bus"; this, however, may be overstating the goal. Clyde Fant urges preachers to use good taste, avoid the exotic, and focus on arousing real interest in the actual content of the sermon itself. In this regard, Rick Warren encourages preachers to ask four questions: "Will the title capture the attention of people? Is the title clear? Is the title good news? Does the title relate to everyday life?" For sermons employing a certain amount of creativity, Mark Galli and Craig Brian Larson encourage some controlled wordplay. Sermon titles such as "Sense out of Nonsense" (David Petersen) and "Doubts in Belief" (Paul Borden) indicate that the sermon is marked by creative energy. It is a good idea to keep this kind of inventiveness on a short leash. Too much creativity can invite disaster as preachers offend people's sense of good taste. Miller especially discourages sacrilegious titles. In this respect, he recalls a sermon title: "Hitch Your Wagon to Jesus and Gee Haw."

It is not likely that sermon titles will disappear from the cultural landscape anytime soon. Preachers who use titles should examine their motives carefully and find ways to turn the business of titling into a modest and helpful way of promoting interest and participation in the sermon.

David Buttrick, *Homiletic: Moves and Structures* (Philadelphia: Fortress Press, 1987); Gardner C. Taylor, "Titles," in William H. Willimon and Richard Lischer, eds., *Concise Encyclopedia of Preaching* (Louisville, KY: Westminster John Knox Press, 1995), 491–92; Clyde E. Fant, *Preaching for Today* (New York: Harper & Row, 1975); Calvin Miller, "Naming the Baby: The Right Sermon Title Makes All the Difference," *Leadership: A Practical Journal for Church Leaders*, Winter 1998, 93–95; Rick Warren, "The Purpose-Driven Title," *Leadership: A Practical Journal for Church Leaders*, Winter 1998, 95–96; Mark Galli and Craig Brian Larson, *Preaching That Connects: Using Journalistic Techniques to Add Impact* (Grand Rapids: Zondervan Press, 1994).

tone   *The overall mood of a sermon.*

The way the preacher speaks conveys a certain mood or atmosphere. It is important that this mood match the preacher's *idea and *purpose. David H. C. Read encourages preachers early on in sermon preparation to decide on the nature of the sermon and strive for a particular tone or mood. Will the tone be argumentative? Declarative? Slightly poetic? Meditative? Reminiscent? Solemn? Light-hearted? Read argues that preachers should not become addicted to a single tone, but should work for variety in order to avoid boredom. Making a decision about sermon tone will add variety to preaching and create more interest in preaching on a week-to-week basis.

David H. C. Read reference from John S. McClure, "Organizing Material," in John S. McClure, *Best Advice for Preaching* (Minneapolis: Fortress Press, 1998), 65–84.

topical preaching   *A *genre of preaching that originates in a topic, issue, or concern within the contemporary world of the listener, and in which some aspect of that topic becomes the sermon's central *idea.*

Before the time of Harry Emerson Fosdick, topical preachers held forth on broad social subjects in a way resembling lecture-circuit speakers or conference orators. The issues or topics these preachers treated often failed to relate to the actual needs and concerns of people in the pews. For this reason, Fosdick created his "project method," a form of topical preaching designed to deal only with subjects that were of vital interest to *listeners. For Fosdick the goal was not to lecture listeners, but to engage people with real topics of deep importance for the living of life.

Although some preachers always preach topically, topical sermons are used by all preachers for *occasional sermons, including *wedding sermons, *funeral sermons, and sermons on special occasions such as Thanksgiving and Mother's Day. Ronald Allen points to several additional occasions for topical preaching: (1) when time is short, such as during a crisis; (2) when understanding a need, issue, or situation, or taking action on that situation, is urgent; (3) when the Bible is silent and does not comment directly on an important issue or concern; (4) when the topic is simply larger than a single biblical text, image, or theme; (5) when a text is suggestive of a topic, but does not treat it fully; (6) when a text is potentially harmful, and must be treated in a larger context; and (7) when there is no decisive Christian viewpoint, so that a range of Christian options should be articulated.

Within the African American tradition of preaching, James Earl Massey argues for "doctrinal/topical" preaching. In this model the preacher chooses a core doctrine of the church that will actually challenge, reinterpret, and redirect the ways listeners think about topics within human society. The driving force for topical preaching is a theological topic, inasmuch as this topic addresses the larger issues of living in the world today, especially issues of suffering, evil, redemption, and hope.

Proponents of *biblical preaching who find fault with topical preaching argue that topical preaching places human needs before the purposes of God found in Scripture. Beginning with the Bible, however, is no guarantee that the result will be a biblically grounded message. Although the topical preacher *begins* with an experiential topic, this does not mean that topical sermons do not interact with biblical texts. The best topical sermons move from a topic at hand toward trajectories within the biblical witness that provide guidance for the preacher in treating the topic. In some cases, as Ronald Allen points out, this is not a possibility. Some topics are simply not addressed directly in the Bible. In this case, the topic can be treated in light of the *gospel. The preacher can search for a thematic substratum within the Bible that sheds light on the topic.

Allen encourages preachers to carefully research the topic and to engage in careful theological reflection on the topic. Theological reflection leads the preacher to the appropriate biblical text(s) for the sermon and to an overall interpretive approach. The preacher should have a very clear sense of the *purpose for the sermon and conceive of this purpose narrowly enough to ensure some success.

Topical preaching should never become a license for the preacher to circumvent the biblical witness or theological reflection. When these elements are carefully integrated in sermon preparation, the topical sermon can be an important way for preachers to bring the Word of God into the closest possible interaction with the difficult issues confronting listeners in their daily lives and confronting society as a whole.

———

Harry Emerson Fosdick, "What Is the Matter with Preaching?" in Mike Graves, ed., *What's the Matter with Preaching Today?* (Louisville, KY: Westminster John Knox Press, 2004), 7–19; Ronald J. Allen, *Preaching the Topical Sermon* (Louisville, KY: Westminster John Knox Press, 1992); Mark Barger Elliott, *Creative Styles of Preaching* (Louisville, KY: Westminster John Knox Press, 2000); Ronald J. Allen, *Patterns of Preaching: A Sermon Sampler* (St. Louis: Chalice Press, 1998); James Earl Massey, *Designing the Sermon: Order and Movement in Preaching* (Nashville: Abingdon Press, 1980).

transition   *A word, phrase, statement, or paragraph that provides connective logic indicating that a preacher is moving on in the sermon.*

At the crucial intersection between one block of thought and another, preachers must provide a transition that both closes out one thought and introduces the next. The preacher needs to summarize briefly, perhaps in a sentence or two, the previous thought, and then use some form of connecting logic (and, but, if . . . then, so, but maybe, etc.) to move the sermon forward. The twin goals of transition building are clarity and subtlety. The listener needs to know clearly when a transition is underway and when it has been completed. This can be accomplished, however, without the jarring cues provided in a lecture: First! Second! Third! Finally!

David Buttrick urges preachers to consider movements of thought within sermons as movements within a conversation. He invites preachers to talk out the logic of the sermon, adding the connectors that would follow from natural conversation. He argues that in some cases, transitions can be accomplished by shifting the listener's perspective, from outward to inward, from one location to another, or from one way of seeing to another.

In all cases, transitions will be dictated by the overall *form of the sermon. If the form is spatial, transitions will be spatial, and will involve spatial gestures: "On the one hand . . . on the other hand . . ." If the logic is conditional, transitions will follow: "If . . . then . . ." Transitions in plotted sermons will be subtle, involving shifts in tone, perspective, action, and time. In order to use appropriate transitions, therefore, preachers must ask themselves, "What is the form of my sermon? What form of logic am I using?"

David Buttrick, *Homiletic: Moves and Structures* (Philadelphia: Fortress Press, 1987); Thomas G. Long, *The Witness of Preaching*, 2nd ed. (Louisville, KY: Westminster John Knox Press, 2005); James W. Cox, *Preaching: A Comprehensive Approach to the Design and Delivery of Sermons* (San Francisco: Harper & Row, 1985); Joseph M. Webb, *Preaching without Notes* (Nashville: Abingdon Press, 2001).

voice   *A metaphor for the preacher's distinctive way of communicating.*

Homileticans sometimes speak of preachers finding their voice in the pulpit. By this, they mean that a preacher is accepted within the congregation and sufficiently confident to claim her or his own preaching identity. Although finding one's voice comes in part from mentors and models, and sometimes from an entire tradition of preaching, the preacher's distinctive voice represents a unique instantiation of that tradition and those influences within a particular situation. Among other things, voice includes the development of a distinctive *style, *tone, *theology, and *purpose.

Gaining one's voice in the pulpit sometimes takes many years of hard work. Mary Donovan Turner and Mary Lin Hudson point out that for women preachers, whose voices have long been silenced within the preaching tradition, discovering one's voice is nothing short of a process of self-discovery.

According to Turner and Hudson, for women the metaphor of voice includes the discovery of a "distinctive self," an "authentic self," an "authoritative expression," a "resistant self," and a "relational self" in the pulpit.

There are three primary contributors to the discovery of one's preaching voice. The first is confidence. Lack of self-esteem can turn preachers away from their own unique way of preaching. In many instances, preachers simply adopt the voice of another. Imitating mentors or models is quite natural and can be empowering, up to a point. If it persists, however, a preacher may never embrace her or his own unique voice. The cult of great preacher personalities tends to feed on lack of self-esteem among preachers. When underconfident preachers return from conferences and large continuing education events, they try out various techniques learned from great orators for a short while, only to run dry after a trial run. This causes them to experience a still deeper loss of confidence, as they realize that they are, in the last analysis, not able to do what these great preachers do. For this reason, it is far better for preachers to work in small, supportive groups where they can be challenged to discover and make use of their own native gifts for preaching.

The second necessary element for finding one's voice in the pulpit is trusting one's experience. A person's voice is an embodied reality, linked to the senses and thus to the way the world is experienced. The more one's words and speaking voice emerge from a larger experience of the world that is honored as important and valid, the more likely it is that one's voice will be strong and unique. Christine Smith and Lucy Rose point out that this is a particularly difficult issue for many women preachers and marginalized persons, whose experiences have been devalued. For Rose, the practice of personal *testimony, in which one claims one's unique experience of God, is an essential practice for those who are marginalized. Anna Carter Florence, examining the long tradition of women preachers, links their practices of testimony to the ways in which women have learned to claim their own experiences of God, narrating those experiences and identifying them with the Word of God found in the Bible. In this way, women preachers learned to trust and assert the importance of their experience and were able to find a voice outside, and in the margins of, the institutional church.

The third contributor to finding one's voice is learning to trust one's judgment. John Henry Newman once called this the "illative sense," or the ability to trust one's own practical *reasoning* in communication. According to Newman, judgment is the faculty whereby preachers become competent to discover the strongest possible elements in any topic and decide best how to communicate those elements using their own native preaching gifts. This form of judgment is achieved only through education and a life devoted to the study of Scripture, theology, the church, and life. It also requires paying attention to one's own ways of thinking about Scripture, tradition, and life, learning to trust one's own judgment to interpret them for preaching.

Again, issues of trusting one's judgment are exacerbated for women in contexts where the competence and *authority of women has been disputed, and where education for ordination and church leadership has been withheld until recently. For this reason, it is important for women to find role models and mentors who will supervise and empower them as preachers and church leaders. It is also crucial to build support networks and small groups of men and women who will work together to change denominational and congregational cultures into institutions where *listeners to sermons fully accept the expertise and leadership of women.

Turner and Hudson encourage several practices for finding one's preaching voice. First, "unlearn not to speak." Preachers can find safe contexts in which they can "break the silence" and begin to voice their own deepest thoughts about Scripture, theology, life, and faith. Second, preachers can learn to trust their own experience. This can be accomplished, in part, by identifying times in life when one felt "voiced" and times when one felt "silenced," and claiming the first set of experiences as normative models for preaching. Third, preachers can imagine a new world in which everyone has a voice, and preach as if they lived and preached in that world, rather than in a world in which some are voiced and others silenced. This is nothing short of claiming a new emotional and spiritual context in which to preach. Fourth, preachers can become listeners, attending to all of the voices around them, and listening especially to their own voice within that context. Finally, preachers can claim their powers to *name* both the sinful world they want to leave behind and the redeemed world they hope for all to inhabit.

Christine M. Smith, *Weaving the Sermon: Preaching in a Feminist Perspective* (Louisville, KY: Westminster John Knox Press, 1989); Lucy Atkinson Rose, *Sharing the Word: Preaching in the Roundtable Church* (Louisville, KY: Westminster John Knox Press, 1997); Mary Donovan Turner and Mary Lin Hudson, *Saved from Silence: Finding Women's Voice in Preaching* (St. Louis: Chalice Press, 1999); Anna Carter Florence, *Preaching as Testimony* (Louisville, KY: Westminster John Knox Press, forthcoming); John S. McClure, "In Pursuit of Good Theological Judgment: Newman and the Preacher as Theologian," in Michael Welker and Cynthia A. Jarvis, eds., *Loving God with Our Minds: The Pastor as Theologian* (Grand Rapids: Wm. B. Eerdmans Publishing Co., 2004), 202–19.

wager   *The tentative or emerging *idea within a *conversational sermon.*

Lucy Rose coined this word to describe the time-bound and interpretive nature of the sermon idea in a conversational homiletic. According to Rose, the conversational preacher's message is not timeless *kerygma* or a response to universal human needs, but a tentative proposal or wager that asserts both its own perspective-laden limitations and the likely need for future correction. This correction will be achieved through further conversation and the reception of a range of wagers brought by the *testimony of others.

Rose adapted the word "wager" from philosopher Paul Ricoeur, who used the term to describe the way in which any active interpretation (*hermeneutic) requires one to wager a belief that something is, in fact, true. Making a wager is like staking a claim in a conversation, asserting that one's perspective contains truth but is not the final word. By making a wager, the preacher takes a stand within a larger ongoing conversation about Christian truth.

Wagers are tentative commitments or working hypotheses that are very much in process. As the situation changes in response to this emergent Word, a new Word becomes possible, moving the individual and congregation into deeper forms of life and witness.

Lucy Atkinson Rose, *Sharing the Word: Preaching in the Roundtable Pulpit* (Louisville, KY: Westminster John Knox Press, 1997).

wedding homily   *A brief sermon preached on the occasion of a Christian marriage.*

Marriage is a solemn ritual of transition that takes place in the context of Christian worship. It is appropriate, therefore, to include a brief sermon based on a scriptural text. It is important for the married couple, embarking on a new life together, to seek guidance from God's Word. It is also important for family and friends to be reminded of the true nature and purpose of Christian marriage. They can also be reminded of the important supportive role they will play in the couple's future. The wedding homily, therefore, is preached not only to the couple but to the whole congregation. It may be that the bride and groom prefer to be seated with the congregation for the duration of the homily.

More than any other aspect of the wedding rite, the role of preaching is to add *reality* to an event within North American culture that has been freighted with unreality and fantasy. The sermon can provide an interpretive theological framework through which the couple and congregation can begin to take a deeper responsibility for themselves and their relationships. The preacher can emphasize several important things in this respect. First, the preacher can highlight the *public and communal nature* of marriage. Christian marriage is not simply a private act, focused entirely on the feelings and sentiments of bride and groom. Marriage is crucial for the welfare of families and society and will require the support of the family, church, and community, in order to fulfill this potential. Second, the preacher can emphasize the role of *promise* in Christian living, as a figure of God's unconditional promise and covenant with the people of God. Marriage is a good gift from God, a part of God's promises of provision and support in the living of life. In marriage, God provides intimacy and companionship to replace loneliness, and family to nurture health, identity, and faith. An accent on promise also suggests the moral dimensions of marriage, especially requirements of fidelity, kindness, and trust in promissory relationships. Third, the preacher can emphasize the *goodness of human sexuality* and intimacy within marriage. When doing this, it is important to remember that singleness is also a valid way to live out one's Christian vocation. It is also important not to overemphasize the significance of childbearing. Infertility is a common human dilemma and should not be stigmatized. Finally, the preacher can emphasize the many ways in which *openness to God's presence* can nurture, sustain, and renew marriage. Faithful living promotes personal integrity, justice and mutuality, honesty, trustworthiness, and a vision of patient, nonviolent care for one another.

William H. Willimon, "Marriage," in James W. Cox, ed., *Handbook of Themes for Preaching* (Louisville, KY: Westminster John Knox Press, 1991), 157–60; Perry H. Biddle, "The Wedding Sermon," in William H. Willimon and Richard Lischer, eds., *Concise Encyclopedia of Preaching* (Louisville, KY: Westminster John Knox Press, 1995), 499–500; J. Randall Nichols, *The Restoring Word: Preaching as Pastoral Communication* (San Francisco: Harper & Row, 1987); Elizabeth Achtemeier, *Preaching about Family Relationships* (Philadelphia: Westminster Press, 1987); Susan K. Hedahl, *Preaching the Wedding Sermon* (St. Louis: Chalice Press, 1999); Scott M. Gibson, *Preaching for Special Services* (Grand Rapids: Baker Books, 2001); David J. Schlafer, *What Makes This Day Different? Preaching Grace on Special Occasions* (Cambridge, MA: Cowley Publications, 1998); Charles Rice, "Preaching at Weddings," *Sewanee Theological Review* 41, no. 3 (Pentecost 1998): 228–40.

witness   *Image of the preacher as one who has had an experience of the gospel and now gives *testimony.*

The word "witness" is the usual translation of the Greek *martyria*, and originally indicated the action of one who, as potential martyr, speaks with one's life on the line. The image of the witness is a courtroom image and thus is linked closely to truth telling in a situation where the only means for determining the truth is through accurate testimony by a witness. The preacher as witness is one whose life has been claimed by an event witnessed. The witness speaks on behalf of a larger community of witnesses, as one called to the witness stand to speak on their behalf. The *authority of the preacher as witness, therefore, is grounded not only in personal experience, but in the way that experience gives accurate testimony on behalf of a larger community or congregation of witnesses. Tom Long points out that the image of witness diverges from the image of *herald, since it incorporates direct personal involvement of the preacher's experience, reason, and belief, along with a more communal form of authority. The preaching of the witness leads ultimately to a more experiential and communal form of preaching than that of the herald, who is the passive carrier of someone else's message.

Current theories of preaching as witness rely in part on the work of philosopher Paul Ricoeur, who wrote two influential essays on the subject of testimony. In these essays, Ricoeur is responding to the philosophical writings of Jewish post-Holocaust philosopher Emmanuel Levinas, whom he calls "the thinker of testimony." Ricoeur identifies two aspects of witness: *testimony as act* and *testimony as narrative* or verbal testimony (affirmation, belief, or confession). Testimony as act refers to the ways the witness's life and social location are wrapped up in the act of witnessing. Testimony as narrative refers more to the actual speaking or truth telling involved in witnessing, and moves from the life and social location of the witness into the communal and courtroom context in which witnessing occurs.

In a way similar to Ricoeur's separation of testimony as act and narration, the image of witness is usually pushed in two directions in homiletic theory. On the testimony-as-act side, witness is linked to experience and authority in preaching. This is not the same thing as the sometimes manipulative evangelistic abuses of testimony as a badge of faith. Lucy Rose stresses the role of personal testimony and *wagers of faith that can bring marginalized experiences or *voices into the pulpit and grant them authority in preaching. David Lose distinguishes a form of confessional practice in which the preacher eschatologically "binds" his or her entire life into a "contractual relationship of mutual fidelity" to Jesus. Anna Carter Florence also accentuates this "sealing" of one's life to the biblical witness to Christ and the importance of one's encounter with the living Christ as the key to authority in the pulpit.

On the other side, Tom Long accentuates the role of preaching as communal witness in the context of the courtroom of believers. For Long, the witness is primarily one who goes to scripture on behalf of a community of believers. Long is careful to caution that the "truth is larger than the witness's own experience of it." Walter Brueggemann also accentuates the way in which the witness gives testimony or countertestimony in a court in which truth is adjudicated.

The difference between these homileticians of witness is usually a matter of emphasis and degree. The groundswell of interest in testimony, however, bespeaks its relevance in today's post-Enlightenment, *postmodern world, in which truth and authority come unmoored from both tradition and science.

In *Other-wise Preaching: A Postmodern Ethic for Homiletics*, I have argued in favor of witness as a helpful *deconstructive element within homiletics. I encourage preachers to travel behind Ricoeur's interpretation of Levinas and listen to the discussion of testimony that took place between Levinas and his

constant conversation partner, the *deconstructionist philosopher Jacques
Derrida. In this conversation, the two philosophers spotted a problem with the
idea of witness. At its worst, witnessing as a way of arriving at what is true creates the possibility of a closed system in which only some *voices are allowed
on the witness stand. At its best, this way of thinking can modulate itself into
a dialectical process between truths established by an accepted core tradition
of testimony and critical forms of countertestimony designed to critique and
improve this core tradition. Walter Brueggemann identified this dialectic
between testimony and countertestimony as fundamental to Hebrew
prophecy. According to Derrida, however, there is a problem with this dialectic: it tends to subtly "other" those who bring countertestimony and inadver-
tently props up core testimony as "core." Derrida worried about the possibility
that witnessing, as the way toward truth, might create a self-sustaining (or
what Derrida calls "auto-immune") rhythm between the center and the margins in which the truth center *needs* the truth margins in order to maintain
itself as the center and, indeed, in order to keep the margins marginal.

Whereas Derrida throws up his hands and asserts that this should lead us
to despair at testimonial forms of reasoning and witness, Levinas sees this as a
hopeful deconstruction that will move witnessing closer to its deepest meaning. Refocusing attention on testimony as act or *ethic*, Levinas points out how
the witness is radically decentered or deconstructed from the very beginning
by the awareness of infinite responsibility for *all* others (not just the court) in
the act of witnessing. Because of this awareness of infinite responsibility as a
witness, Levinas argues that witnessing always intentionally exceeds and
undermines both itself *and the courtroom*. The witness is always a disruptive
presence, subverting dialectical and distributive forms of justice with infinite
unspeakable responsibility to others present and missing. At the heart of witnessing, therefore, is a subversion of all themes spoken on the witness stand,
as well as a decentering of oneself, "tearing oneself up" (*martyria*, or what
Cheryl Bridges-Johns calls being "slain"), in order somehow to open up the
entire communicative situation to an infinite God. Witnessing, for Levinas, is
ultimately an act of *erasure*, through which the witness makes an ethical move
onto the ground of an infinite gathering of others: the infinite "courtroom" of
the infinite God. Levinas's ethical arguments, therefore, suggest that the idea
of the preacher as witness bears within itself the possibility radically to decon-
struct, decenter, and renew proclamation in each generation. Perhaps this is
the deeper reason ideas of witness and testimony are of so much interest in a
post-Holocaust and postmodern preaching context.

Paul Ricoeur, "The Hermeneutics of Testimony," in Lewis S. Mudge, ed., *Essays
on Biblical Interpretation* (Philadelphia: Fortress Press, 1981), 119–54; Paul
Ricoeur, "Emmanuel Levinas: Thinker of Testimony," in Mark J. Wallace, ed.,

Figuring the Sacred: Religion, Narrative, and Imagination, trans. David Pellauer (Minneapolis: Fortress Press, 1995), 115–35; Thomas G. Long, *The Witness of Preaching*, 2nd ed. (Louisville, KY: Westminster John Knox Press, 2005); Lucy Atkinson Rose, *Sharing the Word: Preaching in the Roundtable Church* (Louisville, KY: Westminster John Knox Press, 1997); David J. Lose, *Confessing Jesus Christ: Preaching in a Postmodern World* (Grand Rapids: Wm. B. Eerdmans Publishing Co., 2003); Cheryl Bridges-Johns, "Epiphanies of Fire: Para-modernist Preaching in a Postmodern World," paper given at the annual meeting of the Academy of Homiletics, 1996; John S. McClure, *Other-wise Preaching: A Postmodern Ethic for Homiletics* (St. Louis: Chalice Press, 2001); John S. McClure, "From Resistance to Jubilee: Prophetic Preaching and the Testimony of Love," Yale Institute of Sacred Music *Colloquium: Music, Worship, Arts*, vol. 2 (Autumn 2005): 77–85; Thomas G. Long, *Testimony: Talking Ourselves into Being Christian* (San Francisco: Jossey-Bass, 2004).

Word of God   *The idea that God speaks in the event of preaching.*

Although the idea of preaching as the Word of God existed long before the time of the Reformation in the ancient Hebrew concept of *dabar*, in the idea of the divine **Logos*, and in the writings of Augustine and Chrysostom, this idea was renewed and established as the center of the preacher's self-understanding by the Reformers, especially Luther and Calvin.

The belief that God somehow speaks a Word in and through preaching is an extension of the doctrine of revelation. The church has long held that God is revealed in a variety of ways: in creation, history, Scripture, sacraments, church, apostolic witness, and preaching. The Reformers closely associated the idea of preaching as God's Word with the idea of the Bible as the Word of God. For Calvin especially, preaching is the Word of God in a derivative sense. Just as the Bible derives its *authority from its *witness to Jesus Christ the living Word of God, preaching derives authority as God's Word from both the biblical witness and from the *gospel of Jesus Christ.

The idea of preaching as the Word of God asserts two fundamental things about preaching. First, it asserts that God accommodates to human beings and desires to somehow *communicate*. This is a profound assumption, without which there could be no preaching at all. Second, this idea asserts that God did not speak only during the time of biblical history, but continues to do so now. This means that preaching is not simply *about* God's revelation in Jesus Christ, it actually anticipates Christ's revelation *now*.

There are many views of *how* and *where* the Word of God occurs in and through preaching. These perspectives influence three aspects of homiletics: (1) the model of communication, (2) the theology of the Word in preaching, and (3) the idea of revelation that exists in the preacher's biblical *hermeneutic.

In the first instance, the way the preacher understands the function and location of God's Word influences the model of communication. Some preachers believe that the Word of God actually occurs at the *mouth of the preacher*. Sometimes called an objective view of the Word in preaching, this view is often attributed to Martin Luther. The Word of God in preaching is sovereign when it is spoken and cuts like a two-edged sword. The gates of heaven and hell swing open and closed when the preacher speaks.

Other preachers believe that the Word of God comes into being through the work of the Holy Spirit in the *heart of the listener*. This view is sometimes associated with Anabaptist traditions. In this perspective, the act of waiting, attending, and listening for God's Word becomes most important.

In a mediating model, God's Word occurs in the *communication event* of both speaking and hearing, as the Holy Spirit wills. In this model, both speaking and listening are crucial, as is the work of the Holy Spirit in making the connection occur in such a way that preaching becomes God's Word. Calvin tended to think in this way about the Word of God in preaching.

The second aspect of homiletics influenced by the way the preacher understands *how* and *where* the Word occurs is the theology of the Word in preaching (see *theology of preaching). Some preachers understand the Word of God as a response to questions that arise out of human existence (an *existential* theology of preaching). In a second understanding, the Word is utterly transcendent to both world and human existence (a *transcendent* theology of preaching). In a third understanding, the Word speaks restorative justice and hope into a world of structural evil and oppression (an *ethical-political* theology of preaching). For a fourth group of preachers, the Word is a "whispered Word" in the world that preaching raises to the level of hearing (an *organic-aesthetic* theology of preaching).

Finally, the way that the preacher views the Word in preaching influences the theology of revelation found in the preacher's biblical hermeneutic, determining where and how the Word of God operates with reference to the biblical text. For some, the Word is located in biblical propositions. This is sometimes called a *propositional view of revelation*. For others, the Word of God is located in the history and mighty acts of God located behind the text, to which the text witnesses. This is sometimes called a *historical view of revelation*, or revelation as history. In a third model, God's Word is revealed in and through biblical symbols, literary and rhetorical forms, and language, or what is in front of the text. This is sometimes called a *symbolic view of revelation*. In a fourth model, God's revealed Word is reserved only for the God who self-reveals through the text. The way that the preacher understands God and how God is at work in and through Jesus Christ is crucial to this model. This is sometimes called a theological or *christological view of revelation*. In the fifth model, the Word of God occurs in the fresh ideas and insights sparked by the way in which symbols within the contemporary context draw forth trajectories of meaning when placed next to biblical symbols. This is a contextual form of symbolic revelation, focusing on a correlation of symbols past and present. It is sometimes called a *contextual view of revelation*.

It is very important to reflect carefully on why and how preaching is the Word of God. The doctrine of preaching as the Word of God is, in many respects, the raison d'être for preaching. When preachers take time to consider how and where God's Word occurs in preaching, they become more deeply aware of the divine-human transaction at the very heart of preaching itself.

Ronald E. Sleeth, *God's Word and Our Words: Basic Homiletics* (Atlanta: John Knox Press, 1986); T. H. L. Parker, *Calvin: An Introduction to His Thought* (Louisville, KY: Westminster John Knox Press, 1995); Colin Brown, *Karl Barth and the Christian Message* (London: Tyndale Press, 1967); Richard Lischer, *A Theology of Preaching: The Dynamics of the Gospel*, revised edition (Durham, NC: The Labyrinth Press, 1992); Marjorie Suchocki, *The Whispered Word: A Theology of Preaching* (St. Louis: Chalice Press, 1999); Justo L. González and Catherine G. González, *The Liberating Pulpit* (Nashville: Abingdon Press, 1994); Donald K. McKim, *The Bible in Theology and Preaching* (Nashville: Abingdon Press, 1994); John McClure, *The Four Codes of Preaching: Rhetorical Strategies* (Minneapolis: Fortress Press, 1991; reprinted, Louisville, KY: Westminster John Knox Press, 2003); Burton Z Cooper and John S. McClure, *Claiming Theology in the Pulpit* (Louisville, KY: Westminster John Knox Press, 2003).

Bibliography

Achtemeier, Elizabeth. *Creative Preaching: Finding the Right Words*. Nashville: Abingdon Press, 1980.

———. *Preaching about Family Relationships*. Philadelphia: Westminster Press, 1987.

Adorno, T. W. *The Authoritarian Personality*. New York: W. W. Norton & Co., 1993.

Allen, O. Wesley, Jr. *The Homiletic of All Believers*. Louisville, KY: Westminster John Knox Press, 2005.

Allen, Ronald J. "Assessing the Authority of a Sermon." *Encounter* 67 (2006): 63–74.

———. *Hearing the Sermon: Relationship, Content, Feeling*. St. Louis: Chalice Press, 2004.

———. "How Do People Listen to Sermons?" *Preaching* 21, no. 1 (2005): 52–55.

———. *Interpreting the Gospel: An Introduction to Preaching*. St. Louis: Chalice Press, 1998.

———. "Is Preaching Caught or Taught? How Practitioners Learn." *Theological Education* 41 (2005): 137–52.

———, ed. *Patterns of Preaching: A Sermon Sampler*. St. Louis: Chalice Press, 1998.

———. "Preaching after a Tragedy: Listening to Congregations after September 11, 2001." *Encounter* 66 (2005): 221–32.

———. *Preaching Is Believing: The Sermon as Theological Reflection*. Louisville, KY: Westminster John Knox Press, 2002.

———. *Preaching the Topical Sermon*. Louisville, KY: Westminster John Knox Press, 1992.

———. "Preaching to Listeners: What Listeners Most Value in Sermons." *Homiletics* 17, no. 5 (2005): 7.

———. *Preaching Verse-by-Verse*. Louisville, KY: Westminster John Knox Press, 2000.

———. *The Teaching Sermon*. Nashville: Abingdon Press, 1995.

———. "Three Settings on Which People Hear Sermons." *Lectionary Homiletics* 16, no. 1 (2004–05): 1–3.

———. "What Do Lay People Think God Is Doing in the Sermon?" *Encounter* 66 (2005): 365–75.

———. "What Makes Preaching Disciples Preaching?" *Disciples World* 4, no. 2 (2005): 28–39.

Allen, Ronald J., Barbara Shires Blaisdell, and Scott Black Johnston. *Theology for Preaching: Authority, Truth, and Knowledge of God in a Postmodern Ethos.* Nashville: Abingdon Press, 1997.

Allen, Ronald J., and Mary Alice Mulligan. *Make the Word Come Alive: Lessons from Laity.* St. Louis: Chalice Press, 2006.

Allen, Ronald J., and Clark M. Williamson. *Preaching the Gospels without Blaming the Jews: A Lectionary Commentary.* Louisville, KY: Westminster John Knox Press, 2004.

Altrock, Chris. *Preaching to Pluralists: How to Proclaim Christ in a Postmodern Age.* St. Louis: Chalice Press, 2004.

Anderson, Herbert, and Edward Foley. *Mighty Stories, Dangerous Rituals: Weaving Together the Human and the Divine.* San Francisco: Jossey-Bass, 2001.

Andrews, Dale P. *Practical Theology for Black Churches: Bridging Black Theology and African American Folk Religion.* Louisville, KY: Westminster John Knox Press, 2002.

Asante, Molefi Kete. *The Afrocentric Idea.* Revised and expanded edition. Philadelphia: Temple University Press, 1998.

Aulén, Gustav. *Christus Victor: An Historical Study of the Three Main Types of the Idea of the Atonement.* London: SPCK Press, 1931.

Austin, James L. *How to Do Things with Words.* Oxford: Oxford University Press, 1962.

Bailey, E. K., and Warren W. P. Wiersbe. *Preaching in Black and White.* Grand Rapids: Zondervan Press, 2003.

Bailey, Raymond H. "Ethics in Preaching." *Review and Expositor* 86 (1989): 533–37.

———, ed. *Hermeneutics for Preaching: Approaches to Contemporary Interpretation of Scripture.* Nashville: Broadman Press, 1992.

Barbour, Ian G. *Myths, Models, and Paradigms: A Comparative Study in Science and Religion.* New York: Harper & Row, 1974.

Barnette, James R. "A Time to Laugh: Principles of Good Pulpit Humor." *Preaching* 11, no. 5 (Mar.–Apr. 1996): 1–11.

———. "Using Humor in Preaching: An Interview with Bob Russell." *Preaching* 10, no. 5 (Mar.–Apr. 1995): 5–10.

Barr, Browne. *Parish Back Talk.* Nashville: Abingdon Press, 1964.

Barr, Browne, and Mark Eakin. *The Ministering Congregation.* Philadelphia: United Church Press, 1972.

Barth, Karl. *Church Dogmatics.* Vol. 1, part 1, *The Doctrine of the Word of God.* Trans. G. T. Thompson. New York: Charles Scribner's Sons, 1936.

———. *Homiletics.* Louisville, KY: Westminster John Knox Press, 1991.

Bartow, Charles L. *The Preaching Moment: A Guide to Sermon Delivery.* Nashville: Abingdon Press, 1980.

Beckelhymer, Hunter. "No Posturing in Borrowed Plumes." *Christian Century* 91, no. 5 (Feb. 1974): 138–42.

Berndt, Brooks. "The Politics of Narrative." *Homiletic* 29, no. 2 (Winter 2004): 1–11.

Best, Ernest. *From Text to Sermon: Responsible Use of the New Testament in Preaching.* Atlanta: John Knox Press, 1978.

Biddle, Perry H. "The Wedding Sermon." In William H. Willimon and Richard Lischer, eds., *Concise Encyclopedia of Preaching,* 499–500.

Bieringer, Reimund, Didier Pollefeyt, and Frederique Vandecasteele, eds. *Anti-Judaism and the Fourth Gospel.* Louisville, KY: Westminster John Knox Press, 2001.

Black, Kathy. *A Healing Homiletic: Preaching and Disability.* Nashville: Abingdon Press, 1996.

————. *Worship across Cultures: A Handbook.* Nashville: Abingdon Press, 1998.
Blackwood, Andrew W. *The Preparation of Sermons.* Nashville: Abingdon-Cokesbury Press, 1948.
Block, Jennie Weiss. *Copious Hosting: A Theology of Access for People with Disabilities.* New York: Continuum Publishing Group, 2002.
Blount, Brian K., and Leonora Tubbs Tisdale, eds. *Making Room at the Table: An Invitation to Multi-Cultural Worship.* Louisville, KY: Westminster John Knox Press, 2000.
Bond, L. Susan. *Contemporary African American Preaching: Diversity in Theory and Style.* St. Louis: Chalice Press, 2003.
————. "Taming the Parable: The Problem of Parable as Substitute Myth." *Homiletic* 25, no. 1 (Summer 2000): 1–12.
————. *Trouble with Jesus: Women, Christology, and Preaching.* St. Louis: Chalice Press, 1999.
Bonhoeffer, Dietrich. "The Proclaimed Word." In Richard Lischer, ed., *The Company of Preachers: Wisdom on Preaching from Augustine to the Present,* 31–37.
Boonstra, Harry. "Preaching and Liturgy: The Dance of Worship." *Perspectives* 7, no. 6 (June 1992): 17–20.
Bower, Peter C. *Handbook for the Revised Common Lectionary.* Louisville, KY: Westminster John Knox Press, 1996.
Bowman, Rufus. "Personality and Preaching." *Pastoral Psychology* 5, no. 48 (Nov. 1954): 8–12.
Braxton, Brad R. *No Longer Slaves: Galatians and African American Experience.* Collegeville, MN: Liturgical Press, 2002.
————. *Preaching Paul.* Nashville: Abingdon Press, 2004.
Brekus, Catherine A. *Female Preaching in America: Strangers and Pilgrims 1740–1845.* Chapel Hill: University of North Carolina Press, 1998.
Bridges-Johns, Cheryl. "Epiphanies of Fire: Para-Modernist Preaching in a Postmodern World." A paper given at the annual meeting of the Academy of Homiletics, 1996.
Broadus, John. *A Treatise on the Preparation and Delivery of Sermons.* New York: Harper & Bros, 1926.
Brooks, Phillips. *Eight Lectures on Preaching.* London: SPCK Press, 1959.
Brown, Colin. *Karl Barth and the Christian Message.* London: Tyndale Press, 1967.
Brown, David M. *Dramatic Narrative in Preaching.* Valley Forge, PA: Judson Press, 1981.
Brown, Paul B. *In and for the World: Bringing the Contemporary into Christian Worship.* Minneapolis: Fortress, 1992.
Brown, Teresa Fry L. *Weary Throats and New Songs: Black Women Proclaiming God's Word.* Nashville: Abingdon Press, 2003.
Brueggemann, Walter. *Cadences of Home: Preaching among Exiles.* Louisville, KY: Westminster John Knox Press, 1997.
————. *The Prophetic Imagination.* Revised and updated edition. Minneapolis: Augsburg Fortress Press, 2001.
————. *Theology of the Old Testament: Testimony, Dispute, Advocacy.* Minneapolis: Fortress Press, 1997.
Bryson, Harold T. *Expository Preaching: The Art of Preaching through a Book of the Bible.* Nashville: Broadman & Holman, 1995.
Buchanan, John. "Punch Line: Sermonic Joke-Telling Is a Precarious Business." *Christian Century* 120, no. 16 (Aug. 9, 2003): 3.
Bullock, Jeffrey Francis. *Preaching with a Cupped Ear: Hans Georg Gadamer's Philosoph-*

ical Hermeneutics as Postmodern Wor(l)d. Berkeley Insights in Linguistics and Semiotics. New York: Peter Lang, 1999.

Burghardt, Walter J., SJ. *Preaching: The Art and the Craft*. New York: Paulist Press, 1987.

———. *Preaching the Just Word*. New Haven, CT: Yale University Press, 1996.

Burke, Kenneth. "Dramatism." In *International Encyclopedia of the Social Sciences*, ed. David L. Sills, 7:445–51. New York: Macmillan, 1948.

———. *A Rhetoric of Motives*. Berkeley: University of California Press, 1969.

Buttrick, David G. *Homiletic: Moves and Structures*. Philadelphia: Fortress Press, 1987.

———. "Interpretation and Preaching." *Interpretation*, Jan. 1981, 46–58.

———. "Preaching, Hermeneutics, and Liberation." In Paul Plenge Parker, ed., *Standing with the Poor: Theological Reflections on Economic Reality*, 95–105. Cleveland: Pilgrim Press, 1992.

Campbell, Charles L. *Preaching Jesus: New Directions for Homiletics in Hans Frei's Postliberal Theology*. Grand Rapids: Wm. B. Eerdmans Publishing Co., 1997.

———. *The Word before the Powers*. Louisville, KY: Westminster John Knox Press, 2002.

Campbell, Ernest T. "A Lover's Quarrel with Preaching." In Michael Graves, ed., *What's the Matter with Preaching Today?* 51–58.

Campbell, Ted A. "Itinerant and Open-Air Preaching." In William H. Willimon and Richard Lischer, eds., *Concise Encyclopedia of Preaching*, 274–76.

Capon, Robert Farrar. *The Foolishness of Preaching: Proclaiming the Gospel against the Wisdom of the World*. Grand Rapids: Wm. B. Eerdmans Publishing Co., 1998.

Carl, William J., III. *Preaching Christian Doctrine*. Philadelphia: Fortress Press, 1984.

Carroll, Jackson W. *As One with Authority: Reflective Leadership in Ministry*. Louisville, KY: Westminster John Knox Press, 1991.

Champlain, Mitties McDonald de. "What to Do While Preaching." In John McClure, ed., *Best Advice for Preaching*, 99–115.

Chandler, Daniel. *Semiotics: The Basics*. London: Routledge Press, 2002.

Chapell, Bryan. *Christ-Centered Preaching: Redeeming the Expository Sermon*. Grand Rapids: Baker Books, 1994.

Chartier, Myron. *Preaching as Communication: An Interpersonal Perspective*. Nashville: Abingdon Press, 1981.

Chesebrough, David B. *Phillips Brooks: Pulpit Eloquence*. Great American Orators. Westport, CT: Greenwood Press, 2001.

Childers, Jana, ed. *Birthing the Sermon: Women Preachers on the Creative Process*. St. Louis: Chalice Press, 2001.

———. *Performing the Word: Preaching as Theatre*. Nashville: Abingdon Press, 1998.

———, ed. *Purposes of Preaching*. St. Louis: Chalice Press, 2004.

Chopp, Rebecca. *The Power to Speak: Feminism, Language, God*. Eugene, OR: Wipf & Stock, 2002.

Cicero. *On the Ideal Orator*. Translated and with introduction, notes, and appendixes, glossary, and indexes, by James M. May and Jacob Wisse. New York: Oxford University Press, 2001.

Clader, Linda L. "Preaching the Liturgical Narrative: The Easter Vigil and the Language of Myth." *Worship* 72, no. 2 (Mar. 1998): 147–62.

———. *Voicing the Vision: Imagination and Prophetic Preaching*. Harrisburg, PA: Morehouse Publishing Co., 2004.

Claypool, John R. *The Preaching Event*. Lyman Beecher Lectures. Revised edition. Harrisburg, PA: Morehouse Publishing Co., 2000.

Cooper, Burton Z, and John S. McClure. *Claiming Theology in the Pulpit.* Louisville, KY: Westminster John Knox Press, 2003.

Cox, James W. *Preaching: A Comprehensive Approach to the Design and Delivery of Sermons.* San Francisco: Harper & Row, 1985.

Craddock, Fred B. *As One without Authority.* Revised and with new sermons. St. Louis: Chalice Press, 2001.

———. "The Gospel of God." In Thomas G. Long and Edward Farley, eds., *Preaching as a Theological Task: World, Gospel, Scripture,* 73–81. Louisville, KY: Westminster John Knox Press, 1996.

———. *Preaching.* Nashville: Abingdon Press, 1985.

———. "Preaching: An Appeal to Memory." In Mike Graves, ed., *What's The Matter with Preaching Today?* 59–73.

Craske, Jane V. *A Woman's Perspective on Preaching.* Peterborough: Foundery Press, 2001.

Crawford, Evans. *The Hum: Call and Response in African American Preaching.* Nashville: Abingdon Press, 1995.

Crossan, John Dominic. *The Dark Interval: Towards a Theology of Story.* Sonoma, CA: Polebridge Press, 1988.

Daniel, Lillian. *Telling It Like It Is: Reclaiming the Practice of Testimony.* Herndon, VA: Alban Institute, 2005.

Davis, Ellen F. *Imagination Shaped: Old Testament Preaching in the Anglican Tradition.* Valley Forge, PA: Trinity Press International, 1995.

Davis, Henry Grady. *Design for Preaching.* Philadelphia: Fortress Press, 1958.

DeVito, Joseph A. *Human Communication: The Basic Course.* 10th ed. Boston: Allyn & Bacon, 2005.

Dietrich, Walter, and Ulrich Luz, eds. *The Bible in a World Context: An Experiment in Contextual Hermeneutics.* Grand Rapids: Wm. B. Eerdmans Publishing Co., 2002.

Dodd, C. H. *The Apostolic Preaching and Its Developments.* New York: Harper & Row, 1964.

Drummond, Lewis. "Charles G. Finney and His Impact on Evangelistic Preaching." *Preaching* 7, no. 1 (July–Aug. 1991): 42–43.

Duduit, Michael, ed. *Handbook of Contemporary Preaching.* Nashville: Broadman & Holman, 1993.

Duffett, Robert G. *A Relevant Word: Communicating the Gospel to Seekers.* Valley Forge, PA: Judson Press, 1995.

Eckert, Jerry. *In the Carpenter's Workshop: An Exploration of the Use of Drama in Story Sermons.* Lima, OH: CSS Publishing Co., 1997.

Edwards, O. C. *A History of Preaching.* Nashville: Abingdon Press, 2004.

Ekman, Paul, Wallace V. Friesen, and Phoebe Ellsworth. *Emotion in the Human Face: Guidelines for Research and an Integration of Findings.* New York: Pergamon Press, 1972.

Ellingsen, Mark. *Doctrine and Word: Theology in the Pulpit.* Atlanta: John Knox Press, 1983.

———. *The Integrity of Biblical Narrative: Story in Theology and Proclamation.* Minneapolis: Fortress Press, 1990.

Elliott, Mark Barger. *Creative Styles of Preaching.* Louisville, KY: Westminster John Knox Press, 2000.

Eslinger, Richard L., ed. *Intersections: Post-Critical Studies in Preaching.* Grand Rapids: Wm. B. Eerdmans Publishing Co., 1994.

————. *Narrative and Imagination: Preaching the Worlds That Shape Us*. Minneapolis: Fortress Press, 1995.

————. *A New Hearing: Living Options in Homiletical Method*. Nashville: Abingdon Press, 1987.

Fackre, Gabriel. *The Christian Story: A Pastoral Systematics*, vol. 2. Grand Rapids: Wm. B. Eerdmans Publishing Co., 1987.

Fant, Clyde. *Preaching for Today*. New York: Harper & Row, 1975.

Farley, Edward. *Practicing Gospel: Unconventional Thoughts on the Church's Ministry*. Louisville, KY: Westminster John Knox Press, 2003.

Farmer, Herbert H. *The Servant of the Word*. New York: Charles Scribner's Sons, 1942.

Farris, Stephen. *Preaching That Matters: The Bible and Our Lives*. Louisville, KY: Westminster John Knox Press, 1998.

Florence, Anna Carter. *Preaching as Testimony*. Louisville, KY: Westminster John Knox Press, forthcoming.

————. "Preaching to the Exiles Who Live at Home: Youth, Testimony, and a Homiletic of 'True Speech.'" *Journal for Preachers*, Advent 2000, 23–29.

————. "Put Away Your Sword: Taking the Torture out of the Sermon." In Mike Graves, ed., *What's the Matter with Preaching Today?* 93–108.

Ford, D. W. Cleverley. *The Ministry of the Word*. Grand Rapids: Wm. B. Eerdmans Publishing Co., 1979.

Forde, Gerhard. *Theology Is for Proclamation*. Minneapolis: Fortress Press, 1990.

Forsyth, P. T. *Positive Preaching and the Modern Mind*. New York: A. C. Armstrong, 1907.

Fosdick, Harry Emerson. "Personal Counseling and Preaching." *Pastoral Psychology* 3, no. 22 (Mar. 1952): 11–15.

————. "What Is the Matter with Preaching?" In Mike Graves, ed., *What's the Matter with Preaching Today?* 7–19.

Foster, Charles R. *Embracing Diversity: Leadership in Multicultural Congregations*. Herndon, VA: Alban Institute, 1997.

Fredriksen, Paula, and Adele Reinhartz, eds. *Jesus, Judaism, and Christian Anti-Judaism: Reading the New Testament after the Holocaust*. Louisville, KY: Westminster John Knox Press, 2002.

Furgeson, Earl. "Preaching and Personality." *Pastoral Psychology* 10, no. 7 (Oct. 1959): 9–14.

Galli, Mark, and Craig Brian Larson. *Preaching That Connects: Using Journalistic Techniques to Add Impact*. Grand Rapids: Zondervan Press, 1994.

Gibson, Scott M. *Preaching for Special Services*. Grand Rapids: Baker Publishing Group, 2001.

González, Justo L., and Catherine G. González. *The Liberating Pulpit*. Nashville: Abingdon Press, 1994.

González, Justo L., and Pablo Jiménez. *Púlpito: An Introduction to Hispanic Preaching*. Nashville: Abingdon Press, 2005.

Graves, Mike, ed. *What's the Matter with Preaching Today?* Louisville, KY: Westminster John Knox Press, 2004.

Green, Garrett. *Imagining God: Theology and the Religious Imagination*. Paperback edition. Grand Rapids: Wm. B. Eerdmans Publishing Co., 1998.

Green, Joel B., and Michael Pasquarello III, eds. *Narrative Reading, Narrative Preaching: Reuniting New Testament Interpretation and Proclamation*. Grand Rapids: Baker Academic, 2003.

Greenhaw, David M. "As One *with* Authority: Rehabilitating Concepts for Preaching."

In Richard L. Eslinger, Richard L., ed., *Intersections: Post-Critical Studies in Preaching*, 105–22.

Greidanus, Sidney. *Preaching Christ from the Old Testament: A Contemporary Hermeneutical Method*. Grand Rapids: Wm. B. Eerdmans Publishing Co., 1999.

Greiser, David B., and Michael A. King, eds. *Anabaptist Preaching: A Conversation between Pulpit, Pew, and Bible*. Telford, PA: Cascadia Publishing House, 2003.

Hageman, Howard. *Pulpit and Table: Some Chapters in the History of Worship in the Reformed Churches*. Richmond: John Knox Press, 1962.

Hall, Thor. *The Future Shape of Preaching*. Philadelphia: Fortress Press, 1971.

Hardesty, Nancy. *Inclusive Language in the Church*. Louisville, KY: Westminster John Knox Press, 1988.

Harrell, Danny. "This Is Not Your Father's Preaching Style: How to Speak the Language of the 'Whatever' Generation." *Leadership: A Practical Journal for Church Leaders* (Summer 1998), 83–84.

Hedahl, Susan K. *Preaching the Wedding Sermon*. St. Louis: Chalice Press, 1999.

Henderson, J. Frank. "The Minister of Liturgical Preaching." *Worship* 56, no 3 (1982): 214–30.

Hilkert, Mary Catherine. *Naming Grace: Preaching and the Sacramental Imagination*. New York: Continuum International Publishing, 2003.

Hiltner, Seward. *Preface to Pastoral Theology*. Nashville: Abingdon Press, 1979.

Hjelm, J. Robert. "*Didache* and *Kerygma*: A Preaching Option." *Covenant Quarterly*, Aug. 1981–Feb. 1982, 97–111.

Hoffacker, Charles. *A Matter of Life and Death: Preaching at Funerals*. Cambridge, MA: Cowley Publications, 2002.

Hogan, Lucy Lind, and Robert Reid. *Connecting with the Congregation: Rhetoric and the Art of Preaching*. Nashville: Abingdon Press, 1999.

Hollinger, Dennis. "The Ethics of Persuasion in Preaching." In David B. Greiser and Michael King, eds., *Anabaptist Preaching: A Conversation between Pulpit, Pew, and Bible*, 186–99.

Holmgren, Fredrick C., and Herman E. Schaalman. *Preaching Biblical Texts: Expositions by Jewish and Christian Scholars*. Grand Rapids: Wm. B. Eerdmans Publishing Co., 1995.

Hopewell, James. *Congregation: Stories and Structures*. Minneapolis: Augsburg Fortress Press, 1987.

Howe, Reuel L. *The Miracle of Dialogue*. New York: Seabury Press, 1963.

———. *Partners in Preaching: Clergy and Laity in Dialogue*. New York: Seabury Press, 1967.

Hughes, Robert G. *A Trumpet in Darkness: Preaching to Mourners*. Philadelphia: Fortress Press, 1985.

An Inclusive Language Lectionary. Louisville, KY: Westminster John Knox Press, 1984–87.

Jacks, G. Robert. *Getting the Word Across: Speech Communication for Pastors and Lay Leaders*. Grand Rapids: Wm. B. Eerdmans Publishing Co., 1987.

Jasper, David. *A Short Introduction to Hermeneutics*. Louisville, KY: Westminster John Knox Press, 2004.

Jensen, Robert A. *Telling the Story: Variety and Imagination in Preaching*. Minneapolis: Augsburg Publishing House, 1980.

Jones, Ilion T. *Principles and Practice of Preaching: A Comprehensive Study of the Art of Sermon Construction*. Nashville: Abingdon Press, 1956.

Jones, Kirk Byron. *The Jazz of Preaching: How to Preach with Great Freedom and Joy*. Nashville: Abingdon Press, 2004.

Jones, W. Paul. *Theological Worlds: Understanding the Alternative Rhythms of Christian Belief*. Nashville: Abingdon Press, 1989.

Kay, James. "Reorientation: Homiletics as Theologically Authorized Rhetoric." *Princeton Seminary Bulletin* 24, no. 1 (2003): 16–17, 20–22.

Keck, Leander E. *The Bible in the Pulpit: The Renewal of Biblical Preaching*. Nashville: Abingdon Press, 1978.

Kee, Howard Clark, and Irwin J. Borowsky, eds. *Removing Anti-Judaism from the Pulpit*. New York: Continuum International Publishing, 1996.

Kiefert, Patrick R. *Welcoming the Stranger: A Public Theology of Worship and Evangelism*. Minneapolis: Augsburg Fortress Press, 1992.

Killinger, John, ed. *Experimental Preaching*. Nashville: Abingdon Press, 1973.

Kim, Eunjoo Mary. "Hermeneutics and Asian American Preaching." *Semeia* 90–91, no. 1 (2002): 269–90.

———. *Preaching the Presence of God: A Homiletic from an Asian American Perspective*. Valley Forge, PA: Judson Press, 1999.

———. *Women Preaching: Theology and Practice through the Ages*. Cleveland: Pilgrim Press, 2004.

Koenig, John. *God's Word at Mass*. New York: Hawthorn Press, 1967.

———. *New Testament Hospitality: Partners with Strangers as Promise and Mission*. Philadelphia: Fortress Press, 1995.

Koller, Charles. *How to Preach without Notes*. Grand Rapids: Baker Publishing Group, 1997.

Langford, Andy. "The Revised Common Lectionary 1992: A Revision for the Next Generation." *Quarterly Review* 13 (Summer 1993): 37–48.

LaRue, Cleophus J. *The Heart of Black Preaching*. Louisville, KY: Westminster John Knox Press, 1999.

———. "Two Ships Passing in the Night." In Mike Graves, ed., *What's the Matter with Preaching Today?* 127–44.

Law, Eric H. F. *The Bush Was Blazing but Not Consumed: Developing a Multicultural Community through Dialogue and Liturgy*. St. Louis: Chalice Press, 1996.

Lawless, Elaine J. *God's Peculiar People: Women's Voices and Folk Tradition in a Pentecostal Church*. Lexington: University Press of Kentucky, 2005.

Lee, Jarena. "My Call to Preach the Gospel." In Richard Lischer, ed., *The Company of Preachers: Wisdom on Preaching, Augustine to the Present*, 75–82.

Lee, Jung Young. *Korean Preaching: An Interpretation*. Nashville: Abingdon Press, 1997.

Lewis, Ralph. "Preaching with and without Notes." In Michael Duduit, ed., *Handbook of Contemporary Preaching*, 409–19.

Lindbeck, George. *The Nature of Doctrine: Religion and Theology in a Postliberal Age*. Philadelphia: Westminster Press, 1984.

Linn, Edmund Holt. *Preaching as Counseling: The Unique Method of Harry Emerson Fosdick*. Valley Forge, PA: Judson Press, 1966.

Lischer, Richard, ed. *The Company of Preachers: Wisdom on Preaching from Augustine to the Present*. Grand Rapids: Wm. B. Eerdmans Publishing Co., 2002.

———. "How the Preacher King Borrowed Sermons." *Christian Ministry*, Jan.–Feb. 1997, 19–21.

———. "The Limits of Story." *Interpretation* 38, no. 1 (Jan. 1984): 26–38.

———. *A Theology of Preaching: The Dynamics of the Gospel*. Revised edition. Durham, NC: The Labyrinth Press, 1992.

Loder, James E. *The Transforming Moment: Understanding Convictional Experiences*. 2nd ed. Colorado Springs, CO: Helmers & Howard Publishing, 1989.

Long, Thomas G. "And How Shall They Hear? The Listener in Contemporary Preaching." In Gail R. O'Day and Thomas G. Long, *Listening to the Word: Studies in Honor of Fred B. Craddock*, 167–88.

———. "The Funeral: Changing Patterns and Teachable Moments." *Journal for Preachers*, Easter 1996, 3–8.

———. "Patterns in Sermons." In John S. McClure, *Best Advice for Preaching*, 35–59.

———. "Pawn to King Four: Sermon Introductions and Communicational Design." *Reformed Review* 40, no. 1 (Autumn 1986): 27–35.

———. *Preaching and the Literary Forms of the Bible*. Philadelphia: Fortress Press, 1989.

———. "Preaching in the Prophets." In Michael Duduit, ed., *Handbook of Contemporary Preaching*, 306–16.

———. "Shaping Sermons by Plotting the Text's Claim upon Us." In Don Wardlaw, ed., *Preaching Biblically: Sermons in the Shape of Scripture*, 84–100.

———. *Testimony: Talking Ourselves into Being Christian*. San Francisco: Jossey-Bass, 2004.

———. "What Happened to Narrative Preaching?" *Journal for Preachers* 28, no. 4 (Pentecost 2005): 9–14.

———. *The Witness of Preaching*. 2nd ed. Louisville, KY: Westminster John Knox Press, 2005.

Long, Thomas G., and Neely Dixon McCarter, eds. *Preaching in and out of Season*. Louisville, KY: Westminster John Knox Press, 1990.

Loscalzo, Craig A. *Apologetic Preaching: Proclaiming Christ to a Postmodern World*. Downers Grove, IL: InterVarsity Press, 2000.

———. *Evangelistic Preaching That Connects: Guidance in Shaping Fresh and Appealing Sermons*. Downers Grove, IL: InterVarsity Press, 1995.

———. "Feedback." In John S. McClure, ed., *Best Advice for Preaching*, 135–50.

———. *Preaching Sermons That Connect: Effective Communication through Identification*. Downers Grove, IL: InterVarsity Press, 1992.

Lose, David J. *Confessing Jesus Christ: Preaching in a Postmodern World*. Grand Rapids: Wm. B. Eerdmans Publishing Co., 2003.

———. "Narrative and Proclamation in a Postliberal Homiletic." *Homiletic* 23, no. 1 (Summer 1998): 1–14.

Love, Roger, and Donna Frazier. *Set Your Voice Free: How to Get the Singing or Speaking Voice You Want*. Book and CD edition. London: Little, Brown & Co., 2003.

Lowry, Eugene L. *The Homiletical Plot: The Sermon as Narrative Art Form*. Expanded edition. Louisville, KY: Westminster John Knox Press, 2001.

———. "Preaching or Reciting: Theft in the Pulpit." *Christian Ministry*, Mar.–Apr. 1991, 9–12.

———. *The Sermon: Dancing the Edges of Mystery*. Nashville: Abingdon Press, 1997.

Luther, Martin. "Proclamation versus Moralism." In Richard Lischer, ed., *The Company of Preachers: Wisdom on Preaching, Augustine to the Present*, 115–19.

Maguire, James T. "A Scale on Preaching Style: Hortatory vs. Interactive Preaching." *Review of Religious Research* 22, no. 1 (Sept. 1981): 60–65.

Massey, James Earl. *Designing the Sermon: Order and Movement in Preaching*. Nashville: Abingdon Press, 1980.

———. "Hermeneutics for Preaching." *Review and Expositor* 90, no. 3 (1993): 359–69.

McClure, John S. *Best Advice for Preaching*. Minneapolis: Fortress Press, 1998.

———. "Collaborative Preaching from the Margins." *Journal for Preachers* 22 (Pentecost 1996): 12–14.

————. *The Four Codes of Preaching: Rhetorical Strategies*. Minneapolis: Fortress Press, 1991. Reprinted, Louisville, KY: Westminster John Knox Press, 2003.

————. "From Resistance to Jubilee: Prophetic Preaching and the Testimony of Love." Yale Institute of Sacred Music *Colloquium: Music, Worship, Arts*, vol. 2 (Autumn 2005): 77–85.

————. "In Pursuit of Good Theological Judgment: Newman and the Preacher as Theologian." In Michael Welker and Cynthia A. Jarvis, eds., *Loving God with Our Minds: The Pastor as Theologian*, 202–19. Grand Rapids: Wm. B. Eerdmans Publishing Co., 2004.

————. "Language, theories of." In William H. Willimon and Richard Lischer, eds., *Concise Encyclopedia of Preaching*, 292–95.

————. "Narrative and Preaching: Sorting It All Out." *Journal for Preachers* 15, no. 1 (1991): 24–29.

————. "The Narrative Function of Preaching." *Liturgy* 8, no. 2 (Fall 1989): 47–51.

————. "The Other Side of Sermon Illustration." *Journal for Preachers*, Lent 1989, 2–4.

————. *Other-wise Preaching: A Postmodern Ethic for Homiletics*. St. Louis: Chalice Press, 2001.

————. "The Practice of Sermon Listening." *Congregations* 32, no. 1 (2006): 6–9.

————. "Preaching and the Redemption of Language." In Jana Childers, ed., *Purposes of Preaching*, 83–90.

————. Review of *Preaching Jesus*, by Charles L. Campbell. *Journal for Preachers* 21, no. 2 (1998): 36.

————. "Preaching Theology." *Quarterly Review* 24, no. 3 (Fall 2004): 249–61.

————. *The Roundtable Pulpit: Where Leadership and Preaching Meet*. Nashville: Abingdon Press, 1995.

McClure, John S., Ronald J. Allen, Dale P. Andrews, L. Susan Bond, Dan P. Moseley, and G. Lee Ramsey Jr. *Listening to Listeners: Homiletical Case Studies*. St. Louis: Chalice Press, 2004.

McClure, John S., and Nancy Ramsay, eds. *Telling the Truth: Preaching about Sexual and Domestic Violence*. Cleveland: United Church Press, 1999.

McDill, Wayne. *The Twelve Essential Skills for Great Preaching*. Nashville: Broadman & Holman, 1998.

McDonald, James I. H. Kerygma *and* Didache: *The Articulation and Structure of the Earliest Christian Message*. Cambridge: Cambridge University Press, 1980.

McFague, Sallie. *Metaphorical Theology: Models of God in Religious Language*. Minneapolis: Augsburg Fortress Press, 1997.

McKay, Johnston. "And Finally . . . No Copyright on Sermons." *Expository Times* 115, no. 3 (Dec. 2003): 108.

McKim, Donald K. *A Guide to Contemporary Hermeneutics: Major Trends in Biblical Interpretation*. Grand Rapids: Wm. B. Eerdmans Publishing Co., 1986.

————. *The Bible in Theology and Preaching*. Nashville: Abingdon Press, 1994.

Melloh, John Allyn. "Homily or Eulogy: The Dilemma of Funeral Preaching." *Worship* 67, no. 6 (Nov. 1993): 502–18.

Meyers, Robin. *With Ears to Hear: Preaching as Self-Persuasion*. Cleveland: Pilgrim Press, 1993.

Mickelsen, Alvera, ed. *Women, Authority, and the Bible*. Downers Grove, IL: InterVarsity Press, 1986.

Miller, Calvin. "Naming the Baby: The Right Sermon Title Makes All the Difference." *Leadership: A Practical Journal for Church Leaders* (Winter 1998): 93–95.

Miller, Casey, and Kate Swift. *The Handbook of Nonsexist Writing: For Writers, Editors and Speakers*. 2nd ed. Lincoln, NE: iUniverse, 2001.
Mitchell, Henry H. *Black Preaching: The Recovery of a Powerful Art*. Nashville: Abingdon Press, 1990.
———. *Celebration and Experience in Preaching*. Nashville: Abingdon Press, 1990.
———. "Polishing the Sermon." In John S. McClure, *Best Advice for Preaching*, 85–98.
———. "Preaching on the Patriarchs." In James W. Cox, ed., *Biblical Preaching: An Expositor's Treasury*, 36–52. Philadelphia: Westminster Press, 1988.
———. *The Recovery of Preaching*. San Francisco: Harper & Row, 1977.
Mitchell, Jolyon P. *Visually Speaking: Radio and the Renaissance of Preaching*. Louisville, KY: Westminster John Knox Press, 1999.
Moeller, Pamela. *A Kinesthetic Homiletic: Embodying Gospel in Preaching*. Minneapolis: Fortress Press, 1993.
Montova, Alex D. *Preaching with Passion*. London: Kregel Academic and Professional, 2000.
Mountford, Roxanne. *The Gendered Pulpit: Preaching in American Protestant Spaces*. Carbondale: Southern Illinois University Press, 2003.
Moyd, Olin P. *The Sacred Art*. Valley Forge, PA: Judson Press, 1995.
Mulder, John M. "Call." In William H. Willimon and Richard Lischer, eds., *Concise Encyclopedia of Preaching*, 58–60.
Nelson, Wesley W. "Taking Pulpit Humor Seriously." *Covenant Quarterly* 56, no. 2 (May 1998): 3–14.
Nichols, J. Randall. *Building the Word: The Dynamics of Communication and Preaching*. San Francisco: Harper & Row, 1980.
———. *The Restoring Word: Preaching as Pastoral Communication*. San Francisco: Harper & Row, 1987.
Niebuhr, H. Richard. *Christ and Culture*. New York: Harper & Row, 1951.
Nieman, James R., and Thomas G. Rogers. *Preaching to Every Pew: Cross-Cultural Strategies*. Minneapolis: Augsburg Fortress Press, 2001.
Noren, Carol M. *The Woman in the Pulpit*. Nashville: Abingdon Press, 1991.
O'Day, Gail R., and Thomas G. Long. *Listening to the Word: Studies in Honor of Fred B. Craddock*. Nashville: Abingdon Press, 1993.
Ong, Walter. *The Presence of the Word: Some Prolegomena for Cultural and Religious History*. New Haven, CT: Yale University Press, 1967.
Palmer, Phoebe. "The Great Army of Preaching Women." In Richard Lischer, ed., *The Company of Preachers: Wisdom on Preaching, Augustine to the Present*, 90–97.
Parker, T. H. L. *Calvin: An Introduction to His Thought*. Louisville, KY: Westminster John Knox Press, 1995.
Peterson, Steve. *Drama Ministry*. Grand Rapids: Zondervan, 1999.
Phan, Peter C. "The Wisdom of Holy Fools in Postmodernity." *Theological Studies* 62 (2001): 730–52.
Pitt-Watson, Ian. *Preaching: A Kind of Folly*. Philadelphia: Westminster Press, 1976.
Pope-Levinson, Priscilla, and John R. Levinson. "Evangelistic Preaching at the Beginning of the New Millennium." *Journal for Preachers*, Pentecost 2000, 3–9.
Pound, Ezra. "A Few Don'ts by an Imagiste." *Poetry* (Chicago) 1 (1913): 198–206.
Procter-Smith, Marjorie. "Beyond the New Common Lectionary: A Constructive Critique." *Quarterly Review* 13 (Summer 1993): 49–58.
———. "Lectionaries: Principles and Problems." *Studia Liturgica* 22, no. 1 (1992): 84–89.

Proctor, Samuel D. *A Certain Sound of the Trumpet: Crafting a Sermon of Authority.* Valley Forge, PA: Judson Press, 1994.

Ramsey, G. Lee, Jr. *Care-full Preaching: From Sermon to Caring Community.* St. Louis: Chalice Press, 2000.

Ramshaw, Elaine. *Liturgical Language: Keeping It Metaphoric, Making It Inclusive.* Collegeville, MN: Liturgical Press, 1996.

———. *Ritual and Pastoral Care.* Minneapolis: Augsburg Fortress Press, 1987.

Randolph, David James. *The Renewal of Preaching.* Philadelphia: Fortress Press, 1969.

Reid, Clyde H. "Preaching and the Nature of Communication." *Pastoral Psychology* 14 (1963): 40–49.

Resner, André, Jr. *Preacher and Cross: Person and Message in Theology and Rhetoric.* Grand Rapids: Wm. B. Eerdmans Publishing Co., 1999.

The Revised Common Lectionary: Consultation on Common Texts. Nashville: Abingdon Press, 1992.

Rice, Charles L. *The Embodied Word: Preaching as Art and Liturgy.* Minneapolis: Fortress Press, 1991.

———. "Less Is More: Preaching as a Liturgical Act." *Journal for Preachers* 10, no. 3 (Easter 1983): 14–20.

———. "Preaching at Weddings." *Sewanee Theological Review* 41, no. 3 (Pentecost 1998): 228–40.

———. "Shaping Sermons by the Interplay of Text and Metaphor." In Don M. Wardlaw, ed., *Preaching Biblically: Sermons in the Shape of Scripture*, 101–20.

Ricoeur, Paul. "Emmanuel Levinas: Thinker of Testimony." In Mark J. Wallace, ed., *Figuring the Sacred: Religion, Narrative, and Imagination*, trans. David Pellauer, 115–35. Minneapolis: Fortress Press, 1995.

———. "The Hermeneutics of Testimony." In Lewis S. Mudge, ed., *Essays on Biblical Interpretation*, 119–54. Philadelphia: Fortress Press, 1981.

Ridenhour, Thomas E. "Essential Resources for Preaching." In John S. McClure, ed., *Best Advice for Preaching*, 151–70.

Robinson, Haddon W. *Biblical Preaching: The Development and Delivery of Expository Messages.* 2nd ed. Grand Rapids: Baker Academic, 2001.

Robinson, Wayne Bradley, ed. *Journeys toward Narrative Preaching.* New York: Pilgrim Press, 1990.

Rogers, John B., Jr. "The Foolishness of Preaching." *Interpretation* 45, no. 3 (July 1991): 241–52.

Rose, Lucy Atkinson. *Sharing the Word: Preaching in the Roundtable Church.* Louisville, KY: Westminster John Knox Press, 1997.

Rosenberg, Bruce A. *The Art of the American Folk Preacher.* New York: Oxford University Press, 1970.

Ryan, Halvord R. *Harry Emerson Fosdick: Persuasive Preacher.* Great American Orators. Westport, CT: Greenwood Press, 1989.

Salmon, Marilyn J. *Preaching without Contempt: Overcoming Unintended Anti-Judaism.* Minneapolis: Fortress Press, 2006.

Sample, Tex. *Ministry in an Oral Culture: Living with Will Rogers, Uncle Remus, and Minnie Pearl.* Louisville, KY: Westminster John Knox Press, 1994.

———. *The Spectacle of Worship in a Wired World: Electronic Culture and the Gathered People of God.* Nashville: Abingdon Press, 1998.

Saunders, Stanley P., and Charles L. Campbell. *The Word on the Street: Performing the Scriptures in the Urban Context.* Grand Rapids: Wm. B. Eerdmans Publishing Co., 2000.

Schlafer, David J. *What Makes This Day Different? Preaching Grace on Special Occasions.* Cambridge, MA: Cowley Publications, 1998.

Scholes, Robert. *Structuralism in Literature: An Introduction.* New Haven, CT: Yale University Press, 1975.

Searle, John R. *Speech Acts: An Essay in the Philosophy of Language.* Cambridge: Cambridge University Press, 1969.

Severance, W. Murray, and Terry Eddinger. *That's Easy for You to Say: Your Quick Guide to Pronouncing Bible Names.* Book and CD ROM edition. Nashville: Broadman & Holman, 1997.

Shelley, Carter. "Preaching and Plagiarism: A Guide for Introduction to Preaching Students." *Homiletic* 27, no. 2 (Winter 2002): 1–13.

Sleeth, Ronald E. *God's Word and Our Words: Basic Homiletics.* Atlanta: John Knox Press, 1986.

Smith, Christine M. *Preaching as Weeping, Confession, and Resistance: Radical Responses to Radical Evil.* Louisville, KY: Westminster John Knox Press, 1992.

———. *Weaving the Sermon: Preaching in a Feminist Perspective.* Louisville, KY: Westminster John Knox Press, 1989.

Smith, John E. *Experience and God.* Bronx, NY: Fordham University Press, 1995.

Smith, Ted. *The New Measures.* Cambridge: Cambridge University Press, forthcoming.

Smith, Theophus H. *Conjuring Culture: Biblical Formations of Black America.* New York: Oxford University Press, 1994.

Sonefeld, R. C. *Preaching the Funeral Homily: Proclaiming the Gospel of Heavenly Hope.* San Jose, CA: Resource Publications, 2000.

Soskice, Janet Martin. *Metaphors and Religious Language.* Oxford: Clarendon Press, 1985.

Standing, Roger. *Finding the Plot: Preaching in a Narrative Style.* Carlisle, UK: Paternoster Press, 2004.

Steimle, Edmund A., Morris J. Niedenthal, and Charles Rice. *Preaching the Story.* Philadelphia: Fortress Press, 1980; reissue, Eugene, OR: Wipf & Stock, 2003.

Stewart, Alison, ed. *Drama Team Handbook.* Downers Grove, IL: InterVarsity Press, 2003.

Stewart, Warren H. *Interpreting God's Word in Black Preaching.* Valley Forge, PA: Judson Press, 1984.

Stone, Dave. *Refining Your Style: Learning from Respected Communicators.* Loveland, CO: Group Publishing, 2004.

Stuempfle, Herman G., Jr. *Preaching Law and Gospel.* Philadelphia: Fortress Press, 1978.

Suchocki, Marjorie Hewitt. *The Whispered Word: A Theology of Preaching.* St. Louis: Chalice Press, 1999.

Sutton, Eugene T. "And for Preachers . . . Humor." *Perspectives,* Oct. 1991, n/a.

Sweazey, George E. *Preaching the Good News.* Englewood Cliffs, NJ: Prentice-Hall, 1976.

Taylor, Anita, Teresa Rosegrant, Arthur Meyer, and B. Thomas Samples. *Communicating.* 4th ed. Englewood Cliffs, NJ: Prentice Hall, 1986.

Taylor, Barbara Brown. *The Preaching Life.* Cambridge, MA: Cowley Publications, 1993.

———. *Speaking of Sin: The Lost Language of Salvation.* Cambridge, MA: Cowley Publications, 2000.

Taylor, Gardner C. "Titles." In William H. Willimon and Richard Lischer, eds., *Concise Encyclopedia of Preaching,* 491–92.

Thomas, Frank A. *They Like to Never Quit Praisin' God*. Cleveland: United Church Press, 1997.

Thompson, James W. *Preaching Like Paul: Homiletical Wisdom for Today*. Louisville, KY: Westminster John Knox Press, 2001.

Thulin, Richard L. *The "I" of the Sermon: Autobiography in the Pulpit*. Eugene, OR: Wipf & Stock, 2004.

Tiberi, Laurie. "Borrowing Is OK: Lying Is Not." *Christian Ministry*, Jan.–Feb. 1997, 17–18.

Tisdale, Leonora Tubbs. "The Calling of the Preacher." In John S. McClure, *Best Advice for Preaching*, 1–16.

———. *Preaching as Local Theology and Folk Art*. Minneapolis: Fortress Press, 1997.

Trilling, Lionel. *Sincerity and Authenticity*. Cambridge, MA: Harvard University Press, 1982.

Troeger, Thomas H. *Imagining a Sermon*. Nashville: Abingdon Press, 1990.

———. *The Parable of Ten Preachers*. Nashville: Abingdon Press, 1992.

———. The Poetics of the Pulpit for Post-Modern Times." In Richard L. Eslinger, ed. *Intersection: Post-Critical Studies in Preaching*, 42–64.

———. *Ten Strategies for Preaching in a Multi-Media Culture*. Nashville: Abingdon Press, 1996.

Troxell, Thomas E. "Humor as a Preaching Tool." *Military Chaplain's Review* 15, no. 1 (Winter 1986): 59–63.

Turner, Mary Donovan, and Mary Lin Hudson. *Saved from Silence: Finding Women's Voice in Preaching*. St. Louis: Chalice Press, 1999.

Turner-Sharazz, Diane. "The 'So What' Factor in the Sermon: How the Sermon Connects." *Journal of Theology*, 2005, 45–58.

Turner-Sharazz, Diane, Dawn Ottoni Wilhelm, Ronald J. Allen, and Mary Alice Mulligan. *Believing in Preaching: What Listeners Hear in Sermons*. St. Louis: Chalice Press, 2005.

Untener, Ken. *Preaching Better: Practical Suggestions for Homilists*. New York: Paulist Press, 1999.

Van Der Geest, Hans. *Presence in the Pulpit: The Impact of Personality in Preaching*. Atlanta: John Knox Press, 1981.

Vannorsdall, John. "Humor as Content and Device in Preaching." *Dialog* 22 (Summer 1983): 187–90.

Walker, Alan. *Evangelistic Preaching*. Grand Rapids: Francis Asbury Press, 1988.

Walker, William O. *The HarperCollins Bible Pronunciation Guide*. San Francisco: HarperSanFrancisco, 1994.

Wallace, James A. *Preaching to the Hungers of the Heart: Preaching on the Feasts and within the Rites*. Collegeville, MN: Liturgical Press, 2002.

Ward, Graham. *Theology and Contemporary Critical Theory*. 2nd ed. New York: St. Martin's Press, 2000.

Ward, Richard F. *Speaking from the Heart: Preaching with Passion*. Eugene, OR: Wipf & Stock, 2001.

———. *Speaking of the Holy: The Art of Communication in Preaching*. St. Louis: Chalice Press, 2001.

Wardlaw, Don M., ed. *Preaching Biblically: Sermons in the Shape of Scripture*. Philadelphia: Westminster Press, 1983.

Warren, Rick. "The Purpose-Driven Title." *Leadership: A Practical Journal for Church Leaders*, Winter 1998, 95–96.

Watley, William D. *Sermons on Special Days: Preaching through the Year in the Black Church*. Valley Forge, PA: Judson Press, 1987.

Waznak, Robert P., SS. *An Introduction to the Homily*. Collegeville, MN: Liturgical Press, 1998.

Webb, Joseph M. *Preaching without Notes*. Nashville: Abingdon Press, 2001.

Webber, Christopher L. *The Art of the Homily*. Harrisburg, PA: Morehouse Publishing Co., 1992.

Webber, Robert E. *Ancient Future Evangelism: Making Your Church a Faith-Forming Community*. Grand Rapids: Baker Books, 2003.

———. *Celebrating Our Faith: Evangelism through Worship*. New York: Harper & Row, 1986.

Webb-Mitchell, Brett. *Unexpected Guests at God's Banquet*. New York: Crossroad Classic, 1994.

Welsh, Clement. *Preaching in a New Key: Studies in the Psychology of Thinking and Listening*. Philadelphia: Pilgrim Press, 1974.

Westerhoff, John H. *Spiritual Life: The Foundation for Preaching and Teaching*. Louisville, KY: Westminster John Knox Press, 1994.

Wheelright, Philip. *Metaphor and Reality*. Bloomington: Indiana University Press, 1962.

Whitehead, Alfred North. *Adventures of Ideas*. New York: Free Press, 1967.

Wilder, Lilyan. *Seven Steps to Fearless Speaking*. New York: Wiley, 1999.

Wilhelm, Dawn Ottoni. "God's Word in the World: Prophetic Preaching and the Gospel of Jesus Christ." In David B. Greiser and Michael A. King, eds., *Anabaptist Preaching: A Conversation between Pulpit, Pew, and Bible*, 76–93.

Willimon, William H. "Anti-Jewish Preaching." In William H. Willimon and Richard Lischer, eds., *Concise Encyclopedia of Preaching*, 11–13.

———. "Borrowed Thoughts on Sermonic Borrowing." *Christian Ministry*, Jan.–Feb. 1997, 14–16.

———. "Humor." In William H. Willimon and Richard Lischer, eds., *Concise Encyclopedia of Preaching*, 262–64.

———. *The Intrusive Word: Preaching to the Unbaptized*. Grand Rapids: Wm. B. Eerdmans Publishing Co., 1994.

———. "Marriage." In James W. Cox, ed., *Handbook of Themes for Preaching*, 157–60. Louisville, KY: Westminster John Knox Press, 1991.

———. *Peculiar Speech: Preaching to the Baptized*. Grand Rapids: Wm. B. Eerdmans Publishing Co., 1992.

Willimon, William H., and Stanley Hauerwas. *Preaching to Strangers: Evangelism in Today's World*. Louisville, KY: Westminster John Knox Press, 1992.

Willimon, William H., and Richard Lischer, eds. *Concise Encyclopedia of Preaching*. Louisville, KY: Westminster John Knox Press, 1995.

Wilson, Paul Scott. *The Four Pages of the Sermon: A Guide to Biblical Preaching*. Nashville: Abingdon Press, 1999.

———. *The Practice of Preaching*. Nashville: Abingdon Press, 1995.

———. *Preaching and Homiletical Theory*. St. Louis: Chalice Press, 2004.

Wilson-Kastner, Patricia. *Images for Preaching*. Minneapolis: Fortress Press, 1989.

Wimberly, Edward P. *Moving from Shame to Self-worth: Preaching and Pastoral Care*. Nashville: Abingdon Press, 1999.

Witherup, Ronald D. *A Liturgist's Guide to Inclusive Language*. Collegeville, MN: Liturgical Press, 1997.

Wogaman, J. Philip. *Speaking the Truth in Love: Prophetic Preaching to a Broken World.* Louisville, KY: Westminster John Knox Press, 1998.

Worley, Robert C. *Preaching and Teaching in the Early Church.* Philadelphia: Westminster Press, 1967.

Zimmerman, Gordon I., James L. Owen, and David R. Seibert. *Speech Communication: A Contemporary Introduction.* 3rd ed. New York: West Publishing Co., 1986.

Zink-Sawyer, Beverly. *From Preachers to Suffragists: Woman's Rights and Religious Conviction in the Lives of Three Nineteenth-Century American Clergywomen.* Louisville, KY: Westminster John Knox Press, 2003.

———. "The Word Purely Preached and Heard: The Listeners in the Homiletical Endeavor." *Interpretation* 51, no. 4 (2004): 342–58.